The Plays of
J. P. Donleavy

BOOKS BY J. P. DONLEAVY

Novels
THE GINGER MAN
A SINGULAR MAN
THE SADDEST SUMMER OF SAMUEL S
THE BEASTLY BEATITUDES OF BALTHAZAR B
THE ONION EATERS

Plays
THE GINGER MAN
FAIRY TALES OF NEW YORK
A SINGULAR MAN
THE SADDEST SUMMER OF SAMUEL S

Stories
MEET MY MAKER THE MAD MOLECULE

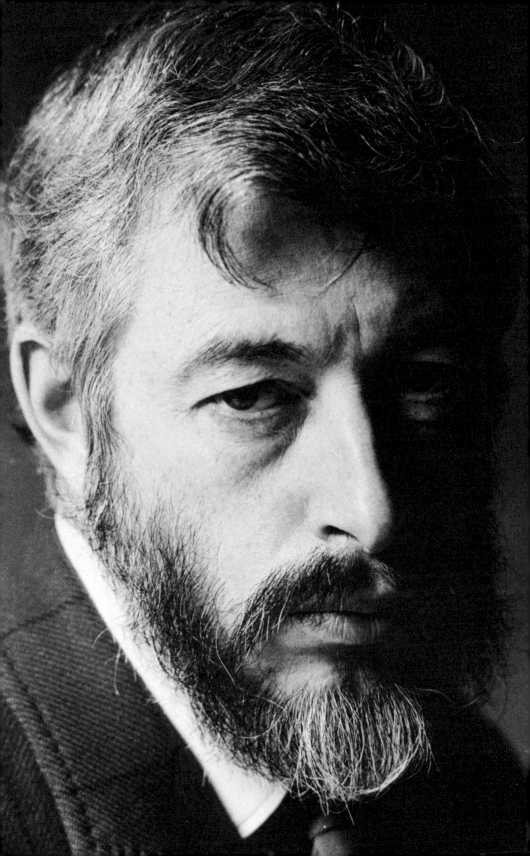

The Plays of
J. P. Donleavy

WITH A PREFACE BY THE AUTHOR

Photographs of the productions by Lewis Morley

DELACORTE PRESS / SEYMOUR LAWRENCE

Library of Congress Catalog Card Number: 73-37660

Manufactured in the United States of America
First printing

Library of Congress Cataloging in Publication Data
Donleavy, James Patrick.
The plays of J. P. Donleavy.
CONTENTS: What they did in Dublin with The ginger man.—The ginger man.—Fairy tales of New York. [etc.]
PS3507.O686A19   1972   812'.5'4   73-37660

TO ALL THOSE FUCKPIGS OF MULTIPLICITIES
WHO HAVE ATTEMPTED TO MOLEST
AND DENIGRATE THESE PLAYS,
WHO TRIED TO STOP
OR SHIFT THEM OFF THE STAGE,
WHO USED THEM UNFAIRLY AS STEPS
TO STARDOM AND BIGGER CONTRACTS,
WHO PANNED THEM, WHO HATED THEM,
WHO COUGHED DURING THE TENDER MOMENTS,
WHO LEFT BEFORE THE FINAL CURTAIN,
OR CAME LATE FOR THE FIRST,
AND NOT LEAST,
TO THOSE WHO DON'T KNOW THEY EXIST,
I HEREBY DEDICATE THE CONTENTS
WHICH STILL BRING ME AND MINE
SO MUCH GOLD.

CONTENTS

PREFACE

The theater is full of amusing wise guys and dedicated girls. Everyone casting an eye around looking for someone. Past whom they might sneak. Out into the sunny joy of riches and celebrity. To stand on their heads wagging their legs on top of a smash hit.

Of all the arts there is nowhere where charmcoated bullshit flies thicker. Especially from directors who think they are playwrights. And women married to men who put money in plays. And from people who have opinions because they've been in the theater for the last continuous fourteen years. And they know how it should work.

The secret to the theater. Is a deep desire to get flush and famous out of it as fast as possible before you get poor and unknown even quicker. The next thing is to let the playwright do the talking. Don't call his work "material." Just say "O my god your play, it turns my knees to jelly I love it." Soon as you make him feel good then you've got a chance to sneak past. But watch it. Because he's watching.

Now take this author. This is his third production. Notice the good quality sole he has on his shoe as he puts his feet folded up on the back of the seat in front. Just think of the great thoughts going through his head. The immense passions through which he has suffered. Let that inspire you. Never feel that that son of a bitch is getting all the publicity. Your turn will come. Much later. When he's being read from textbooks and pounded into schoolchildren's heads the world over with little fees trickling into his vast river of royalties. As his worldwide team of lawyers relentlessly track down and bring to book infringers and pirates.

Now there's a small select group in the theater. Maybe two or three chaps. They wear camel haired coats and they come down from Oxford, Cambridge, or Harvard. In early youth they were lovers of the ballet. On their inheritances keeping chauffeured cars waiting while they sat evenings entranced in the stalls. To them the world of the theater is a world of beauty away from the grit and grime of trustees and bankers who oversee their annual allowances and frown. The first thing they do when they see the playwright is to smile. Like a big cat with a mouse on a square mile of linoleum. They bring you into their best office, the one with the maroon satin casting couch and autographed pictures of the old Hollywood stars on the walls. Perhaps the next hour is as splendid as any mankind can ever know. Over China tea and macaroons rushed in from the nearby sweet emporium. Each chappie staggering the other and the author with a casual stream of drawling compliments.

Then come the contracts. Often the boys of Harvard and Cambridge have been introduced to you by other boys. From the Bronx, Brooklyn, Stepney, and Clapham. Who have come pounding at your down at heel door trying to get you to part with the rights. They tell you to keep away from the big name producers. That they're insensitive bastards. Sign up with us. Meet Prince L whose grandfather just dropped him a packet of bullion when he was climbing the steps to the next world assisted by his gamekeepers. And Prince L doesn't know what to do with it. Except he's out of his millionaire mind in love with the theater.

Of course all these chaps above I allude to are absolutely fictitious. But I remember others who stood around, gentle, sober members of the community, who smiled a little warily after we signed our contract but were always glad to see me. Rushing to brush off the seat where I sat. As I watched and listened to the wild, desperate struggle to crowbar funds out of each other and any distant or near rich relative. As an amused typist pounded out addresses from mailing lists of investors. These lists were as antique as the letters were cheeky.

Dear Sir,

The management of Bilk Bilk and Bilk are proud to announce the acquisition of the theatrical, film, and favorable ancillary rights to "It Was a Long Way to Fortnums Yesterday" by the well known and fashionable author Cornelius Christian. We are further most proud to welcome a selected few investors to take an interest in three of the remaining shares of £1,000 each. The limit of £1,000 has regretfully had to be imposed because of the overwhelming response to subscribe to this production. However, the producers will make every effort to accommodate larger investments but we know you will understand that we cannot undertake to do so. After deduction of management fees and unavoidable overheads we offer the full 30 percent of the producer's profit.

Yours sincerely,
THE MANAGEMENT

After most of the letters are returned marked deceased, the management rush to clasp the lapels of friends. Who with bankrolls previously scalded now clutch them tightly as they return cold hearted looks. And the management's eyes turned slowly toward the cast. Who in terror of their careers beg their friends for money. These were the dazzling afternoons of panic. The last ditch telephone numbers rang. Sunlight fading on the tasseled chaise longue. Phones grabbed up and plonked down. Five seconds away from ruin or fortune. Where sometimes there wasn't even time to watch female tourists undressing in the hotel window across the street.

I had worked out a routine. At two P.M., finishing my novelist's work for the day, I'd go out my little doorway and stroll by quiet side streets to Eel Brook Common to catch the Twenty two bus along King's Road heading east out of Fulham. My favorite seat up front on the left downstairs. These rides were very homey. With the same conductress who wore a peaked cap over her blond hair, who'd rode the route for eleven years, greeting her older customers with inquiries after their health and their day's demeanor. And calling out the stops in her high, serious voice. Past the familiar antique shop fronts. Through World's End. Where snazzy film producers and stars were these days setting up house. And farther on, dowagers with walking sticks were helped aboard. The neighborhood increasing in affluence every yard. Then deep in Knightsbridge I would leap off at a building site, a fire, a motorist's argument, or just to stretch the legs in the afternoon sunshine. Knowing at the end of the journey a busy little group of producers would be catching the pieces as they fell from a new explosion of panic. Erupted often by a chap who ratted. On his absolutely sworn word given yesterday afternoon.

Rehearsals would take place in strange rooms in strange parts of town, above pubs, in school halls, or sometimes in the theaters. Drinks were had with members of the cast. With everyone bound up with their dreams of that pillowy plateau up there of news photographers, moguls, and fans, all of them begging to please one with a best profile, juicy contract, and cries of You were wonderful. And a world would grow up of these familiar faces. Collected together with a shipboard fate. Not including those of course who thought they were in for a resounding flop and were busy negotiating better contracts where they could star solo with their own unique banjo played by toes.

As opening night approached, ratting smoldered everywhere. Behind each pair of charming eyes. But again there were moments of single-minded courage. As subtle battles ensued among the cast for the best dressing rooms. It was an astonishingly pleasant way of life. Studded with moments watching the calipeige of some actress bending with a spotlight upon her pear shaped backside mounds.

The long lonely walks as the final rehearsals raged on back at the theater. While one stood in the cool of old churches reading the wall memorials. And outside, covering further bereft distances, to spy an elegant, agreeable looking lady of contented years and stand watching her hesitate as one worked up the courage to make an approach.

"I beg your pardon, madam, but are you lost."

"I beg your pardon."

"Oh I thought perhaps from the expression on your face you were lost and that I might assist you in your desired direction."

"I don't think so."

"Oh. I'm sorry to hear that. I had the temerity to think that one might, after increasing our acquaintance somewhat, shoulder you gently through a blizzard of beguilements into a parkside suite at the Ritz and after certain vintages and underdone beeves throw a resounding fuck into you, madam."

"I see. Well as a matter of fact I am lost."

And return to the darkened theater just as the players were packing up to take beers at a familiar local. Everybody feeling at home sailing on the same ship. Some wondering if it was time to get off. Listening carefully to any slip of tongue, whether investors were pulling out or not putting in. And then the sowing of the seeds of blame. The director isn't helping us. The author falls asleep at his own lines. So and so simply isn't up to it. And suddenly the full mutiny explodes. The leading man takes a swing at the director. And lands. Awful language is used. Loudly. Actresses stand in tears. The cast deserts.

But all of them are back for the fatal opening. Critics wearing their dead serious faces. This could be the last night that folk rush up to one and say something gushingly. Or widen their eyes and part smiling lips widely. One goes through those breathtaking agonies as a prop teeters readily to crash in a cloud of dust at some most tender moment of underplayed drama. Ah but the more experienced members of the cast are ready to grab it with a quip that brings the house down and hands clapping. Some of those actors are really something.

And as the anticlimactic night wears on, the author waits for the morning scurrilities. The snide shots at one's integrity. And the sense of urgency between the lines to kill it off before it goes too far. And plays to full houses. And which if they are two thirds full begins the Chinese torture. At least that means the guillotine has not yet fallen. But now comes the anxious visits to the box office. The phone call to get the night's gross. The pencils and paper and the scribbles to work out the precedents for opening night takings. The box office returns of previous hits scrutinized. And the present meager bookings ahead. Protestants attend heavily on Tuesday. Jews on Thursdays. The awful seesaw that goes on during the week toward that fatal figure of the weekly total. Upon which the theater owners contract to throw you out or not. Hungrily waiting, some of them, to put their own show in as soon as it's ready and the hope to keep you there at their mercy till the time is ripe. And out you go. With only the later dismal compensation that their show fell flat on its face and the producers had to sell their cars to pay creditors.

Bankruptcy stalks producers. To stay afloat on this treacherous sea of show biz requires keeping your disasters and hand trembling out of sight. As the cyclist continues over the tightrope. The telephone in one hand and a pneumatique check in the other. A little book to put names in of shits who lost faith and signed up to get out of the show. Those bastards who wouldn't paint the scenery till they were paid the further sums in cash. The whole city around one fades, all attention zeroes in on the box office where some of your chaps actually sit huddled counting as the customers come in and the phone rings for bookings. One watches the skies on a Wednesday matinee, desperately hoping it will piss down in torrents half an hour before curtain time and drive in thousands of dowagers desperate for shelter.

And then that day that always comes too soon. The posting of the notice to the cast. The show will close and Saturday evening will be the last performance. The smiles and handshakes. Folks not as enthusiastic as usual at the confrontations. Suddenly one is left lonely without meetings and plans. Far at the bottom of the plateau one thinks is up there. Upon which you roam carefree, picking blossoms, staying at the best hotels, with the breakfast orders of pancakes, maple syrup, and sausages.

But there is always the magic moments that live on. Tucked up in the mind where they starrily simmer with exquisite reverie. A voice, sound, a moment heartfelt and tragic or even funny. That makes you want to go through it all over again. The crushing insult, the bitter burning envies, the praise and worship and eyes that light with laughter and glow with tears. It calls to you to come out. Please. Make more magic. And you smile. At all those dirty bastards, turncoats and fair weather friends. Who want you to shake hands again with the world. Before they try to bust you one. And you do. And they bust you one.

> And
> So help
> Me god
> You smile

J. P. DONLEAVY
November 1971

WHAT THEY DID IN DUBLIN

with

The Ginger Man

a play

ACKNOWLEDGMENTS

We wish to thank the editors of the following newspapers for their permission to reproduce, in full, their comments on the Dublin production of *The Ginger Man:*

The Irish Times
The Irish Press
The Irish Independent
The Evening Herald
The Dublin Evening Mail

1

Have you ever heard of Dublin, a city of half a million souls. On a
moonlit country lane in Dorset I was told they were going to see *The
Ginger Man.*

I took the train to London and went to the Fortune Theatre to the
last performance of this play. Sadly spying the standing room only.
Backstage at the final curtain I said goodbye to the players. Later retiring to a nearby pub where the bar was awash.

Next morning I was in no fit condition to take the plane to Dublin.
Feeling sick, my stomach churning, but as we approached Ireland in this
motor bird I saw a rainbow in the sky and a ship beneath making a white
wake on the green water. I was counting the seconds away. Next to me,
an enormous American with spatulate fingers and tiny clean nails on
monstrous ham hands holding a picture magazine.

I was sheepish about vomiting next to these well groomed fellow
countrymen. And did so into a little bag, hiding my head away by the
window. The American's wife, so blond and diminutive, which made me
think in my lonely sadness what she thought when he was all over her.

Below, the white sandy beach of North Bull Island, the gorse head of

Howth and soft mossy fields of Raheny and Baldoyle. The cows looked up as the great motor bird flew over their dewy backs to settle on the long glistening runway.

Glass doors, polished floors and an autumn wind blowing gently over these white airport buildings. Women in furs and careless hair with legs folded waiting for customs to dig and prod the baggage. Dark men with bright eyes. Big Italians and some wayward French. Richard Harris, the actor, the star of *The Ginger Man*. Walking with giant shoulders, the back of his hand brushing his hair.

There were three cars to take this group of people into Dublin City, on this empty Sunday in Ireland. Along the Swords Road lined with fields as green as green and candy houses. Past the great old gates of past great old houses. Sad sentinels of the claret days of this gracious city.

A winter low weather over Ireland. The colored glass and bright paint on the new suburban villas. The road dipping down to Dublin across the River Tolka. The houses go tall, dark and tattered. Lights burn in the corner grocery shops, open an hour in the afternoon for sweets. Huddled in belted overcoats, figures peddle by from pub to Sunday dinner.

The metropolis lies around the spine of O'Connell Street, an emporium where newsboys, country cousins and hopeful citizens lurk for the sight of something doing. Behind the windows of the smart Gresham Hotel, alcohol burners flaming for the crêpes suzette. And down these narrow side streets are forlorn railway stations and wastelands of markets and dank abattoirs. And the lonely rooms of Dubliners who crouch over their dark tea.

2

The River Liffey divides Dublin with six churches along its city banks. Coming a clear water from the west of the Wicklow mountains. Swans at night all white, glide under the penny bridge. Chug chug of Guinness boats. And the slow ancient commerce of giant horses trundling heavy carts across the cobbles. South of this stream lies the Gaiety Theatre where came *The Ginger Man.*

Grafton Street is a short small world. Of fragrant coffee houses and the sheen and shank of Dublin women gaily ready for laughter and perhaps, years later, for love. Early morning poets taking their earnest ways to the better betting shops, making a conversational exchange with a clerk to ask what's a good thing today. Then the morning's tension till the crazy afternoon when the nags are let loose and the poets pray.

This October Sunday with migration birds and gale warnings in the area of the Irish Sea. The three cars stop by an alley the top of Grafton Street and nine folk get out. They go talking down this dark passage and into the stage door of the Gaiety Theatre.

In the wings backstage the sound of hammering. Later in the afternoon there would be a concert. Polite people stepping out of Georgian doors to sit in the crimson plush as the musicians bow, blow and pluck. Now the panelled bar and carpeted foyers are empty. Balconies held like graceful hands out toward the stage. Welcome.

And in this black alley facing the stage door is another door. Which when pushed opens to two more doors and if you go in the right one you will be standing at the bar of Neary's licensed premises. A room ringing with the solid sound of tall full glasses touching the marble counter. Here are citizens with wit and some with less. A neat row of them along the wall talking in each others' ears. While loneliness is outside beyond the pale, cows and beasts huddling against the hedgerows under a gray sky.

A wisp of a man went whispering from group to group leaving each with nodding heads. And as he passed we heard the message.

"The Jews and Irish are teaming up to take over the world."

This prophet in his gray belted overcoat and cap over the tips of his ears scurried from sight. Someone laughed that it was a good joke.

A blushing girl from Iowa was introduced. Large eyes, fidgeting body, crossing her toes, saying she had only meant to stay in Dublin a week and stayed a year. A large man came forward with a green homespun tie and rumbled that good manners and diction were disappearing and vulgarity was rife. Someone said, "Sit down."

A cold misty rain was descending mottling all the empty shop windows down Grafton Street. Trinity College sat baleful with its great iron gates, a light in the porter's lodge. Dame Street and the massive porticoes of the Bank of Ireland. Fallen leaves staining the way ahead. For Dame Street is a haunted road where you walk for weeks and as it goes west, strange windows open, curtains part and a voice says.

> Do not mind
> Do not care
> Take a toothbrush
> And go to Adare.

Men going this way have never been seen again. Perhaps just turning to look back over a shoulder with a weather eye or a hope to hold them back. By the side of the road they walk. Six in the last thirty years. Two of whom had been scandalized in Dublin. The other four, men who had never amounted to much except when they took this road, they did so bravely.

Jury's Hotel has colored glass around its bottom front windows. With a lobby that is generally brown. A cage rises from floor to floor bringing passengers up and passengers down. In the dining room, white tables spread with condiments held in silver. Down some stairs, a lounge cocktail bar walled with walnut tree. And another upstairs with wicker chairs and glass topped tables. Coffee is brought here with ham and beef sandwiches and the best of pot still whiskeys.

This is where I came to stay. A porter in a brown uniform taking my tiny case and up we went in the vertical machine. Past a lounge of flowered stuffy chairs, a television set flickering. Several elderly folk glued. The door of my room was stuck, a gentle shove and the lock broke. Later a man came up and put things right.

Out the window, the back end of Dublin. The green breasty roof of the Four Courts. On the bed the curious counterpane tucked up in a rosette. Scalding water from the tap and music from a loudspeaker on the wall. I twirled a switch and a voice came out. And there was a voice telling a story. About a girl who had been raised by the nuns and left them and went to London to the big lights, to return in loneliness after two years, broken in health. And she was nursed in her last illness by the kind sisters until she had to be sent away for special treatment.

After a bath in a cavernous tub I took the vertical machine down for victuals. In the center of the dining room sat the cast and managers. I tiptoed by and down the stairs to the gentlemen's. I heard a voice behind me saying, "I take drops to calm me down, pills to pep me up and drink brandy in between." These were strange words in this old fashioned new republic.

In the dining room I sat by the wall alone. Ordering a confection of fresh cream and a compote of fruit. Waitresses in uniforms of convent colors. Waiters with stiff collars, black ties and tails. Sauce boats went by. Across the room sat a young blade from the country who sniffed a sample of wine for the waiter and said it was marvelous and his two girl companions smiled.

The Sunday quiet evening passed whitely, warmly. *The Ginger Man* cast went up to a small reception room to have a rehearsal at eight o'clock. Farther down the hall there was another babbling of voices. An assembly of elderly women and some clergy playing cards.

I went out for a walk. A priest spoke to a little crowd near the Liffey. Green lighted buses to and fro over O'Connell Street bridge and a barrel organ played. Downriver the masts of ships and one midstream making for sea. Along the wide boulevard, ice cream palaces with white coated, fawn eyed country girls in attendance, standing hands held behind back, while the odd person bent over a plate of ice cream.

As I stopped to peruse each doorway and building, thinking of my student days in Dublin, I noticed a figure behind a newspaper. Each time I stopped and happened to look in his direction he would put his head back and look directly up at the sky until I looked away again. He was a silent Dublin shouter.

I hurried back to the hotel. Now ten o'clock. I pushed quietly through the door into the rehearsal room. Five tired people. Going through movements and lines over and over again. Trying to touch some aesthetic ultimate. Green drapes closed over two windows. A table, two chairs and wide green carpet. The floor trembling as Richard Harris struck his forehead with the palm of his hand when a line slipped his mind. Philip Wiseman squatted seated on his heel as Harris said, "Don't tell me, don't tell me, whatever you do."

Then the line would come and relief to the watching faces. Later all of us taking refreshments, a pot of thick rust colored tea. And Wiseman and I went for a walk down the Quays. Past a dredger, the Customs

House across the river in the moonlight. The mailboat moored and dark waiting to set sail tomorrow. Along the banks of the Grand Canal, the empty lonely black cobblestone streets. We stopped to look in the great barred opening of the gas works, a dark pit, catwalks, pipes and blackness. A blue flame belching, and men working in this darkness go home to steamy lives over kitchen kettles.

Returning to the hotel along a barren Ringsend past the high gray wall and fence of Trinity College. The night porter, unlocking and admitting us, said a cheery good night and hoped we had enjoyed our stroll. The radiators were cooling. Dublin lay still. At the end of Sunday. And tomorrow would be the first night of *The Ginger Man*.

3

The spidery bikes were out on this windy Monday morning in Dublin. In the newspaper a small headline. Unending battle with rats. That the Dublin corporation employed eight men full time in this relentless war, tactics changing daily, as the rats were amazingly cunning.

The papers carried the announcement of the opening of *The Ginger Man*. At eight fifteen A.M. I went for a walk through Trinity College. Passing by the porters' lodge, porters rolled up sleeping near the embers of a fire. The gray tiny cobblestones of the front square. The green aprons of grass, old trees with their Chinese crooked branches. Lunatic and cold.

In the old days, many unsanitary conditions prevailed. But new water closets were installed and now a certain item no longer flies from the apertures. Nor do sneaky stains appear down the granite beneath various windowsills. The chapel today all silent with the peace of Protestantism. Rows of pews, crimson kneeling pads. A great attendance book lies open. Two names neatly writ of persons present last Saturday at devotion.

Students could be seen steaming up their windows with early morning kettles for tea. Sea gulls screaming near the slop pails carried by servants. Gravel paths lead to the back playing fields through flowerbeds and some trees with leaves this late autumn. Buildings of zoology, pathology, medicine, gray, large, windowed and cold.

I walked slowly back to the hotel for breakfast. Sitting at a white table in a sunlit corner. Pots brimming with coffee and hot white plates of eggs and rashers. As I chewed I counted fifty five deaths and eighteen memoriams in the morning paper. In another column was listed one birth. Evidence enough there had been two citizens unable to control themselves nine months ago in Dublin town.

In another column an item that Catholics were in a minority number-ing barely one fifth of the human race, that Islam was on the march and that its increase in the last thirty years had been the most dominant and bewildering statistical fact of this century. Traffic of new visitors in the lobby this morning and two lonely Moslems. Hoot of horns outside on the street. A red and black placard hung by the reception desk saying nightly at eight P.M., the Dublin play that startled London, Richard Harris, in *The Ginger Man*. Dress Circle, 10/; Parterre 7/6; Grand Circle 4/ and 6/—now booking 10 A.M.—9 P.M.

Backstage at the Gaiety Theatre, hands lifted scenery into position. Piles of chairs in the wings from Sunday's concert. A man on a high ladder and another way up in the darkness shout back and forth, light-ing the set. Batteries of switches, the hum of electric current. Light floods down. In green, yellows. One of lime.

A vacuum cleaner pushed by a white aproned woman across the car-pets, a gentle dust rising in the sunlight. Across the street, Monday publicans lining up pints for customers. A pedestrian passing the glass doors of the theater, stopping vaguely to look. Two schoolgirls giggling by. A motorized bicycle sputtering to a stop, its rider dismounting, re-moving headgear, looks at theater, puts back head and laughs. Later kicking his two wheeler into life and making off rapidly in the direction of the hospital at the end of the street.

They said business at the box office was as usual, neither sad nor glad this Monday. The man on the motor bike had bought two tickets saying to the clerk, "I wouldn't miss this bash for anything." A free ticket had been reserved for the director and author. And were pink and pretty.

I went for a walk through St. Stephen's Green and beyond up the

Georgian Streets past the bright painted doors. Sparsely peopled this morning. At the canal bridge, the country sound of water slipping through the sluice gates. There were sometimes dead domestic animals floating. Cattails and swamp grass growing by the shore. Along here I met a man. Arms folded largely across his chest. Sandals over the white thick socks on his feet. We stopped in front of a butcher shop as we met and he told me of an attempted murder. He said that when the hands of death suddenly make a grab for you, the strength to resist is almighty and comes up from the bottom of the being. We stepped into a chilly public house for a drink.

Later catching a bus back into town. Riding on a bench facing a phalanx of women shoppers. They had flung him, a drugged man, into the canal. To stop his voice and write a legend that he had drowned intoxicated. A plotted violence in this city. Where citizens stop to pat the better dressed little children's heads and smile. Or the sorrows of an infant death. As they carry the tiny coffin aloft on shoulders through tattered streets and sit nights as last hours lurk over the old. The color is blue. Faces white and fearful. Where death is holy, an act of faith as well as one lonesome terror.

After lunch and a word with Wiseman in Neary's public house, I took a green bus south to wile the afternoon. A winding road passing over ancient battlefields. Past a little white door, the entrance to Dundrum Criminal Lunatic Asylum. Cattle being driven on the road. Damp cottages in fields along the River Dodder. Something made me turn my head in the bus. There were eyes on the back of my head. A man in dark regalia writing something in his lap. I'd been straining to see over the asylum's high wall, at a building in the distance with bars on the window.

It began to rain. Bus now making a turn through a more green and open countryside. The last stop at the top of a hill in an isolated street of squat stucco houses each with four panes of stained glass, lace at the bedroom windows and concrete path down to a little front gate. Woman comes out to take in wash off the line. In the distance a manor house without a roof, bullocks walking in and out of the ground floor ballroom. The bus driver and conductor had a smoke, idly saying it looked to be a wild night.

Now dark back in Dublin. The homeward bound swarming up the

streets. Protestants carrying black umbrellas. Newsboys holding out the urgent papers to passersby. There's a Victorian glass canopy over the entrance to the Shelbourne Hotel. A spacious high ceilinged lobby where diminutive pages with mock deep voices go crying triple barreled names through the public rooms. I ordered a tomato juice from the circular bar of the cocktail lounge and sat with my newspaper in a red leather seat.

A woman with a pheasant feather in her hat said she was from Texas and liked the friendly atmosphere she encountered on all her travels through Europe and that in her experience if you treated people right they treated you right. Her words drifted to many ears, most clientele paying sudden attention to their fingernails.

Near me a group of two ladies and gentlemen, one of whom, a woman, discussing her chest.

"I am wheezing."

"Are you now."

"Lungs in a shocking state. It's the night air."

"Fancy that."

"Don't mind telling you this weather's no good for the chest."

"That's a fact."

"It's the catarrh. I've been taking the lung linctus. Miracle medicine. Been no miracle with me."

"You don't say."

The husbands of this group in their camel's hair coats progress to the bar, touching glasses of whiskey and flashing them back. The drone of the chest sufferer, brown monstrous breasts, leaning into her companion's ear, whispering, "Charles, the dear boy, plays with these like toys."

Shocked at this remark I edged away. And when husbands joined the women again, I heard the word "ginger." Then the word "man." And the name "Harris." I put the three together, gathered up my coat and took a sharp right in the lobby to where one retreats for natural acts and to flowing wide basins, rare scented soaps, and warm fresh towels. Attendants stand idly by ready to leap forward with brush to remove specks from the person.

And the evening is born. Tall curtains drawn on windows. Central-heating pipes getting warm to the touch. Eaters assembling around the white linen. Grouse shooters scanning the lobby. Taking a bead on the possible indiscretion. Their spare taut wives, cigarettes hanging from lips, make their ways from the ladies' to follow the human hawthorn into the dining room.

Guarding against the night air, taking a leisurely pace along St. Stephen's Green, I stopped to look down South King Street. No sign of life in front of the Gaiety Theatre. I felt a distinct chill and stood in rigid silence. My first reactions to hearing in a lane in Dorset of the production of *The Ginger Man* in Dublin had been that it was the ultimate act of bravery. Or madness.

I turned away from the darkened theater, my chill and silence turning slowing into a teeth clenched mumbling fury. I had walked but a few steps when there was a sudden flood of light behind me. I turned and looked at the brightness spilling over the street and lighting up the façade of shops across the road. I found myself looking down upon my right hand doubled in a hard fist which I put quietly away in my pocket. And made my sheepish steps back to Jury's Hotel.

In the lobby I wrote notes of good wishes to the four performers. Took the vertical machine up four floors, changed my shirt, listened briefly on the Irish Radio to a discussion of the proper time for the eating of mushrooms, one correspondent maintaining they should never be consumed out of season, another that if mushrooms were there on the plate before you, season or no season, and you had a fancy for fungi, only a fool wouldn't eat them.

4

Tonight the lobby of Jury's Hotel was lively. Rich ham handed red-faced farmers from the country. Salesmen from England in their gent's natty suiting. Outside the swing doors in College Green the wind was high. The evening paper said a westerly air stream covers Ireland with cold rain, gale gusts and cloud, high water mark in Dublin at 6:48 P.M., further outlook was variable.

A minor headline about the increased drunkenness, which the authorities now considered endemic. Inside page two, a column concerning the theft on a Sunday of twopence half penny by thieves who left children's comics behind them so as to mislead the police but the latter were not fooled by this false clue, having taken note of the expert removal of a window to gain entrance and the further evidence of a telephone directory torn in half, the police thought, possibly as a show of strength by the thieves.

Crossing College Green I made my way by dark back streets and an alley to Neary's licensed premises. Passing on the way modern coffee houses with candles burning on the tables. Stopping several times with an uncontrollable desire to look behind and find an empty bleak street. Except once when I thought I saw the white of a newspaper against a dark figure stepping up backwards into a doorway. The two globes of light burning outside of Neary's were a comforting sight and I passed between them into the packed interior. I met Mr. Wiseman, who was having a nonalcoholic beverage, sitting alone at the bar. Together we pushed our way out the pub's back entrance and I delivered my notes of good luck and best wishes for tonight to the stars, leaving them with the porter inside the stage door across the alley.

In front of the theater there was a modest line for seats. A preponderance of women in their thirties. It was whispered in the foyer that the plainclothes police were already in their seats, most of them holding the rank of sergeant. The Lord Mayor of Dublin stood with his chain of office round his neck talking with an ease befitting his station. A large man passed by letting loose wind. And a remark, "Up the Republic."

Many camel's hair coats, gentlemen with their own gray abundant hair slapped back with, as the smell indicated, reputable hair lotion. The women in the middle thirties held boxes of chocolates, light lipstick on lips, sensible coats on backs with perhaps just a dash of fashion. A poet, of whom another poet had said his verse glittered, smiled like he had caught a fish from a muddy river where it had been reputed the natives had poisoned the lot to death long ago. He looked over his shoulder advancing up the stairs, stopped, took a silver lighter to a cigarette and blew a smoke ring which floated down over the heads, encircling finally and to his embarrassment, a prominent member of the Dublin Corporation.

Eight o'clock, the chatter quieted as the house lights dimmed. A Chinese music of reeds and strings melted sadly out over the audience. The curtain rose. The plainclothes police were ready with pencil and pad. From a private box came a guffaw followed by head turning and mouse murmurings. High in the unreserved seats at 2/6 a skull, there was a brief commotion followed by another guffaw emitting from the private box. Then a comment too loud for a whisper was heard, "Ah, well the first fifteen seconds have gone by now uneventful enough."

The curtain plunging down on the first act to a spattering of claps. The audience rising and making for the bars, leaving a sprinkle of women in the middle thirties who dipped further into their chocolate goodies. Elderly ladies making their turtle journey to the coffee lounge, fanning their perfume about them with a program. A silver haired captain of an English industry, holding out an arm for his wife, who looks up from her diamonds and down her nose at the way ahead through a group of well known meter readers from the Gas Company Alliance and Electricity Supply Board.

Four prominent members of the artistic population of Dublin had convened at one end of the bar, one of whom was loudly using the word balderdash, another shouting the singular word ball, which, a sentence later regrettably became plural. There was some friendly pushing followed by the remark Would you mind keeping your hands to yourself. At which point a man in uniform advanced and said, "Now, now, there's a time and place for everything."

A pretty blue eyed woman, her cigarette in a long ivory stem, parted her lips and said far out over the heads of many people, "I have never wanted my body to become the plaything of others." A few seconds later most conversations were resumed and some jocularity was prevalent. A bell rang for the second act. Drinks were put back smartly, the meter readers returning as a unit, one stopping briefly in the corridor to tie his shoelace, finding himself rather embarrassingly bumped from behind. Dublin audiences being well known for their playfulness.

Several harmless minutes had elapsed in the second act when a loud shout was heard from a skull in the seven and six penny seats of the parterre.

"This has gone far enough."

There was a distinct slowing of action on the stage. The shouter looked around him and taking a step backwards slowly sat down. A witness reporting that seen from behind, his ears looked very large and his hair cut close to the head. He wore a belted overcoat from a pocket of which protruded the *Irish Independent,* a newspaper widely circulated among the Irish, after whom it is thought to be named.

Backstage the hands, having got engrossed in the play, had to be roused several times to move the scenery. The plainclothes police had been seen during the interval standing quietly apart shrugging their huge shoulders, one of them, reaching for a chocolate from a lady's box and taking a bite, was heard to say, "Very tasty." The latter remark, he said, could not, however, be applied to the show in question but he was keeping an open mind in the matter.

Tonight seemed to resemble other first nights, insofar as after the final curtain there was clapping. And an informant sitting behind the skull who had said it had gone far enough, said that this gentleman was applauding heartily while his ears wagged.

After a drink in the bar, Philip Wiseman and I went backstage. Through the long corridor, up and down staircases. There was a group around the stars. I was exchanging some words with a Dublin producer and his wife. Out the corner of my eye I saw Philip Wiseman and Mr. Elliman, owner of the Gaiety Theatre, in conversation. And there seemed to be no smiles. And Mr. Wiseman, who rarely smiles, had a silent look on his face. I heard the word "contract" and knew what it meant. The word "cut."

Richard Harris stood surrounded by people. And had said, as a long stream of folk entered the stage door, "So you've all come." This was Richard Harris's family from Limerick. Mostly my eyes and ears were tuned to Philip Wiseman and Mr. Elliman who seemed to be getting on less and less well together. And Mr. Wiseman finally came in my direction and said:

"They want us to cut the show."

"Whoops."

"I told him there were to be no cuts in this show. That we have a contract with the author to this effect."

"I see."

"Nothing is coming out of this show."

Slowly the crowd backstage drifted into the drinking lounge nearby called the Green Room. A small hatch in the wall through which drinks were served. Wicker chairs to sit on. An American in sneakers slipped up to people and made strange remarks. He came up to me and asked if I had faced reality.

"No."

"Say, you're a smart cookie."

"Thanks."

"I'd like to talk to you at length sometime. Maybe you got it figured out."

And the American drifted away to other little groups where I heard him say with a thumb pointed back to me,

"Hey that cookie, back there, you think he's got it figured out."

The first night came to a close. The audience slowly making their way back into their own lives. The meter readers mounting their two wheelers to record the units once more. Others back to their damp rooms and solitary breakfasts of rasher, egg and thick tea. The buses green and laden making ways out of Dublin, the respectable spinsters in the late thirties aboard. The audience had clapped. Some had made comments, carefully couched, that it was a nice evening.

Others had gone off into the drinking dens, where caged up close by other elbows they put back the dark liquid. Suburban citizens of this city. Some with clubs up under their coats who said the yellow horde would one day be on its way across Europe from the East and it was only sensible that they go out for a night's drinking prepared. Meanwhile perhaps, laying open a few heads of any cheeky upstarts from the minorities.

Grafton Street empty and silent save for the odd cyclist with drink taken, mounting a curb and passing through a plateglass window where he engaged the plaster male models in fisticuffs, screaming as they went down before his swinging arms, "You stuffed shirts, I'll teach you proper manners." A crowd of newsboys gathered round, faces wreathed in smiles, clapping as a blow from this citizen took a head off and sent it bumping across the street. Grave exception was taken, however, when the man set upon the female figures in the window, a newsboy shouting, "Ah now, enough's enough, leave the women from harm."

Dame Street wide and endless, deserted now. Philip Wiseman and I asked the porter at the front door of Jury's Hotel where we could eat. He said there was an all night eatery five minutes' walk away. We passed under the great portico of the Bank of Ireland, the only spot in Dublin for sheltering out of the rain. Westmorland Street with its coal and shipping offices, the premises of the *Irish Times,* a soothing daily journal in this elfin city. Number 10 Westmorland Street, one more of Bewley's Oriental Cafés, blue pottery in the windows, and the smell of newly roasted coffee lurking in the night air.

We made our way into a narrow entrance with the touches of a South Sea island. Up another flight of stairs past bamboo fences, candlelight lapping over the empty tables. Waiters swarming from all directions to usher these only customers to a central table. Menus were flourished. A large jug of fresh water was brought forth and with a bow, placed on the table. Commands whispered back and forth. A young stout woman emerged and sat at the piano, tinkling out a rendering of "Raggle Taggle Gypsy."

Great slabs of steak arrived with garnishings green and fulsome. Golden potato chips. Empty handed waiters standing watching these two solitary meat eaters. Dublin asleep save for those strange voices of newsboys that wander all night over the city crying *Herald* and *Mail.* All transport stopped, with children wrapped ten in a bed in the secret rooms of the Combe.

A stormy night rattling the big Georgian windows. The thick walls of the houses suck the oxygen out of the wind. Just before dawn in Dublin there's a sudden peace when the night citizens step out of the drinking dens and take a sniff of the fresh country air. Retching briefly they steal away in the horse cabs. And the only moving thing left are dogs lifting legs and a little ship floating out toward Dublin Bay.

5

The papers said it was the wildest night of the year, Ireland swept by gale force winds, trees uprooted, telephone lines toppled and scores of ships scurrying to harbors. But inside Jury's Hotel there was the same warm tranquility. The murmuring movements in the kitchens as the trayloads of breakfasts were delivered to the mouths in the dining room.

Opening up a copy of the *Irish Times* bought from the news vendor on College Green across from Trinity College.

"THE GINGER MAN," AT THE GAIETY THEATRE

The Globe Theatre has enterprisingly captured the current production of J. P. Donleavy's play, *The Ginger Man*, in transit between two London theatres, temporarily and partially recast it, and put it on display at the Gaiety for a week. Like the sheeps' heads which are the hero's main item of diet, this is strong and often rancid meat, but a theatrical experience on the same level as *Look Back in Anger*.

In this stage version the resemblance to *Look Back in Anger* is strongly and unfortunately marked—due to the superficial likeness of the four main characters to which the novel has been cleverly reduced. Jimmy Porter, however, is a babe in arms compared with the psychopathic Sebastian Balfe Dangerfield, whom Mr. Donleavy obviously regards as a true romantic hero. The picture of student life on a G.I. grant, an expense of spirit in a waste of gin, is all too true within its squalid limits.

The mingled love and loathing of Dublin, expressed in words that glitter and cut like a welding torch, is not a pastiche of Joyce, but a recreation. And in this truncated version, shorn for pragmatical reasons (as Mary McCarthy would doubtless put it) of the novel's more luridly antisocial episodes, Mr. Donleavy almost achieves his ambition of turning Dangerfield into a latterday Hamlet. At any rate, while the novel brought down the wrath of the French Government on its publishers, last night's stage presentation brought only a few shouts from the audience.

For this, of course, production and acting take much of the credit. Philip Wiseman's production is brilliant, and so is Richard Harris in the central part which demands extraordinary physical and emotional reserves. Genevieve Lyons and Rosalie Westwater deal excellently with the feminine side of the quartet, and Godfrey Quigley, as the pathetic O'Keefe, gives the performance of his life. O'Keefe is the play's one frail link with our own lives of quiet desperation—lives which, after such vicarious excitements, seem infinitely more desirable, but undeniably tame.

M.K.

The conversations in the dining room over the wild weather across the country. Toilet article representatives sit blue suited and lonely, reaching out to adjust their toast in the silver rack, looking up now and again to catch the blue eyes of the waitress to bring a spot of marmalade. An instant later a jar comes brimming.

Sunlight flashing on and off through the stained glass window, splashing suddenly on two columns of print in the *Irish Press*:

GOOD ACTING IN DISTASTEFUL PLAY

J. P. Donleavy's *The Ginger Man* which opened at the Gaiety Theatre last night is slightly lunatic, more than slightly brilliant and considerably distasteful.

There is one scene near the end of the second act which is probably the most offensive ever performed on a Dublin stage and which I sincerely hope will never again be repeated.

In a short five minutes a travesty is made of everything that stage entertainment is supposed to mean, morals are mocked at and indecency is flaunted. It is all very well to talk of art and freedom of expression in the theatre, but I think we have gone far enough.

Up to this scene, the play had been rude, vulgar and even offensive to a degree, but I think we might still have stomached it but for this intrusion. I thoroughly agreed with the gentleman in the gallery who shouted, "You have gone far enough."

The play deals with the life and loves of an irresponsible and permanently impecunious Trinity student, Sebastian Dangerfield, a "mystic maniac" who cloaks his unwillingness to face up to life with liquor and his deeply sensitive awareness of nature with boyish clownings.

His wife, in desperation, is forced to leave him, and the girl who might have helped him finds that her sense of religion is too strong to permit a continuous liaison.

There is also an Irish American student friend who rambles on and off stage periodically, who is very interesting and at times amusing, but whose incursions have little bearing on the plot of the play.

For me, however, this Irish American, splendidly played by Godfrey Quigley, helped to relieve a good deal of the tedium of the Ginger Man's ramblings. Not that they were all ramblings; there was quite a lot of sensitive writing in the Ginger Man's part and Richard Harris captured much of it.

Indeed, he was magnificent at times but, very often, his antics were boring and exaggerated. Genevieve Lyons and Rosalie Westwater both contributed good performances.

M.M.

Opening up the *Irish Independent*, searching the columns. No review of *The Ginger Man*.

At noon on this Tuesday the cast were assembling in the Green Room in the Gaiety Theatre. Newspapers opened across their laps. A dingy cold interior by day. The manager of the theater presented his compliments to Mr. Wiseman and asked for his decision in the matter of cuts in *The Ginger Man*.

Philip Wiseman said there would be no cuts in the play. The theater manager said he had his instructions and that he would have to act accordingly. Under the circumstances the play would have to be taken off and Spur Productions Limited would be responsible for any damages.

Philip Wiseman's stage manager, brought from London, suddenly made for the door where he said he was phoning to London to inform the business manager of Spur Productions of what was happening in Dublin. Mr. Wiseman said that it wouldn't be necessary as the business manager of Spur Productions was employed by him and would only have to phone back again to him. The stage manager insisted, however, that it was his duty to inform those directly above him. Mr. Wiseman finally saying that if it makes you feel any better, phone London. And the stage manager was gone.

The manager of the Gaiety Theatre presented a copy of their standard contract. Further asking if the decision not to make any cuts was final. Mr. Wiseman said it was. The manager said very well he would inform Mr. Elliman and let Mr. Wiseman know of any further steps to be taken.

Richard Harris sat with a newspaper open in his lap, which he slowly began to fold between his outstretched legs. He said, "Well, what's going to happen? Are we going on, or aren't we? Whatever you do, I'll play it. I'll go on a soap box on O'Connell Street Bridge, if necessary. Just let me know when there's a decision."

The Bailey, an eating and drinking establishment in Duke Street, has figured for many years in the conversational life that is Dublin. Its proprietor John Ryan, an Irish painter, had invited Philip Wiseman and myself to lunch. We sat at a bar and ate crustaceans with chablis. In another room a thick murmur of voices, and some sad morning after faces. Business leaders, higher members of the civil service, one well known porter from the Dublin abattoir, a leading corrector of crossword puzzles and a sprinkling of meter readers from the Dublin gas board.

Sitting next to me, a small man with a red beard and sparse dark hair engaged me in conversation. He said that he was visiting Dublin and was setting up a transmitter from which television signals would be sent to the people of Ireland. He said that he was a Dubliner himself and as a child his nanny wheeled him in a pram in St. Stephen's Green. He said that Ireland was an inaccurate country and functioned inefficiently with no regard for the facts. He himself had started a small factory making plaster models of Jesus Christ as a baby, a youth and finally a grown man. At each stage he lost money. And lastly made casts of Jesus crucified which finally drove him into bankruptcy. These articles now come from Japan.

Back in the Green Room of the Gaiety Theatre there was a brief exchange between the manager and Mr. Wiseman concerning any further developments regarding cuts. Mr. Wiseman stating there was no change in his decision, both himself and the author having agreed to make no cuts in the play. The manager informed Mr. Wiseman that his instructions were that if the cuts were not made in the play, there would be no performance tonight and that Spur Productions would be served with a writ for damages.

Godfrey Quigley, the actor playing Kenneth O'Keefe, came into the Green Room with an early edition of the *Evening Herald* with a review of *The Ginger Man.*

AMERICAN STUDENTS IN DUBLIN

Sebastian Balfe Dangerfield, the Ginger Man of J. P. Donleavy's play at the Gaiety, is an American student in postwar Dublin who should never have been allowed out of the U.S. in the first place. He is obviously a mental case.

As such, his behaviour is not funny, whatever the English (who have been looking at him for the past five weeks) may think.

Completely irresponsible and almost always drunk, he treats his young English wife so atrociously that she leaves him.

He then has an affair with a woman lodger. She in turn leaves this lecherous buffoon.

And so he is left alone, spouting poetry of a sort and feeling terribly sorry for himself. He is about to depart for England; he should be locked up.

Sketched in episodically from the novel, *The Ginger Man* makes a sordid and repulsive evening in the theatre. The transfer of this play from London to Dublin is no feather in the Globe Company's cap.

The pace is murderously like a film in slow motion. Richard Harris acts authoritatively in the title role.

What laughs there are come from Godfrey Quigley's way as a fellow American.

Genevieve Lyons portrays the English girl and Rosalie Westwater, the Irish girl.

                                                        J.J.F.

In the Green Room this afternoon, the drama of cuts went on. Philip Wiseman standing thinly as well fed folk went back and forth with messages. It being finally decided that the cast would be present that evening in the theater and await a decision as to whether there would be another performance.

This group with their newspapers stood up and made a slow winding way through the dark of the backstage out into the narrow alley and down past Woolworth's this chilly late afternoon. They stopped on the corner of Harry Street and Grafton, a well known meeting spot for all sorts of raconteurs most of whom were capable of soaking up a good dozen pints of porter while engaged of an evening in their happy pastime. For many years this spot has also been made famous by windmakers who have vied with motor contraptions in fouling the air. And although Ireland has changed these last years, there are still some old-timers who carry on this great sport. A few of them using matches to explode their issue. Police taking a poor view of some of the bigger bangs as being a menace to shopkeepers' windows as well as to innocent private pedestrians.

The group made a right turn in Harry Street and went down some rather fancy stairs into the Zodiac lounge. Richard Harris sat widely along the wall. Godfrey Quigley with Philip Wiseman and myself at a nearby table. Quigley telling stories of his visits to America, which sounded like strange pioneerings in the new world and which brought New York, Florida and the Middle West into the room. And as this town of Dublin always does, it stopped life. And one could look back over the yesterdays. And take a deep breath in the present.

The *Evening Mail* turned up, which was opened on the various laps.

"THE GINGER MAN" AT THE GAIETY IS EMPTY, TRIVIAL

If I had to choose the most tasteless, trivial and empty play that I have yet seen I think my choice would be J. P. Donleavy's *The Ginger Man* presented last night at the Gaiety.

First and foremost it is a piece about a drunken, dissolute Dublin student who plainly belongs to what has come to be known as the "beat" generation, apparently because they are beaten before they start. We know there are drunken wasters in every condition of society but to have a whole night of drunken maunderings is too much. Richard Harris may be a good actor, I could not tell by his staggering and muttering from chair to door which made up most of last night's performance.

Little Plot

There was practically no plot, nothing to give the audience any of the mental anguish of thought. I had hoped there would be some scintillating dialogue, some smart, even if risqué, repartee. There wasn't. It was all dull and dreary with a touch of the disgusting.

Having seen Genevieve Lyons at the Gaiety in such a fine play as I Am a Camera, and many others, I know she can act well, but here, as the wife of a student drunk, she revealed just one mood of hostility to her husband. We never got to know her real character. The same applies to Godfrey Quigley, who is another American student, dressed like a battered cattle drover, whose function appears to be to stagger in at intervals, drink out of glasses and bottles and utter words of despair. I sympathized with him. It was how I felt too.

A Real Character

The only real character that emerged was that of Miss Frost, the boarder, sensitively played by Rosalie Westwater. Every phrase and intonation was right. It was a study of pitiful frustration though I do not think she would so easily have become the victim of the student drunk. She would probably have left the house when his wife died. That scene seemed to owe something to John Osborne's Look Back in Anger, an infinitely better play. If one takes out the bad language, the squalid and sordid appeal of The Ginger Man, there is nothing left. Yet there are, of course, the jeers at Ireland made by the drunks. Direction, Philip Wiseman.

R.M.F.

Back stage at the Gaiety there was distinct hostility in the air as Philip Wiseman and myself made our way across the dark stage and to the steps which led up to Mr. Elliman's office.

We rapped on the door. The manager in evening dress came and bade us wait a few minutes. In a way it was reminiscent of high school days waiting outside the principal's office before one was expelled.

The theater manager told us to come in. A beautiful office. A fat coal fire glowing in the grate. Mr. Elliman facing us behind his desk. To our right was Mr. Ryan, business manager of the Globe Theatre Company. Philip Wiseman and I sat on a soft sofa. And for our little group of two, Mr. Wiseman became the spokesman.

I suppose, breaking down the facts, it was a strange little meeting. An Irishman and a Jew against an Irishman and a Jew. The Irishmen it seemed were the seconds. Mr. Wiseman and Elliman meeting head on.

In a moment of curiosity I had asked Philip Wiseman why the proposition of cuts had incensed him so, since for myself, although I would have refused the cuts, I couldn't get steamed up. Mr. Wiseman said, "Because I feel that they are trying to cut off my balls." I agreed that fury on that account was reasonable enough.

The curtain was due to go up in twenty minutes, at eight o'clock. The manager had popped in to say that the crowds were gathering on the footpaths outside.

Mr. Elliman put the facts before us. He said cut or else no play tonight. We said no. There was the pause that does not refresh and a few impatient exchanges. Throughout the theater were hands resting on switches, usherettes at doors and a cast waiting for calls. Mr. Elliman said, "I have no alternative, gentlemen, but to close the play and serve you both with writs for damages." We said OK.

Mr. Ryan said that the church on City Quay is mentioned in the play and that this church was in the diocese of the Archbishop. I said the audience didn't object and laughed happily. However, I pointed out that Dangerfield never mentioned a church on City Quay but referred only to the church on the quays and that according to a recent map there are five or six churches on the Dublin quays, some of which may not have been of the Catholic persuasion.

At eight minutes to eight these four people sat facing one another. Mr. Elliman said, "There are people out there tonight, waiting to get into this theater, I don't care, I'll turn them away if I must, these are reasonable cuts you are being asked to make. If I saw this play in London, I would never have agreed to put it on in this city."

At three minutes to eight Mr. Elliman looked at his two Bronx citizens across on the sofa and said for the last time, "Gentlemen, are you going to make these cuts?" And for the last time Mr. Wiseman said no.

The manager in evening dress was at the door. He peeked his head in at one minute to eight. Mr. Elliman looked at us and then to the manager and said, "Raise the curtain, the show goes on."

The lobby bustling with people who were released into the seats. The Chinese music came gently seeping under the door. In the office the tension was momentarily gone. Mr. Donleavy talked easily about the history of the play. How Mr. Wiseman had persisted day after day to get the rights. How Mr. Donleavy had gently refused to part. And then Mr. Wiseman in a last desperate effort had come to Mr. Donleavy's house in desperate Fulham and made him one last final offer while the author ate his spaghetti. And when Mr. Donleavy refused it, he left the house more cheerful than he'd come, saying, as he parted in the street, that he could sleep that night with a clear conscience knowing he had gone as far as he could to get this play and now that he didn't get it would have no regrets.

Mr. Donleavy, having always been fascinated by people without a pot to piss in, has always been a great one for handing out the pot. So back in Dublin in that office and after Mr. Donleavy's little tale it was obvious all were touched and the group nearly came to handshakes before being led out by the manager to seats to view proceedings on the stage.

But uneasiness was in the air. Some dark shadow. During the interval a man lashed another across the chops in the bar, setting him on his arse. And when the person was asked why he had hit the other, he said the man had made a discreditable remark about Sebastian Dangerfield. Dublin always being a cantankerous place, where folk are likely to see both sides of a question so long as it can result in a fight.

Late that night as Philip Wiseman, John Ryan, and myself sat on stools in an all night eatery relishing various types of burgers with coffee, a newsboy came in, with the early morning papers. Wiseman spread out the *Irish Independent* of this 28th October day, 1959, and read:

"THE GINGER MAN" AT THE GAIETY

The current production in the Gaiety Theatre, Dublin (*The Ginger Man*) is one of the most nauseating plays ever to appear on a Dublin Stage and it is a matter of some concern that its presentation should ever have been considered.

It is an insult to religion and an outrage to normal feelings of decency.

Now that it has shocked everyone with an average sense of values who has seen it, the best course open to all concerned is to withdraw it with the greatest possible speed.

D.R.

Back in the early morning in Jury's Hotel as I bolted the lock on my door and gathered my little possessions together. My two shirts. Some bits of paper and pencil and a notebook. I thought perhaps tomorrow I would take the motor bird back to London. There was a sense of something, a black wire cage being wound around one. And I lay myself down to sleep a little fitful in this unhappy land.

6

This morning I read a fresh new copy of the *Irish Independent* over coffee in Bewley's Oriental Café in Grafton Street and gave Philip Wiseman an opinion. I said it looked like an invitation to incite a breach of the peace as well as a general unfriendliness. And then a telegram was dispatched to the *Irish Independent,* from a new post office in Ann Street.

Dear Sir,
Your article concerning the play *The Ginger Man* in your October 28, 1959, issue we consider a deliberate attempt to incite a breach of the peace. We are, therefore, giving you notice of our intention to protect our interests in the matter and to hold you directly responsible for any damages resulting from such a breach.

Yours faithfully,
Philip Wiseman, Director
Spur Productions Ltd.
Coventry House
London W. 1.

In the rest of the paper there was news of a warehouse fire stacked with wines and spirits in Liverpool. The ships, *Weybridge*, from Calcutta with tea, the *Fisko* from Alicante with tomatoes, the *Donau* from Antwerp with sand, the *Almaden* from Palma with locust beans. There was also renewed buoyancy of Gilt Edge Securities. In Dublin market two to three dozen lobsters and six boxes of herrings had arrived. There was an appeal for an old folks home to clean up the prison-like appearance of the front entrance hall. And there were fifty nine deaths and one birth in Dublin.

Following a walk through St. Stephen's Green, Philip Wiseman and myself mounted a bus for Enniskerry, a village nestled in the Dublin mountains. The bus making its way south through Donnybrook and Milltown. Past Dundrum and the asylum with its little innocent white door.

The bus emptied its passengers until, arriving at the outskirts of Enniskerry, there were only three of us left on the top of the bus. One, a person in dark regalia, seated in the back. I somehow felt the eyes and turned around. The bell rang for a stop. I turned again and the personage of the dark persuasion was gone.

In front of Enniskerry's Protestant church we dismounted, giving the open demeanor of visitors to a foreign country, climbing a steep hill and through an ancient graveyard. Tall cedars and pines. Dark low clouds and a sprinkle of rain.

We made for a hostelry in the town, and ordered two pints of draft stout and roast beef sandwiches in this dark interior. The bartender and a customer playing darts, mentioning the names of girls they knew from time to time. Outside the wind had got up and the trees were moaning. Inside, a coke fire, brown walls, the long dark mahogany of the bar glistening with brass porter taps. One sadly reflecting that even these would, when a meeting of old or new friends came to blows, be used in the battle to bring unconsciousness to the innocent.

Windy uneasiness swept through this dark afternoon. Night was falling. As the bus bumped back to Dublin, weak winking lights popped on in the little suburban houses. All like candy boxes. It was cold. Harsh sight of Dublin buildings. A little group marched along the street. Their faces bitten, thin lipped and gray.

Entering Jury's Hotel. Getting keys from the porter. Waiting for the elevator. I looked as I often did for reassurance from the poster of *The Ginger Man*, which had read:

GAIETY

The Dublin play that startled London. Spur Productions Ltd. in association with The Dublin Globe Theatre Company

Present

Richard Harris

in

THE GINGER MAN

by

J. P. Donleavy

with

Rosalie Westwater
Godfrey Quigley
Genevieve Lyons

There are two plays in London through which blows the wind of genius. One of them is *The Hostage*, the other is *The Ginger Man*.

—HAROLD HOBSON, *The Sunday Times.*

The poster was gone. There were dark looks everywhere. The brown interior was browner. Eyes avoided eyes. New customers were coming in for whom there seemed some welcome. I told Philip Wiseman I would see him at the theater and would stop off at the Bailey for a drink on the way.

As I set forth from the hotel there was a personage in the dark regalia reading his breviary as he paced back and forth in front of the entrance. Farther away on the street corner I saw a young clean cut type standing with arms folded next to a motor scooter. As I passed he leaped on this machine and roared off in the direction of Grafton Street, which was also the direction of the Gaiety.

I went up these so familiar streets. Past silversmiths with their windows bulging with richness. Across the road where there was a polite tea and coffee house which now was no more. The work folk had gone home. The evening folk were coming out to the sparse pub life.

The Bailey's bar had collected little knots of people. Whitecoated waiters went to and fro. Some hand seemed to pull me and I said to John Ryan that I felt that I ought to be moving toward the Gaiety.

As we turned the corner of Duke Street into Grafton a white faced Wiseman was coming down the opposite side of the street at an apprehensive pace, calling across the cobbles, "They're closing the show."

Three figures shot into the back alley of the Gaiety. And as Wiseman and I made our way backstage a voice shouted after us, "What did I tell you, the Archbishop is closing the show, his secretary is up in the office right now with Mr. Elliman."

Wiseman and I made for the stairs. Rapping on the door of Mr. Elliman's office they said inside, "Who is it." Wiseman said, "It's Mr. Wiseman and Mr. Donleavy." A voice inside said to us outside, "Would you wait a few minutes." Wiseman said, "We'll wait."

Five minutes passed, the door opened and we were ushered in. A shallow faced, quiet man was introduced and we shook hands with a Father Nolan, secretary to the Archbishop of Dublin. Mr. Elliman said, "The show is having its last performance tonight. Since there are so many people waiting outside, this evening's performance will be held but will be the last."

A brief moment of silence and these two American figures withdrew. Passing backstage and out the stage door, moving, as usual, like visiting tourists to the country who found the customs and way of life, Greek. Knowing, of course, it was Irish backed by German ingenuity.

In front of the theater thronged a rather pushing public. The lobby was jammed. Along side the queue for the box office shuffled a bowler hatted figure, wasted, hawk nosed, rheumy eyed, who muttered a strange little song.

> He was a chancer
> He was a cad.
> He was a rogue
> He was a dad.

Up the soft carpets and into this long gracious bar of the Gaiety Theatre. John Ryan, Philip Wiseman and myself sat at a table. The last performance of *The Ginger Man* in Dublin had begun. The bar empty save for these three customers who were eyed by the barmaids with silent hostility.

John Ryan, long a native of the country, said it was the first time in the history of the Irish theater that a play had been stopped. Both he and Philip Wiseman suggested to the author that he get up on the stage at the final curtain and announce to the audience that this was the last performance and the play was being withdrawn. I demurred. Ryan said, "Well, you better get in touch with the papers before they do."

Alas two reporters were already in the lobby with a statement from the theater.

> The management of the Gaiety announce that the run of *The Ginger Man* will be discontinued after tonight's performance because of the lack of cooperation by Spur Productions Ltd., of London, who refused to make cuts as demanded by the management on Monday.

John Ryan said he would put me onto the correspondent of the *Daily Mail* and went to call from a booth downstairs in the lobby. He came back and said he had them on the phone.

I went down the stairs. There were silent groups standing in the lobby, their eyes following me into the telephone booth. More reporters collecting in the lobby. I saw John Ryan lurking on the staircase to see that I was not molested, which chilled me somewhat. Surely the Irish public would never attack a visitor.

Wiseman, Ryan and myself went back to see the final minutes of the play. Coming out with the audience who flocked into the bar. A photographer approached and asked us to go down and pose in front of the theater.

Cold and dark outside. A little warmth in the windows of the pub across this South King Street. The photographer suggested we look stricken in this Somaliland. He followed us backstage to get pictures of the cast. Harris was in his dressing room surrounded by people. A bottle of refreshment on his table. A loud chatter of voices in the hallways. A man came out, said there could be no pictures in the theater. Cast then trooped outside again around to the front of the house where we stood coldly in the windy street. And as the flash bulbs popped, out of the theater stepped the Archbishop's secretary who passed whitefaced up the street. As the man of the dark persuasion went by, Harris said, "There goes a battleship."

A sad group made ways back to Jury's Hotel. In Wiseman's room we made telephone calls to London. We were told that Mr. Tony Walton's line in London was out of order. We tried other numbers and found that phones were out of order all over London. Great gray gates seemed to be closing. However, the bedroom door flew open and in stepped Richard Harris, a bottle of refreshment in his fist.

We asked for sandwiches and while they were delayed Richard Harris spoke of previous theatrical terror in Dublin. How the public would ransack the seats doing the worst damage to the better quality materials, set fire to the stage and while it burned, beat the bejesus out of the author.

A boy in a white coat peeked in the door. Asking were we the gentlemen as wanted the sandwiches. And what variety was being requested. Ham. He would ask the chef but he might be in his bed. Voices were raised and the boy left saying he would see what he could do.

More attempts to phone London, all lines still out of order. The gates got bigger and darker. Harris sat on the bed. Wiseman on his dressing table. The moon was out across the top of the four courts. Clouds still racing over the sky. Faint sound of the Belgian National Anthem as its station closed down for the night.

7

A black hand tightening over the world. Suddenly the smiles shut down. Corners of the mouth were sour and eyes blank. Favor withdrawn.

Breakfast time. The lobby filled and busy. Whispers and huddled shoulders. These dark spinster waitresses in their black garb and chalk white faces. Granite walls outside, drying in the morning sun. A priest with rabbit ears. A porter fat faced whose sister in law might be a bridge champion. And feet taking newly polished boot leather out the swing doors.

Two overcoated figures, cameras slung over shoulders, come through the door. A man standing in the corner of the lobby. Eyes looking at this playwright, as I collected my bill.

In Philip Wiseman's room the phone began to ring. Knocks on the door. People with pads came in. Reporters from the papers. The room was filling. The room was full. Smoke rising from cigarettes. The crowd pushed into the hall and finally overflowing down it and into my room.

Richard Harris surrounded, took a seat in the middle of my bed and announced, "This play has ruined my life and health, wrecked my marriage and nearly killed me. But I think it's a classic."

The situation in the hotel was becoming untenable. There was an exodus to the Bailey restaurant in Duke Street. Already on the newsstand the headlines of a London newspaper,

"THE GINGER MAN" OFF AFTER THREE NIGHTS

The Bailey was jammed. Desmond MacNamarra, the Irish sculptor seated at the bar, next to him, Brendan Behan, Irish playwright, both of them sipping vintage soda water. Behan announcing, "This is a sad day for this country. My uncle wrote the National Anthem and he might just as well have written, 'We Ain't Got No Bananas.' "

Patrick Kavanagh, Irish poet, appeared in the front entrance, arms stretched wide, head back, "The city's alive. Breathing. Donleavy's taken over where Yeats and the rest failed. The city lives again." Naturally no one present had seen the play.

Several nondescripts were edging into the limelight of the flash bulb. Tony Walton finally got through to Philip Wiseman after six hours of attempted phone calls, having been told the phone at the Bailey had been out of order for two years.

A reporter came from the phone and said that his editor had just rung him from London where he had heard I was trying to escape from Ireland and was hiding out under an assumed name at the Bailey.

Richard Harris announced he was going to see the Archbishop. And if that didn't succeed he would fly with the script to the Pope in Rome. But from the Archbishop's secretary came the reply that if he were in need of spiritual advice or aid they would recommend someone to whom he could go.

Philip Wiseman and I went to a Georgian house in the north of Dublin. We talked to a calm man behind a sea of desk. Yes, one could sue the Church. But stepping out into a thronged street of these rough dark faces, a dark tide. Drown you.

O'Connell Street filling with evening laden buses. The tomb of the General Post Office where the derelict stand rubbing thin shoes on the worn cement. Crouching, shawled women peeking out of their darkness to ask, "Sixence for the nice bunch of violets."

Making a way south, O'Connell Street Bridge, Westmorland Street. Memories of a Dublin which could ache with loneliness as one searched the lanes and snug bars across town looking for familiar faces. Often to go back to barren cold college rooms and lay fetal in the bed, feet searching for some tropical spark from somewhere.

The Irish laugh and sing. They raggedly march and sometimes pray. They even have eyes and ears and pumping parts as they walk backwards into the world. And three Finns on the bridge play the mechanical musical machine. Standing solemn, waiting, faceless and blond.

Wiseman and I met his stage manager and assistant. Always sad to part from people. One more thread gone, and less left. The bicycles were streaming up Grafton Street. Meter readers advancing pubwards. A poster at a newsstand.

DUBLIN PLAY IS STOPPED

Farther along in a narrow alley a newsboy wearing inch thick lens on eyes, toothless, tongues of shoes flapping in the low cold breeze. Had his own little sign which brought tears.

DANGERFIELD IS DEAD

For this last time up between the shop fronts of Grafton Street, the coffee smell and roasted bean of Bewley's Oriental Café. Down the narrow lane of Clarenden Street where they went under the iron arch through the sacred vestibule to kneel and pray in the incense. A darkling city. Touched with little candles of light, women's hearts.

In the Bailey we said goodbye to the folk who were now turning back into their own lives. They were laughing, some of them happily. Others rocking back on their heels. All around the coast of this country a gray-green sea. A lonely lighthouse. And a white ribbon flickering on the shore.

A suicidal man, who missed the oncoming traffic rather cleverly at times, drove us to the airport. Richard Harris hanging forward like a gigantic gorilla asleep. Mr. Wiseman too polite to ask for a reduction in speed. Crystals of rain. Our hospitable driver leaning in close to the front glass making out the way ahead. Which was noted with some concern to be confused.

Motor birds on the runway. Moist green way out on the dark country fields. The engines were roaring. In Dame Street in Dublin, a man hummed a little tune.

> O what
> O what
> Tell me what
> Can I say.

The Ginger Man

THE GINGER MAN was first presented by Spur Productions, Ltd., at the Fortune Theatre, London, on September 15, 1959, with the following cast:

SEBASTIAN BALFE DANGERFIELD   *Richard Harris*
MARION DANGERFIELD   *Wendy Craig*
MISS LILLY FROST   *Isabel Dean*
KENNETH O'KEEFE   *Ronald Fraser*

And presented by Spur Productions, Ltd., in association with the Dublin Globe Theatre Company at the Gaiety Theatre, Dublin, for three performances, first on October 26, 1959, with the following cast:

SEBASTIAN BALFE DANGERFIELD   *Richard Harris*
MARION DANGERFIELD   *Genevieve Lyons*
MISS LILLY FROST   *Rosalie Westwater*
KENNETH O'KEEFE   *Godfrey Quigley*

Both productions were directed by Philip Wiseman
And designed by Tony Walton

ACT ONE

SCENE 1

June in a warm year. A south suburb of Dublin City. In the house that SEBASTIAN DANGERFIELD *rents, he sits in a stuffy arm chair, feet folded on a stool, hands gently crossed in his lap. He watches three chairs in front of him in which are signs: twelve o'clock, three o'clock, six o'clock. That large celestial telescope stands lonely at the window. On an orange box sits an old Gramophone. On the wall are three pictures of ships in distress. The rays of the sun shine just past the chair with the twelve o'clock sign. And a trolley car roars past the window and screeches to a halt up the street. Shadows pass the window. One stops, bends and peers in. Then a sudden loud rapping on the door.* DANGERFIELD *freezes. Slowly he eases out of the chair to floor, crouches and waits.*

O'KEEFE [*More knocking, harsh Boston voice outside the door*] Open up, I know you're in there. It's me.

DANGERFIELD [*Peeking over chair*] Who's me.

O'KEEFE Me. Open up.

DANGERFIELD [*Going to door*] Why, my dear Kenneth, didn't you say it was you.

O'KEEFE I said it was me.

DANGERFIELD So you did, Kenneth, so you did. [O'KEEFE *enters*] I'm just a little nervous this morning [*Looking over shoulder at the sun on the three chairs*] or is it afternoon.

O'KEEFE [*Pointing at three chairs*] What's that.

DANGERFIELD [*Mock Irish accent*] You wouldn't be knowing now what that was, now would you offhand.

O'KEEFE [*Eyeing* DANGERFIELD *suspiciously. Stands mumchance, deerstalker on his head, eye patch on one eye, fur collared greatcoat and high laced boots*] What is it.

DANGERFIELD A clock.

O'KEEFE You gone Asiatic.

DANGERFIELD [*Rubbing hands between knees in a paroxysm*] More. [*Laughs*] More, more of same. Can't get enough. Not enough. Must have more.

O'KEEFE Where's Marion.

DANGERFIELD She'll be back.

O'KEEFE [*Opening a cupboard*] You got any real food.

DANGERFIELD   I beg your pardon, that sheep's head simmering cost me sixpence.

O'KEEFE   Can't we eat something real.

DANGERFIELD   I assure you that head was only lately munching grass. It even has two eyes.

O'KEEFE   That all you got to eat.

DANGERFIELD   Kenneth, you're welcome to whatever I possess.

O'KEEFE   Which is nothing.

DANGERFIELD   I wouldn't put it that way. I think you wear too many tight clothes in this town of temptation. [*The wide eyes of* DANGER-FIELD]

O'KEEFE   I haven't had these clothes off for three months. Since I've been here, everything has been down and these guys at Trinity think all Americans are loaded with dough, and I'm starving. You get your check yet.

DANGERFIELD   Going to see about it Monday.

O'KEEFE   If mine doesn't come I'll croak. Hey, any loose women around here.

DANGERFIELD   The beauty of the world passes here, Kenneth.

O'KEEFE   [*Peering in telescope*]   Ever see any women with this.

DANGERFIELD   Heavenly bodies only.

O'KEEFE   Tubs of fat Irish lard.

DANGERFIELD Unfair words.

O'KEEFE I can't even find out where they hold my Greek lectures. But I'm too hungry to study anyway. Much as I like your company, Dangerfield, I'd prefer it on a full stomach. With that English accent of yours you ought to be able to get some credit.

DANGERFIELD [*Smile of benignity*] I've got credit, Kenneth [*Horizontal hand held under eyes*] right up to here and I can just see out.

O'KEEFE You couldn't get credit wearing those clothes.

DANGERFIELD [*Taking a moment of gentle contemplation. A holding up of the singular index digit*] Danger desires credit. Wait. [*Using the tricky skip once*, DANGERFIELD *mounts the stairs. From above a sound of tearing.* O'KEEFE *with a step back folds arms on chest.* DANGERFIELD *slowly descending, a pink volume of scarf around the pearly neck*] Kenneth, how do I look in Trinity's rowing pink.
  [DANGERFIELD *slowly placing sunglasses in front of his eyes*]

O'KEEFE You shrewd bastard, I must admit it looks good.

DANGERFIELD Always best to provide a flippant subtlety when using class power. Now we'll see about a little credit.
  [DANGERFIELD *steps out into the streets of strife*]

O'KEEFE [*To the cupboard. Puts a slack hand on a piece of stale bread and gnaws it. A general nosing into all recesses. Picks up a pile of letters. Reads.*] Dear Sir, we beg to remind you of your account now outstanding of eight pounds sixteen shillings and will be obliged for an early settlement of same. [*Leafs through letters. Emits the whistles on the high note and comes slowly down to low. With a hand slapping them back on the mantel. Stretches out his hands and flaps from wrists*] Whoo hooo.

DANGERFIELD [*Entering laden and victorious. Extracting a bottle from box by neck. Holds it up*]   The large size. Kenneth, I've always been put off by half bottles of anything.

O'KEEFE   How you do it, Dangerfield, I don't know. The first time I went looking for credit they told me to come back with a letter from my bank manager.

DANGERFIELD   It's the blue blood, Kenneth.

O'KEEFE   Where's the food. What made you get all that damn booze.

DANGERFIELD   Dear Kenneth, to warm us up. I think in spite of the sun a tricky cold front is on its way from the arctic. [*Brings forth chunk of cheese and loaf of bread*] Let there be bread. Let there be cheese.

O'KEEFE   Let there be fury when Marion gets back.

DANGERFIELD   Kenneth, these English wives are great. Know their proper place. Wear cheerful chains at the stove.

O'KEEFE   [*Getting up to cheese and bread*]   How you do it, Dangerfield, I don't know. I'm hungry and celibate. And virgin.

DANGERFIELD   Take a wife, she's got to let you touch flesh as a matter of common law. Oh yes, I know the law. [*Opening and pouring from gin bottle*]

O'KEEFE   [*Making a sandwich*]   All I want is my first woman. Plenty of time to get snowed under with a wife and kids. Sometimes I think the only work I'm suited for is cooking. One summer when I was working in Newport, I thought of giving up classics to become a cook.

DANGERFIELD   A noble calling. [*Points to boiling pot*] How about that head in there, make something nice out of that. Hee, hee, Kenneth, do you think you're sexually frustrated and maladjusted and that lust has disturbed your imagination.

O'KEEFE Yeah.

DANGERFIELD You'll find opportunities in this fine land.

O'KEEFE For unnatural acts with farm animals. The only time I forget about it is when I'm hungry. When I eat I go mad. Read every book on sex. Did me no damn good. I repel women and there's no cure for that.

DANGERFIELD [*Leaning back in the calm early afternoon*] Patience now. No woman ever been attracted.

O'KEEFE [*Filling a glass*] Give me some of this gin, have some while it's free.

DANGERFIELD Never even held hands, Kenneth.

O'KEEFE A girl pressed against me once and I ran out of the room. She was too ugly. Another thing against me. I'm attracted toward beautiful women. Only thing is for me to grow old and not want it any more.

DANGERFIELD You'll want it more than ever.

O'KEEFE [*Confronts* DANGERFIELD] That's not true, is it.

DANGERFIELD [*Leaning further back in the calm of the afternoon*] Wooo hooo.

O'KEEFE I may as well die right now.

DANGERFIELD Nonsense, live on.

O'KEEFE Thanks.

DANGERFIELD My advice is always free. Until people need it.

O'KEEFE What's it like to get it steady.

DANGERFIELD Get used to it like most things.

O'KEEFE I could never get used to it.

DANGERFIELD You will.

O'KEEFE What's up with Marion.

DANGERFIELD She and the baby need a little rest. [*A generous replenishing of drink*]

O'KEEFE From you.

DANGERFIELD Could be worse.

O'KEEFE I think her old man must be wise to you. How did he screw you out of that nice little dowry of two hundred and fifty pounds. That interests me.

DANGERFIELD He just led me into his study and said sorry, son, things are a little tight at the moment.

O'KEEFE Should have said dowry or no marriage. He must have dough, an admiral. Give him the stuff, like to provide for Marion the way she's accustomed to. Get him to sail one of those rosy dreamboats of yours.

DANGERFIELD Too late. 'Twas the night before the wedding. I even refused a drink for strategy. That nice man waited a good five minutes after the butler left before pleading poverty.

O'KEEFE See, he's shrewd. Saved himself two hundred and fifty nicker notes. [*The pointing finger*] If you had been on your toes you could have told him you had Marion up the pole and with a birth imminent you needed a little nest egg. Now look at you. All you need to do is flunk your law exams and bingo.

DANGERFIELD I'm all right, Kenneth. Little money and everything's all right. Got a house, a telescope, keep track of the planets, a wife, a daughter.

O'KEEFE You mean you pay rent for a house. Stop paying rent and no house.

TWO BOYS [*Appearing at window, shadows through the curtain. Shouting in*] Jews. Jews.

O'KEEFE [*Pointing with a relaxed thumb*] That's what I like about this country. So open about hatreds. [*Shouts back*] Irish. Irish.

DANGERFIELD [*Getting up to bottle*] I think we need drinks, Kenneth. [*At a near church the Angelus bells ring*] Ah, the Angelus. [*Moves chair with six o'clock sign to catch a ray of sun*] Little error here, half an hour slow.

O'KEEFE [*Raising glass of gin*] This, Dangerfield, is your blood for which your family will starve and which will finally send you to the poorhouse. Should have played it cozy and married strictly for cash. Come in drunk, have a quick one and whoops, another mouth to feed. You'll be eating spaghetti as I had to as a kid, till it comes out of your ears. Or else you'll have to take your English wife and kids and screw back to America. [*Gets up, removes sign*] This thing's getting me nervous, people will think you're cuckoo. [*Rotating shoulders, calming the nerves*] Gee. I want a full sex life.

DANGERFIELD A nice round ambition.

O'KEEFE [*Confronting DANGERFIELD*] Do you know, at Harvard, I finally got Constance Kelly in my power. There was a girl who strung me along for two years till I found out what a fraud American womanhood was and I squeezed her right under my lascivious thumb. Boy, I used to love watching her cry. But I can't figure it out. She'd do anything but let me in. Holding out for wealth on Beacon Hill. Didn't want to get stuck on the bottom of the social ladder marrying me.

One of her own kind. God, she's right. [*Striding, picks up a curtain rod leaning against wall*] But do you know what I'm going to do. [*Pointing curtain rod at* DANGERFIELD] When I go back to the States, fat with dough, wearing my Savile Row suits with my black briar, M.G. and my man driving, I'm going to turn on my newly acquired English accent full blast. Pull up to some suburban house where she's married a mick, turned down by all the old Bostonians, and leave my man at the wheel. [*Striding*] I'll walk up the front path, knocking the kid's toys out of the way [*Raps wall*] with my walking stick and give the door a few impatient raps. She comes out. A smudge of flour on her cheek and the reek of boiled cabbage coming from the kitchen. I look at her with shocked surprise. I recover slowly and then in my best accent, delivered with devastating resonance, [*Long pause*] I say, Constance, [*Holding back aloof*] you've turned out just as I thought you would. Then I spin on my heel, give her a good look at my tailoring, knock another toy aside with my cane and roar away.

DANGERFIELD [*A cackle with a rub of the hands between the legs*] More. I tell you I want more. More of same. Whee. But supposing, Kenneth, you slip on a toy and break a backside bone.

O'KEEFE Never. [*Takes loaf of bread and tears off chunk with teeth*] And Constance's mother hated my guts. Thought I'd suck her down socially. Would open all my letters I'd write her daughter, and I'd sit in Widener thinking up the dirtiest stuff I could imagine, I think she loved them. I had to laugh thinking she'd read them and then have to burn them up. [*A large sweep of curtain rod through air*] I repel women. Even this winter down in Connemara visiting the old folks, my retarded cousin who looked like a cow wouldn't even come across. I'd wait for her to go out and get the milk at night and go with her. At the end of the field I'd try to nudge her into the ditch. I'd get her all breathless and saying she'd do anything if I'd take her to the States and marry her. I tried that for three nights running, standing out there in the rain up to our ankles in mud and cow flop, me trying to get her in the ditch, knock her down, but she was too strong. So I told her she was a zombie and I wouldn't take her to East Jesus. Have to get them a visa before you can touch an arm.

DANGERFIELD [*All smiles and help*]   Marry her, Kenneth.

O'KEEFE   Get tangled with that beast of burden for the rest of my days. Be all right if I could chain her to the stove to cook, but to marry the Irish is to look for poverty.

DANGERFIELD   I suggest the matrimonial column of the *Evening Mail* for you. Put no encumbrance. Man of means, extensive estates in West. Prefers women of stout build, with own capital and car for travel on Continent. No others need apply.

O'KEEFE   I want to leave my problem uncomplicated. [*Surveys room*] This sad room. Dark gloom. We live like beasts.

DANGERFIELD [*Reclines further in the sinking day, holds drink high*] Patience, Kenneth, we'll see the green grass some day. Inside the walls of the estate it'll be green all right. Nurse for baba. A little morning run, barefoot in the dew.

O'KEEFE   Running from the rent collector.

DANGERFIELD   Maybe that, too. But there's going to be a bit of the corporation law. And that thing they call investment banking. Oh, I'll see it all right. Secret is, Kenneth, got to watch the lust. Got to watch that. Never let it sneak up on you. Passion of the moment a disaster over the years. You are listening, Kenneth.

O'KEEFE   I'm listening.

DANGERFIELD [*The deep chuckling*]   Oh, I admit it, I slipped up once. Be changes though. Big changes. Some day. Sebastian Bullion Dangerfield. Chairman of Quids, Incorporated. Count on it. Change the interest rates. [*Leaning forward with the wide eyes*] Lower them. No. Make them higher. Forward with the rich.

O'KEEFE   I'm getting stinko.

DANGERFIELD Take off your coat and hat, Kenneth.

O'KEEFE Drink clouds the brain, I'm leaving. Anyway these clothes don't come off unless it's for an act of passion.

DANGERFIELD You're a man of strong convictions.

O'KEEFE Appetites is the word. So long.

DANGERFIELD Don't go. Stay. While the sun sinks.
[*Up to Gramophone*]

O'KEEFE And you with it. I'm going to read a book.

DANGERFIELD But listen to these girls sing.

[*Girls' choir singing "On an April Evening"*]

O'KEEFE [*Listens. Spins on heel*] So long.

[*Exits.* DANGERFIELD *hands folded on belly, watches* O'KEEFE *go. Peers in telescope, pats it. Reclines in his chair, trusty bottle by his trusty hand. Music and light fade. Night. And morning comes.* MARION *enters with bag and baby bundled in her arms. She stands surveying room and sleeping* DANGERFIELD. *She exits up stairs with baby and returns, stands over* DANGERFIELD *and tugs at him*]

DANGERFIELD [*Shouts in sleep*] All engines full astern. [*Abruptly awakens*]

MARION Why weren't you at the station to meet me. Look at you. Gin. This is horrid. I had to take a taxi out here, do you hear me. A taxi.

DANGERFIELD [*Covers face in hands, a walrus groan*] For God's sake have some patience and let me explain everything.

MARION I say, explain. Explain what. There's nothing to explain, it's all quite evident. [*Holds up gin*]

DANGERFIELD All right, I'm not blind, I see it.

MARION Oh dear, this is frightful. Why, you honestly are a cad. If Mummy and Daddy could see what I've got to come back to. What are you doing on the table.

DANGERFIELD Goat dance.

MARION Who's been here.

DANGERFIELD Shut up.

MARION I won't shut up and don't look at me like that. Who bought this drink. Where did you get the money. Didn't meet me at the train. Why, answer me.

DANGERFIELD Shut up. Be quiet for the love of Jesus. The alarm didn't work.

MARION You're a liar. You were drinking, drinking, drinking. The mess, the filth.

DANGERFIELD Shut up.

MARION Who paid for all this. You had smelly O'Keefe out here. I know you did. [Sniffs] I can smell him.

DANGERFIELD Just leave me alone.

MARION Did you pay the milk.

DANGERFIELD Yes, and now, sweet Jesus, shut up, my head.

MARION [To mantel, holds up bill] So you paid it, did you. Here it is. Here it is. Exactly where I left it and the money gone. Lies. You blighter. You nasty blighter.

DANGERFIELD Call me a bugger, I can't stand the gentility on top of the yelling.

MARION Oh, stop it, stop it. I don't intend to go on living like this, do you hear me. Your lies. One after the other and I was trying to get my father to do something for us and I come back to this.

DANGERFIELD Your father. Your father is a sack of excrement, genteel excrement, as tight as they come. What was he doing, playing battleship in the tub. [MARION *lunging, slaps* DANGERFIELD *across jaw.* DANGERFIELD *slaps her back. Upstairs, a child's crying.* DANGERFIELD *makes for stairs*] I'll kill that kid, God damn it, I'll kill it, if it doesn't shut up.

MARION [*Screaming and grabbing* DANGERFIELD *at stairs*] You madman, leave her alone, I'll get the police. I'll divorce you, you blackguard, coward, coward. [*On stairs*] No, you bastard.

DANGERFIELD [*Comes down stairs, hands over ears. Door slams up in bedroom*] Vulgar blood in her somewhere. Mother's father worked in a shop. Bad blood leaks out. And I ought to get out. One way on the boat. Let her rot up there. Face the facts of life. A few days without food will weaken her. [*Slowly to wall, fists clenched, raising and pressing them toward ceiling; shouts*] I'm still a young man in the late twenties. The father of a child. They tell you. Caution you. Don't get married without money. Without a degree. They're right. [*Sits, the sad, sorrowing sit*] And the world was made for me. Here long before I arrived. And they spent years getting it ready. [DANGERFIELD, *that sinner, looks up at heaven*] Dear God. Give me strength. To put. My shoulder. To the wheel. And push, like the rest.

[*Curtain*]

SCENE 2

A week later in the One Mohammed Road. DANGERFIELD *stands at the window, arms folded across chest. A hearse and horses go by.*

DANGERFIELD [*Sings softly*]
        Sleep thy last sleep
        Free from care and sorrow
        Rest where none weep
        And we too, shall follow.
[*A rubbing of the hands, and hoarsely whispering*] Green greedy mouth is dead. Green greedy mouth is dead.

MARION [*Comes down stairs*] You ghoul.

DANGERFIELD [*Cheerful*] You don't like that.

MARION No.

DANGERFIELD You don't like to see them taken away. Free from care and sorrow.

MARION Why don't you go with them.

DANGERFIELD I am. Starting next week I'm taking up the rear on my black rented two wheeler.

MARION [*Making for front door*] The baby is asleep. I'm going into town to shop. [*Leveling the housewife eyes at* DANGERFIELD] And I can't bear much more.

DANGERFIELD Of me.

MARION And a broken lavatory.

DANGERFIELD Oh, they just put in some harmless rubber pipes. Guess they rotted. Skully the landlord is an economizer.

[MARION *exits tight faced, steps into the street of passersby.* DANGER-FIELD *from his little orange crate of books extracts a bottle of gin. With bottle at lips, a head peeks in.* O'KEEFE *enters wrapped up tightly. Deerstalker squarely on head, a satchel slung over his shoulder.*]

O'KEEFE Just what I thought.

DANGERFIELD Come in, Kenneth. Have a little something.

O'KEEFE [*Indian chief hand held high*] Nothing.

DANGERFIELD What's the satchel for.

O'KEEFE I'm leaving.

DANGERFIELD I say, Kenneth.

O'KEEFE Leaving. Getting out. Do you want some ties. Bow ties. [O'KEEFE *pulls out handful of ties from pocket and chucks them to* DANGERFIELD]

DANGERFIELD Thanks. Ah, I need a little color. But this is sad news, Kenneth.

O'KEEFE I think it's great news. I'm off to France. Got a job.

DANGERFIELD Can only say I'm delighted, Kenneth. Join me in a bit of this fine liquid, good for bowels, chastity, repression, giggles, gangrene and glowering. [*Joining himself in a drink*] So you're really leaving.

O'KEEFE   In exactly an hour from now. And if you're watching very carefully, you'll see me fill this sack with four packs of cigarettes. [*Taps pack*] Got one pair of socks, two shirts, a bar of soap and a towel. Maybe a spit on a shoe, little wipe [*A foot up on chair*] with the sleeve. Then a cup of coffee in Bewley's alone, I might add, unless you've got money to pay for your own. Then if you're still watching, I'll saunter down O'Connell Street past the Gresham, take a sharp right at the corner and you'll see my slender form disappear into a green bus marked airport and finis. You see what I mean.

DANGERFIELD   Kenneth, I'm baby sitting at the moment but I wish you God's speed. [*Points to jug slung with string on o'keefe's back*] What's the jug for.

O'KEEFE   This. [*Releasing it*] It's yours. Do you know what this is. I'll tell you. A year ago I was full of big ideas. Things like rugs and easy chairs in my college rooms with the footman to make breakfast and a fire. I was going to have a few paintings on the walls and have some of those pukka public schoolboys up to tea to look at my objets d'art. I thought things would be like Harvard, only I'd be able to crack into a few of the clubs as I was never able to do at Harvard. I felt it would be best to start the furnishing with a few bedroom items, so I bought the jug for one and four and that was that. Needless to say, I never cracked or rubbed shoulders with these public schoolboys. They talk to me but think I'm a little coarse.

DANGERFIELD   Pity.

O'KEEFE   Yeah, pity. I'll give you the jug to remember my by when I'm gone from the ould sod, sacked in with some lovely French doll. Jesus. If I had your accent I'd be set here. That's the whole thing, accent. I'm beat even before I get my nose in. Anyway it won't stop me in France.

DANGERFIELD Kenneth, I don't want to be personal—

O'KEEFE Yeah, I know. Where did I get the money. That, my friend, is an affair of state which is top secret.

DANGERFIELD Pity.

O'KEEFE This is the last I'll ever see of this dreary setup. Never even had a fire in my fireplace. I'm twenty seven years old and I feel like sixty. I don't know, I think I'd die before I'd go through this again. Wasted time. No degree. I think I got to four Greek lectures and two in Latin in the last six months. Trinity is tough, not like Harvard. These boys work. [With a hunch of shoulders into the mouse position] I'll be as poor as a church mouse for the rest of me days.

DANGERFIELD Now now, cheer up.

O'KEEFE One thing I'm sure of, I'm nothing but a hungry sex starved son of a bitch. Cooking is my trade. [Expands his arms to world] But I'm out. On the move again. Best feeling there is. How does it feel, Dangerfield, to be loaded with wife and child. It's a problem for you even to get out the door.

DANGERFIELD One manages. Be better days. I promise you that.

O'KEEFE Be the looney bin.

DANGERFIELD Did you know, Kenneth, that Trinity undergraduates get preferential treatment in Irish mad houses.

O'KEEFE Good, you'll need it.

DANGERFIELD [Offering O'KEEFE a glass of gin] Take this, Kenneth, soften your heart.

O'KEEFE Thanks. But you know, Dangerfield, I don't dislike you as you might think. I've got a soft spot somewhere. [Takes a nip of the spirit]

I can't wait to get to Paris. [*The glow of vision*] Maybe I'll make a rich contact on the plane. Rich Yankee girl coming to Europe for culture who wants to see the points of interest.

DANGERFIELD And perhaps your own, Kenneth.

O'KEEFE Yeah, if she saw that I'd make sure she saw nothing else. Why is it that I can't have something like that happen to me. Like getting in with a theatrical crowd, a lot of beautiful women looking for guys like me who haven't got looks but brains and wit. I've got charm. Make a magnificent husband. [*A raised hard fist*] And I've been beaten, beaten.

DANGERFIELD Nonsense.

O'KEEFE I think, looking back, that the only time I've ever been happy was in the Army.

DANGERFIELD You're overwrought, Kenneth.

O'KEEFE It's true. Except for being stationed down South with those miserable Southerners. And I'd hear all those bastards groaning about the lousy food and gee I miss my mom's cooking and I told them my mother could never cook this good. They wanted to beat me up. The food almost made me weaken to the point of an Army career until I discovered you could get this food outside if you made money.

DANGERFIELD Talking about money, Kenneth.

O'KEEFE [*Jaw clamping. A low grown of discontent*] Yeah.

DANGERFIELD Look, Kenneth, I know this is rather an impromptu request, but could you possibly let me have ten quid.

O'KEEFE I'm getting out of here.

DANGERFIELD Beg you, Kenneth, stay. Don't let me drive you like this out of my little oasis of refreshment and joy. Kenneth, ten quid, promise to have it to you in four days, be right there when you arrive. No question about that. Airtight loan. My father's sending me a hundred quid Tuesday. I say, Kenneth, airtight, your money is safer with me than in your pocket, may get killed on the plane.

O'KEEFE   Thoughtful of you.

DANGERFIELD   Make it eight.

O'KEEFE   You're making it eight. I'm making it nothing. I haven't got it. I'm hounded through streets, beaten to the wall, scratching up pennies, and for the first time in months I've got a few beans to have a bath and haircut and get out and you come and push me to the wall again. Jesus, why do I know poor people. They smell it when you've got money. (DANGERFIELD *mumchance with evil eye*) All right, all right, watch me, go ahead. Yeah, you're right, I've got money. You've put me up, fed me, all right, but now you're beating me.

DANGERFIELD   I've said nothing, Kenneth.

O'KEEFE   [*Reaching into his pocket*]   I come out here to say goodbye. [*Takes two large white five pound notes from his roll, flicks them to* DANGERFIELD] And it costs me ten pounds. Well damn it, take it [*Throws fivers*] for Christ's sake. And get drunk. Throw it away, tear it up, do anything but there's one God damn thing, I want that money there when I arrive. You've beaten me.

[DANGERFIELD *delicately retrieves money from floor*]

DANGERFIELD   [*Tucking fivers into shirt pocket*]   Now Kenneth, no need to feel this way.

O'KEEFE   I'm a fool. If I were rich I could tell you to go to hell.

DANGERFIELD   Kenneth, you lack love.

O'KEEFE [*Hand in sky*]   Poor crippling the poor.

DANGERFIELD   Poverty is temporary, Kenneth.

O'KEEFE   With you it may be but I'm not fooling myself, I know damn well I can go down forever and stay. This whole damn setup exists to keep me in penury. And I can't stand any more. I had to break my ass to get this dough. Work. Use my head.

DANGERFIELD [*That plaintive voice of reason*]   I'd like to know how you did it, Kenneth.

O'KEEFE   Sure you do, here. Read this. [*Pulling sheets from his pocket. Hands them to* DANGERFIELD]

DANGERFIELD   Rather scruffy, Kenneth.

O'KEEFE   Read it, go ahead. A circular letter to all my relatives in Ireland. Loud. Does me good just to hear it.

DANGERFIELD [*Reading*]   Dear Relative. This is my position. [O'KEEFE *adjusts himself against wall, leans back, thumbs in armpits, head to heaven*] I am going to make a public stink to the newspapers that I am starving in the old country, ignored by my relatives. To avoid this shame send me money by return. Yours truly, without scruples, Kenneth O'Keefe.

O'KEEFE [*Taking a letter from his pocket*]   Here's the reply from Father Moynihan. He's the one my mother gave me the shoes for. Jesus, will I ever forget this bastard. How did God ever create the Irish. Read this.

DANGERFIELD [*Reading*]   I find myself incapable of even addressing you since this is the most despicable letter I have ever had the displeasure to receive, and it amounts to blackmail. It is difficult to believe that you are the product of a good Catholic home or for that matter, my nephew. You are an insult to the American people. However, there seems always to be an element, the scum and evil minds bred in the gutter, who are a threat to those decent people who have devoted their lives and sweat to rearing ungrateful blackguards. How dare you threaten me with such insolence. It is only that you are my sister's son that I have not brought your filthy correspondence to the attention of the police. Enclosed are your thirty pieces of silver and let it be understood that I shall not tolerate hearing from you again. While here as my guest you violated my hospitality and also the dignity to which I am accustomed in this parish. I am also aware of your efforts to corrupt the purity of one of my parishioner's daughters. Let me warn you, should I again hear anything of you, I shall send the details of this execrable outrage to your mother. J. Moynihan, P. P. Kenneth, this is fantastic. What did you do down there.

O'KEEFE [Hands in air] Oh me, I don't want to remember. Told the girl who worked in the library she ought to liberate herself. Probably told that old bastard in the confessional that I had touched her arm. Same old thing. Nothing new. Same damn pattern, despair, frustration, misery. That sneaky old fraud with his bottles of whiskey and dignity neatly misered away. I was never so damn cold in all my life. House was like a morgue. Wouldn't put an extra piece of turf on the fire. Soon as he found out I hadn't a bean and I'm living on his charity, there's no fire at all and the cigarettes that were lying around the house disappear and the housekeeper watches the kitchen like a hawk. However, no cause to be bitter, that letter of abuse arrived with ten quid in it. When I asked him for money before he sent me half a crown.

DANGERFIELD [Rubbing of the pink hands] One thing that can be said for you, Kenneth, you're resourceful. If you ever go back to America, you'll be rich.

O'KEEFE I want money here. Stay here till my last breath if I had the necessary nicker. But what tight bastards. Stay out of the countryside. After my visit with the Reverend Moynihan I thought I'd see what could be had in the way of hospitality on my father's side. A bunch of damn phonies. But when I first arrived they gave me the best of what they had but it was embarrassing. I'd be sitting at the other end of the table with a tablecloth and napkin and they'd be gobbling off the bare boards. I'd say, look why can't I be the same as you and eat off the bare boards, and they'd tell me, oh no, you're from America and we want you to feel at home. They even kept the pigs and chickens outside which I didn't mind. But then they wondered when I'd be going and like a jerk I said I was broke. Boy, was that a quick change of scene. The chickens and pigs in the house, tablecloth and napkin gone. They even prodded me into church one Sunday, said the neighbors would talk. But I hung on till Christmas Eve when my uncle says now let's all kneel down and say the rosary. There I was, on hard, cold stone, mumbling Hail Marys thinking of the good atheist parties I was missing in Dublin. I beat it the next day after Christmas dinner. I thought it was the least I could do to eat the dinner.

DANGERFIELD   A fine concession.

O'KEEFE   I guess all I want out of this life is a decent fire in the grate, a rug on the floor and a comfortable chair to sit in and read. And just a few quid I don't have to slave for and mix with people with money, not, I may add, in your exact circumstances.

DANGERFIELD [*Joyful ears flapping*]   Woo hoo.

O'KEEFE   But, Jesus, when you don't have any money, the problem is food. When you have money, it's sex. When you have both, you want more. When you get more, you worry about health, whether you can get it up any more or a rupture or something. If everything is simply jake, then you're frightened of death and you start giving money to charity. [*Points out window*] Look out there at those faces, all stuck with the first problem and will be for the rest of their days.

DANGERFIELD   What's mine, Kenneth.

O'KEEFE   You just sail dreamboats. You think because you were born rich you're going to stay that way. Too many guys like me around waiting for a slip up. Get your degree, passport to security. Use contraceptives. If you get snowed under by kids you're whipped.

DANGERFIELD Woo hoo.

O'KEEFE Keep in with these rich Trinity students. They all like you. I'm crippled by my accent but as soon as I have my phonetics taped, watch my smoke. I'll come back from France a new man. Where's your sundial.

DANGERFIELD Having it repaired.

O'KEEFE Yeah. Time for me to go.

DANGERFIELD Me and my baba will see you off, Kenneth.

O'KEEFE Against my principles to have people see me off.

DANGERFIELD Just as you wish. I'd like to thank you for the money.

O'KEEFE Don't make it painful. Just send it to me. I'm counting on it. [Leaving] Let there be no bungling.

DANGERFIELD No bungling.

O'KEEFE So long.

DANGERFIELD Take care of yourself and wear armor.

O'KEEFE I want nothing between me and flesh the first time. God bless.

DANGERFIELD [Wags hand. Refills from his trusty bottle. Sings]
    Oh, the wine tavern street is the silliest
    Of the streets full of fury
    Oh the very very best
    For this moo from Missouri. Ding dong.

MARION [A package in her blond arms]   God.

DANGERFIELD   Ding dong.

MARION   Why don't you take some responsibility.

DANGERFIELD   Me big mountain of that.

MARION   I can smell the lavatory. Who's going to fix it.

DANGERFIELD   Marion, I beg of you. Do you want to give me ulcers.

MARION   Yes.

DANGERFIELD   Don't drive me up the wall over Irish plumbing, it's new to the country and the pipes got mixed.

MARION   And who'll pay.

DANGERFIELD   Skully out of his little gold egg.

MARION   And the smell, what are we going to do about that.

DANGERFIELD   It's just a healthy smell of life.

MARION   It's not. It's ugly.

DANGERFIELD   It's us.

MARION   It's you.

DANGERFIELD   As you wish.

MARION [Rattling with the pots, the nervous vein flames on her neck] The foulness of this place.

DANGERFIELD Take it easy, Maaa. It's just adjustment. Got to get used to it here.

MARION Children running barefoot in the streets in the middle of winter and men wagging their things at you from doorways.

DANGERFIELD Untruths. Lies.

MARION You weren't like this before we came to Ireland. This vulgar filthy country.

DANGERFIELD Easy now.

MARION I know now why they're only fit to be servants.

DANGERFIELD Oh, bitterness.

MARION You know it's all true. O'Keefe's been here. I can still smell him. America doesn't seem to help them. He's not even fit to be a servant.

DANGERFIELD I think Kenneth's a gentleman in every respect.

MARION He has the revolting lechery of an Irish peasant. And he tries to give the impression of good breeding. Watch him eating. It's infuriating. Grabs everything. That first time we had him to dinner he just came in as if we were servants and proceeded to eat even before I had time to sit down. And pulling hunks out of the bread. How can you be blind to these things.

DANGERFIELD [To telescope] Testing my sight.

MARION That damn stupid thing.

DANGERFIELD How dare you. How would you like it if I missed a comet.

MARION   We've only got thirty shillings left.

DANGERFIELD   Interesting foreign body here.

MARION   Did you hear me, we've got thirty shillings left.

DANGERFIELD   I heard you. Our good accents and manners will see us right. Didn't you know, Marion, they can't put Protestants in jail.

MARION   And to have my child raised among a lot of savage Irish and be branded with a brogue for the rest of her life.

DANGERFIELD   Marion, do you ever think of death.

MARION   No.

DANGERFIELD   Marion, do you ever think you're going to die.

MARION   Would you mind awfully stopping that sort of talk. You're in that nasty mood.

DANGERFIELD   Not at all.

MARION   You are. Coming down here every morning to watch the funerals of these wretched people. Dreadful and sordid. I think you get a perverse pleasure out of it.

DANGERFIELD [Pink hands in prayer]   Beyond this vale of tears, there is a life above, [Head to heaven] unmeasured by the flight of years and all that life is love.

MARION [Cooking]   You think you're frightening me with these sinister, boring and repulsive airs of yours.

DANGERFIELD [Outstretched arms of innocence]   For the love of Oliver, look at me. Look at my eyes. Go ahead, come on.

MARION   I don't want to look in your eyes.

DANGERFIELD   Honest globes they are.

MARION   You can't talk seriously about anything.

DANGERFIELD   I just asked you about death. Want to know how you feel, really get to know you. Or maybe you think this is forever.

MARION   Rubbish. You think it's forever, I know you do. You're not as flippant as this for your law lectures I notice.

DANGERFIELD   I'm very careful with my imagination.

MARION   Screaming in your sleep last night.

DANGERFIELD   I beg your pardon.

MARION   You were shouting how do I get out of this. And you thought there was a white thing in the corner. That's your careful imagination.

DANGERFIELD [Laughing]   Woo hoo.

MARION   You can laugh, but I think there's something serious at the root of it.

DANGERFIELD [Doing spider dance]   What's at the root. Can't you see I'm mad. Can't you see. Look. See. Madness. E. I'm mad. [Ogling and wagging tongue]

MARION [Wearily arranging foodstuffs, bread, salt, sugar and tea]   Always willing to clown but never to do anything useful.

DANGERFIELD [Peeks in telescope]   Ah, see a ridge of blue approaching from west. Marion, I think I'll go and study in the park.

MARION   Take the baby with you.

DANGERFIELD The pram is broken.

MARION Carry her.

DANGERFIELD She'll piss on my shirt.

MARION Take the rubber sheet.

DANGERFIELD How am I going to study watching her. She'll crawl into the pond.

MARION Can't you see I've got my hands full with all this, the mess. Look at the ceiling. And there you are with that damn telescope. Why don't you get Skully to fix that loathsome toilet. I know why. You're afraid of him, that's why.

DANGERFIELD [*Slight expansion of chest for bravery*] Not a bit of it.

MARION You are. All I have to say, Skully, and you're off up the stairs like a frightened rabbit, and don't think I can't hear you crawling under the bed.

DANGERFIELD Just tell me where my sunglasses are, that's all.

MARION You look for them. And you're wearing my sweater. I don't want you wearing my sweater.

DANGERFIELD I absolutely refuse to go out of this house without my sunglasses. [*Kicking at the helpless furniture*]

MARION Well, look.

DANGERFIELD [*Pointing at his face*] Do you want me to be recognized. Do you.

MARION I'd love it.

DANGERFIELD God damn this house. The size of a closet. Can't even find my foot in it. I'll break something.

MARION Don't you dare. You've done enough.

DANGERFIELD Silence.

MARION Who started the account in Howth. Who was the one who bought whiskey and gin. Who was.

DANGERFIELD I want my sunglasses.

MARION And pawned the fire irons. And the electric kettle.

DANGERFIELD [*With hunched shoulders, twisting hands grieflike on the chest*] Let us have Christian silence.

MARION Your sarcasm. Why do we have to live like this.

DANGERFIELD [*The pose of the supplicant beggar*] My glasses. [*Points to ceiling*] Up there the malodorous things, the punctured pipes. Hee hee, our lives are twisted.

MARION Yours is. Vulgar too.

DANGERFIELD [*Bravely straightens, shines his lamps to world. Holds chin high*] I'm cultured.

MARION From your chromium plated life in America.

DANGERFIELD I'm distinguished looking. Speak the king's English. Impeccably tailored. [*Looking down the perpendiculars*] Few little lines need attention.

MARION What rot. I don't know how I ever let you meet Mommie and Daddy.

DANGERFIELD Your Mommie and Daddy thought I had lots of money. And I, for that matter, thought that they had lots of money. Neither had nicker, no notes, no love.

MARION That's a lie, you know it's a lie. There never was a question of money until you started it.

DANGERFIELD All right, get the baby. I can't stand any more. I need a long trolley ride in the womb to take me out of this.

MARION Take you out. I'm the one who ought to be taken out. And it may be shortly, too.

DANGERFIELD What do you mean, shortly.

MARION Never mind.

DANGERFIELD [*Takes good lungful of air*] All right. Let's be friends.

MARION It's easy, isn't it. Just like that.

DANGERFIELD Pop'll be dead in autumn. We'll be rich. Big golden udder. Just wait till me big Q.C. [*Raps mantel*] Boy, what an udder that will be. I'll see justice gets done, by God. I'll put a stop to these outrages on private property. By God.

MARION Shut up.

DANGERFIELD Oh, so you don't want to see thievery put down. And fraud. And forgery. So.

MARION I'd be satisfied if you took a bath.

DANGERFIELD I beg your pardon. [*Delicately sniffs beneath a shyly lifted arm*] New mown hay.

MARION [*Investigating a bundle of wrapped newspapers. Screams*]   Oh God. What's this.

DANGERFIELD   I'm saving it.

MARION   One of those damn revolting sheep's heads. Get this revolting thing away.

DANGERFIELD   Don't you dare. I need that to nourish my brain. [*Takes newspaper covered head. Holds it in crook of arm. Gently sways*] Poor little head. [*Pats it*] Going to take you away from me. I need you to pass my exams. And grow a few curly hairs. [*To* MARION] Marion, do you like men with hairy chests.

MARION [*Slicing the bread. Laying plates for the late, late lunch*]   Yes.

DANGERFIELD   Biceps.

MARION   Oh, stop.

DANGERFIELD   How about the shoulders.

MARION   So that he can wear a suit.

DANGERFIELD   Would you say now, that I'm your man.

MARION   No.

DANGERFIELD [*Cocked arms. Inflates air pumps in chest*]   Look here a minute. I say. Look here.

MARION   No. Cut some more bread.

DANGERFIELD   Not a bad body. [*The one two spider skip to table*] Note the youthful use of legs.

MARION   About the only thing you can do. Cut the bread.

DANGERFIELD   Of course, darling.

MARION   Don't say that if you don't mean it.

DANGERFIELD   I mean it.

MARION   Doesn't sound like it.

DANGERFIELD [*Sits at table*]   Ah, nice white plates. Why don't we buy a radio. I think we need a radio.

MARION   Buy it with what.

DANGERFIELD   A system for people like us. Little a week.

MARION   Yes, and that could pay our milk bill.

DANGERFIELD   We can have milk, too.

MARION   Why don't you take a part time job then.

DANGERFIELD   I'm learning law.

MARION   Of course. Oh, yes.

DANGERFIELD   Do you want thievery to triumph. [*Reaches to feel* MARION] Come on, little kiss. On the lips.

MARION   Get away from me. And get another chair.

DANGERFIELD   Let's go to the cinema tonight.

MARION   Have you forgotten. We have a child you know.

DANGERFIELD [*Carrying chair, crashes it down*]   Shit.

MARION   Stop it. Stop it. Stop using that ugly word to me.

DANGERFIELD   Shit.

MARION   I'll leave this house. Use that language with your working class friends, but I shan't stand for it.

DANGERFIELD   Leave.

MARION   It's always like this. All our meals.

DANGERFIELD   What meals.

MARION   My God, what did I marry.

DANGERFIELD   You certainly didn't have to marry me.

MARION   I wish I hadn't. Father was right. You're a wastrel. You drink. Spend your time with wretched useless people.

DANGERFIELD   That's my business.

MARION   Yes, and will they help you to get on.

DANGERFIELD   Get on where. Where to.

MARION   To make something of yourself. You think it's easy, don't you. You'll never get a degree. Cheat on your exams. Don't look shocked. Don't think I don't know it. And then go and butter up your professors. How long do you expect to get away with it.

DANGERFIELD   Absurd.

MARION   You've insulted every friend I have. People who could have helped you. Do you think they'll help an absolute rotter, a rotter.

DANGERFIELD   Rotter. Me. Me, a rotter.

MARION   And a liar.

DANGERFIELD   Liar.

MARION   You needn't smirk. My friends could help us. Lord Gawk could have introduced you to a firm in London.

DANGERFIELD   What's stopping him.

MARION   You. Your insulting manner. You've ruined me socially.

DANGERFIELD   Don't blame me if your pukka friends ignore you now.

MARION   Blame you. My God, how can you say I can't blame you, when you called Lady Gawk a whore, ruined her whole party and shamed me. Blame you.

DANGERFIELD   The woman is stupid. A moral decadent.

MARION   And you haven't had a bath for a month. And you smell. [*Hand to brow*] Oh, God. What's happening to us. [*Head into hands, elbows on table*] What. We don't talk. We shout, we fight. You're never with me. I'm so cut off. You've never loved me.

DANGERFIELD   I say, stiff upper lip.

MARION   Don't mock me. Please. I've got feelings just as you have. I can't help being English. Nor can I help feeling desperate and alone. I don't want to fight and argue. What's going to become of us. And Felicity.

DANGERFIELD   [*Fingers playing piano on chest*]   I think maybe I'll slip out for a minute. [MARION *looking up slowly, eyes sad nor glad*] Just slipping out.

MARION   You've got money.

DANGERFIELD Money. Me. What money.

MARION You've got money.

DANGERFIELD What do you mean I've got money.

MARION God, all I'm asking for is that we be honest with each other. You're going out to get drunk. I stay in this dreary house day after day. You've got money and you're going out to get drunk.

DANGERFIELD What makes you think I've got money.

MARION [*Screaming*] Because you have.

DANGERFIELD Very well. I'll stay here.

MARION [*Shouting*] I want to be free instead of hiding behind these walls. With that hideous Skully coming alone here any time he wants to look for rent. Daddy was right. He was right about you.

DANGERFIELD Daddy. Daddy.

MARION He was.

DANGERFIELD Right. He was right. God's teeth, shut up. Daddy, Daddy. Sterile bastard. That Daddy of yours is merely a leech. On the Admiralty's bottom [*Shouting*] and a pompous lot of shit.

MARION I'm going to leave you.

DANGERFIELD You're going to leave me.

MARION I mean it.

DANGERFIELD Oh, you mean it.

MARION Yes, I do.

DANGERFIELD   Marion. I'm upset. Now do you know what upset means. It means that I'm capable of doing anything. I'll kill you here and now unless I'm given some peace. I want peace. You know what I want. [*Shouting*] Peace, God damn it.

MARION   Don't shout at me, I'm not afraid of you.

DANGERFIELD   You're afraid of me, Marion. It's better that way. You'll keep away from my hands.

[*Afternoon gets old and dark*]

MARION   You don't frighten me in the least.

DANGERFIELD   You're really upset. Blinking your eyes. Lie down, get you a little prussic acid to soothe your nerves.

MARION   Let me soothe yours. Just one little thing I'd like you to know while you've got that horrid grin on your face. I've wired your father. I told him that both my child and I were starving.

DANGERFIELD   [*All muscles tightening. The slow hard voice*]   You've made a big mistake, Marion. A big mistake. A big big one.

MARION   Don't.

DANGERFIELD   A big mistake. You're forcing decisions.

MARION   Don't for God's sake go on like this. I can't bear it.

DANGERFIELD   You had no right, absolutely no right. Do you understand. No right.

MARION   Stop it.

DANGERFIELD   What did you say. [MARION *weeps*] I repeat, what did you say. Answer me.

MARION   You're hideous.

DANGERFIELD   What did you tell him, God damn it.

MARION   I told you what I told him. [*Screaming*] That my child and I were starving.

DANGERFIELD   Cost you a pound to say that.

MARION   [*Child's cries from upstairs*] My baby has rickets. Because you've drunk every penny we get. You've slapped and punched me when I was pregnant. Threw me out of bed and pushed me down the stairs. You're hundreds of pounds in debt. Why shouldn't I tell him we're starving.

DANGERFIELD   You shouldn't have done that, Marion. Do you hear me.

MARION   What do you want me to do. Go on like this forever. Until there is no hope. Live on your dreams of becoming a great barrister when you never work and cheat on your exams. And you never intend to work. I know you don't. Spend your time in the slums. I hate this house. I hate it all, Ireland, everything in it. And left to cope with this wretched hole.

DANGERFIELD   Shut your damn mouth.

MARION   I won't.

DANGERFIELD   Shut it.

MARION   I won't.

DANGERFIELD [*Takes shade off lamp. Holds lamp by base*] Are you going to shut up.

MARION No.

DANGERFIELD [*Smashes off bulb of lamp on table*] Now shut up. You're rotten. Bloody British blood. Damn stupidity. Hear me. Go ahead, cry. You've done the one thing for which I would kill any man. You're a scheming slut. Did you hear what I said. I said you were a scheming slut.

MARION Don't say that to me. Please.

DANGERFIELD That wire cost you a great deal of money. Hear me. Money. Contact my father again and I'll strangle you.

MARION Oh, for God's sake stop it.

DANGERFIELD I'm driven mad. [*Waving clenched fists*] This on top of every damn thing. I want to tear this house down. Everything in it. I'll smash everything in it. You won't have a house then. You'll be in the gutter. You belong in the gutter. Your damn vulgar father. Slutty mother. And your uncle is a sniveling title sneak. Do you hear what they are. Human garbage and rubbish, not fit to be alive.

MARION Please, I beg of you to stop it.

DANGERFIELD Get out.

MARION Please, Sebastian.

DANGERFIELD Get out, God damn it. Do as I say. Get out or I'll strangle you here and now.

MARION What's made you like this.

DANGERFIELD You've made me like this. That's what. You.

MARION I haven't. You can't blame me. I'm sorry I wired your father. I'm sorry for it.

DANGERFIELD Get out.

MARION Can't you see I'm sorry. Can't you see anything.

DANGERFIELD I can't see a God damn thing. I'm mad and I'm blind. I'm mad.

MARION Please stop it. [*Walks toward* DANGERFIELD] I beg of you. Please stop.

DANGERFIELD Stay away. Get away from me. Jesus, what ever made me come to this damn country. I'm finished. Finished. Not a hope. A God damn snake can't live here. Nothing can live here. Every Christ botched thing on top of me. Every side. Every minute. What are you trying to do to me. Finish me for ever? Do I actually have to suffer this now. Do I. Will you shut up about work, study, work. I'm not going to work. Never. Hear that. Never. That wire cost you thousands. Damn you.

MARION How was I to know. Can't you see, even for a second, that I'm sorry for it. I didn't mean to do it. Can't you see I've been driven to·it.

DANGERFIELD Thousands.

MARION When you've left me here day after day in this sordidness. No gas, no hot water and the toilet and roof leaking. I'm the one to be angry and upset. But have I.

[*Baby's cries from upstairs*]

DANGERFIELD I don't want to hear it. Just stop that right now. I don't want to hear it. You've disinherited me.

MARION It won't be for years and years.

DANGERFIELD Shut up. I know when it will be.

MARION It will. You'll wait for years.

DANGERFIELD So what. You're alive. You're not dead. You're not sick. Can't you wait a year.

MARION I'm not well either. We may be dead by then. Listen to my child up there. She's yours, too. Think of her. [*Exits up stairs*]

DANGERFIELD [*Hands over ears, spins slowly across room*] I just want no more. Take it all away. I'll poke out the windows. I'll beat it to the ground. I want no more. [*Slumping in chair. Viewing a panorama*] They're carrying me from the cradle to the grave. In a basket. [*The day dims and goes.* DANGERFIELD *takes up his sheep's head, comfort to journeys everywhere*] Little item. Sheep's head. [*Nestles head in arm*] Take you with me here while we go through the night. [*Pats head*] Can't go gobbling grass no more. [*In the midnight, voices sing softly*]
> Down in Dingle
> Where the men are single
> Pigwidgeon in the closet
> Banshee in the bed
> An antichrist is suffering
> While the Gombeen man's dead.
> Down in Dingle.

[*Morning comes, rising up the window. Letters are shoved in the door,* DANGERFIELD *gives a twitch in his sleep.* MARION *in dressing gown. Gently past the sleeping* DANGERFIELD. MARION *ripping open an envelope.* DANGERFIELD *lifts back a blanket covering his head. Eyes on envelope*] Hey what's that.

MARION Your father.

DANGERFIELD [*Making move from chair*] I'll get my glasses.

MARION   I'm afraid this is addressed to me.

DANGERFIELD   What do you mean you're afraid.

MARION   Just that. You're not going to read it.

DANGERFIELD   Now just a minute, that letter is from my father and I intend to know what's in it.

MARION   And I intend you shan't.

DANGERFIELD   Don't get snotty.

MARION   I'll be as snotty as I want. I no longer have to tolerate your nastiness.

DANGERFIELD   What's this mumbo jumbo. Don't act as if you have a secret file on me.

MARION   It's not mumbo jumbo. I'm leaving this house.

DANGERFIELD   Now look, Marion, I don't feel well. I'm not up to kidding about at this God forsaken hour of the morning. Now just what the hell do you mean you're leaving this house.

MARION   Leaving this house.

DANGERFIELD   There's a lease.

MARION   I know there's a lease.

DANGERFIELD   For three years.

MARION   I know it's for three years.

DANGERFIELD Ah, for Jesus' sake, now let's not get started. I only wanted to know what you're talking about. You know, just for the sake of making things clear. I'll never get this damned exam if I have to face more misunderstandings. Now what is it. Has my father made you an offer of money or something.

MARION You're not reading it.

DANGERFIELD All right, I'm not reading it. Now tell me what the hell it's all about.

MARION Your father is on my side.

DANGERFIELD Look, Marion, all right. Now we know that you have everything your way. I know this drivel, what's he done, sent you money.

MARION As a matter of fact, he did.

DANGERFIELD And told you I was a bastard and have always been a bastard.

MARION Yes, he did.

DANGERFIELD That I've been expelled from schools. Lot of that. Oh, a lot of that. All right, what are you going to do.

MARION Move from here, instantly.

DANGERFIELD Where.

MARION I'm going to see an agent this morning.

DANGERFIELD What about the lease.

MARION   That's your doing.

DANGERFIELD   You stupid bitch.

MARION   Go right ahead. Say anything you want.

DANGERFIELD [*Blanket over head of this American Indian*]   Now, Marion, let's have a little pow wow, let's understand each other. I don't feel this fighting is going to get us anywhere.

MARION   It's certainly not going to get you anywhere.

DANGERFIELD [*The reasonable voice of the mediator*]   Now look, how much money has he sent you.

MARION   That's my business.

DANGERFIELD   I've got to get my typewriter out of the pawn. I must have it for my notes.

MARION   Ha ha ha.

DANGERFIELD [*Huddling cold in blanket*]   Suppose I admit to a few indiscretions.

MARION   Indiscretions. Ha ha.

DANGERFIELD   Now that we have a chance to start all over again.

MARION   We do, do we. Oh, we. It's we now.

DANGERFIELD   I'm naturally thinking about the lease.

MARION   You signed it. You got us into this wretched place. Now you can get yourself out. Because I'm leaving. [DANGERFIELD *slowly*

hunches over to wall, cowers there] And you'll never treat me again the way you've done. Never. Never. Never.

DANGERFIELD [*Raising arms slowly, turns, outstretches his back in a cross against the wall*]   Put in the nails.

[*Curtain*]

ACT TWO

SCENE 1

*Eleven Golden Vale Park, The Geary. The dining room, sitting
room of a suburban villa.* MARION *arranging flowers. The front
doorbell rings.* MARION, *opening door, looks and slams it shut.
The voice of* DANGERFIELD *from outside.*

DANGERFIELD Please let me in for God's sake, Marion. [MARION *goes
back to flowers*] I say, Marion, are you alone. Really, this is ridiculous
behavior. You can't do this.

[*The window opens.* DANGERFIELD *wearing a bowler hat, scrabbling
in*]

MARION Why don't you leave me alone. You desperate bastard.

DANGERFIELD Don't call me a bastard when I'm breaking my damn neck
trying to get in this window. For Christ's sake help me on to the floor.
Why didn't you let me use the door.

MARION Because I don't want you in the house. This is my house and I can call the police and have you thrown out.

DANGERFIELD For the love of God, Marion, have you no mercy. Look at me, I'm soaked.

MARION Where have you been, drinking. With that hat.

DANGERFIELD [*Straightening with dignity*] I beg your pardon. A frightfully decent chap asked me to play squash. Always wear this when I play, case I bust my head on the fall. Damn good player, but I just managed to beat him.

MARION Oh, get out why don't you!

DANGERFIELD Just for taking some healthful exercise. I say, let's play the game.

MARION Get out. I spent all last week packing and moving. I'm tired. And I'm not going to listen to you lie.

DANGERFIELD Forgive me. It's such a nice house. Just let me look around. Are you here alone. All this.

MARION Yes.

DANGERFIELD How much.

MARION My business.

DANGERFIELD Skully is hounding me down there. One Mohammed Road is under siege by that incredible bastard.

MARION You can still live there.

DANGERFIELD How can I study with that ghoul sticking his repulsive skull in the door. [*Looking around*] Nice. Rather respectable area I gather. [*Rubbing hands*] Golden Vale Park. Wow. Bank clerks and stone masons must live out here.

MARION   But you're not.

DANGERFIELD   Oh Jesus. Come on, Marion. Look, just five minutes peace. I smell running water. [*Approaching a closed door*] Can I see in here. [*Opening door*] Real beds. [*Sings in the quavering voice*] I'm just a Christian soldier, weary on my way—

MARION   You're not ruining this for me.

DANGERFIELD   Just a bath, Marion. I'm chilled. Then drive me out. Feel chills. I may die.

MARION   Die, but this is my house.

DANGERFIELD   [*Holding out two upward palms*]   At your mercy, Maaaa.

MARION   Don't call me Maaaa.

DANGERFIELD   Right, captain. Where do you sleep.

MARION   None of your business.

DANGERFIELD   Let me stay, Marion. Please. I promise to abide by anything you say. But I've just got to have a little security.

MARION   Ha ha.

DANGERFIELD   That's true. Just because I'm big and strong. Just look at this muscle. But it doesn't mean that I can't be stricken by the insecurity that's in it. Please.

MARION   This is my house now.

DANGERFIELD   Absolutely.

MARION   If there's even a suspicion of drink I'm having you put out.

DANGERFIELD   You're wonderful, Marion. Oh, I know it's your house and I like it that way. [*Examining house with renewed fervor*] This is really frightfully good of you—

MARION   That's enough of that.

DANGERFIELD   Anything you say, Marion.

MARION   And be quiet. Felicity isn't asleep yet.

DANGERFIELD   Mum's the word. Oh, mum is the word all right. [*Slightly twitching*] You know, Marion, just maybe a little touch of some brown bread and jam. [*Pats belly*] Little short down here at the moment.

MARION   Do you good.

DANGERFIELD   Oh, there's truth, there's truth in what you say. [*Using the rotary step across room, lifts aside a curtain*] My, my. A garden. Marion, there's food out there for sure. Oh, I see rhododendrons. And oh for joy, rhubarb. It's there, I tell you, I see it, plain as day. [*Quick rubbing of the hands*] Oh, we'll get a reputable gardener in. Oh, I can see it all—

MARION   Your official residence as far as I'm concerned is One Mohammed Road.

DANGERFIELD   Marion, don't put me back there. It's too much for my nerves. Skully was creeping outside all morning, slipping notes under the door. [*Sees photograph on mantel*] Ah, and who are these nice ladies.

MARION   My landladies.

DANGERFIELD   Ah, Protestants. I can see that. Four honest eyes. Get those from living on investments. Can see they're faithful to their king. [*Inflates lungs*] Ah, I can breathe again.

MARION   I can breathe again you mean.

DANGERFIELD   Of course, of course, Marion. [*A figurine on mantel*] Ah, and do I see Wedgwood. Ah, Wedgwood. Marion, you can't send me back there.

MARION   I'm taking in a boarder.

DANGERFIELD   But there's room for me.

MARION   And she'll be here any minute.

DANGERFIELD   Marion, there's room for me. I'll have manure laid on the garden. I'll cook the boarder's breakfast. Promise. I'll sweep up. Promise I'll be good.

MARION   I'm not slipping back into poverty. Have our lives hounded day in and out.

DANGERFIELD   [*Picking up blanket, wrapping in it*]   Be none of that. But just let me ask you one question. Just one question. Is the boarder Catholic.

MARION   Of course she's Catholic. The whole country is Catholic. I hate them.

DANGERFIELD   Marion, that's absolutely preposterous. Let's have a little democracy here, I say.

MARION   They can't be trusted. Nor do they bathe.

DANGERFIELD   Little spiritual scruffiness never hurt anybody. [*Spins round with blanket*] Yes. Oh, yes. I think a boarder would be happy here. Golden Vale. Quiet and select. Convenience. Suit a nice non-dancing teetotaler. Oh, but we won't tolerate any indecency, none of that. But otherwise, a house of freedom. Marion, do you think God will ever forgive the Catholics.

MARION [Shouting]   Get out of that blanket.

DANGERFIELD   Just trying to store up a little security. Now, let's not have that uncontrolled bitterness. What does the boarder do.

MARION   She works in a seed shop.

DANGERFIELD   Ah, a horticulturist. A woman who must know her stuff about plants. The back garden out there. A piece of ground that looks to be in good heart.

MARION   What do you know about it.

DANGERFIELD   The earth has always interested me. I think we ought to make it available for her work.

MARION   Oh, you do, do you. This is my house.

DANGERFIELD   Of course, Marion, of course. Only trying to help. [Rubbing hands] She could be out there after work with that spade. See a few bits of the food coming free. [Approaches a chair] Ah, a rather fancy item, this. [Sits and adjusts back, lies supine] Ah, this is refreshing. What a nice ceiling. Makes you take stock. Look at things in retrospect. You know, Marion, we've come a long way. From One Mohammed Road to the Eleven Golden Vale, [MARION, who has begun to sew, stops] The Geary. From low to middle. From coal in the closet to coal in the bin. From water outside to water in. Away from broken doors and walls. To carpets and Wedgwood. I only miss the trams going by the window. Lovely stiff track to Dublin and back. Ah, no doubt Mr. Skully is a little apprehensive to find me gone. Maybe he's a little upset by the odd pound outstanding. Oh dear, it's a selfish world.

MARION   Are you finished.

DANGERFIELD   Skully will have his hands full to find me here.

MARION   In another second I'll call the police. Get out of that chair and get out of that blanket.

DANGERFIELD   Anything you say, Marion, anything at all. So pleasant here, I forgot myself. [*Getting out of blanket*] But, Marion, why don't you live from day to day and enjoy life.

MARION   [*Doorbell rings*]   There she is, you go.

DANGERFIELD   Not me, please.

MARION   Go.

DANGERFIELD   If you insist. What's her name.

MARION   Miss Frost.

DANGERFIELD   [*At door*]   Ah. Miss Frost. Do come in, let me help you. [*Takes bag*] Ah, has there been some rain.

MISS FROST   I'm afraid there has.

DANGERFIELD   [*Spotting another bag*]   It can be beastly at times. Do allow me.

MARION   Please, let me take your coat. And sit down, Miss Frost.

MISS FROST   I really mustn't put you to any trouble, Mrs. Dangerfield.

DANGERFIELD   [*Madly wiggling fingers over diaphragm*]   Miss Frost, forgive my sudden question, but I'm intensely interested in Irish boarding houses.

MARION   Miss Frost has hardly had time to take off her coat.

DANGERFIELD   Do forgive me, Miss Frost, I suffer at times from the odd bit of impetuosity.

MISS FROST   Oh, I don't mind. Really.

MARION [To DANGERFIELD, *introducing him to* MISS FROST]   This is Miss Frost, this is my husband, Mr. Dangerfield.

MISS FROST   How do you do.

DANGERFIELD   Charmed [*Bows. Nifty click of heels*]

MARION [*Low voiced*]   I'm sure.

DANGERFIELD   You did stay in an Irish boarding house, Miss Frost.

MISS FROST   I did, Mr. Dangerfield. It doesn't bear repeating, but one gets used to them.

DANGERFIELD [MARION *takes bags out*]   Now, how is that, Miss Frost.

MISS FROST   Well, Mr. Dangerfield, some of them are nice enough people but it was hard to get a proper night's rest with goings on.

DANGERFIELD   Now what sort of goings on, Miss Frost.

MISS FROST   It would be embarrassing to tell you, Mr. Dangerfield.

DANGERFIELD   Are you happy here, Miss Frost, do you like Ireland.

MISS FROST   Well, to be honest, Mr. Dangerfield, I guess I'm so used to it. I worked in England as a land girl. But I've always wanted to go into business for myself.

DANGERFIELD   I take it, Miss Frost, that you're rather go ahead.

MISS FROST   Well, Mr. Dangerfield, [*Her pale eyelids drop*] I'm not the sort who doesn't want to get on.

DANGERFIELD   Now how would you say the seed business is, in a grand country like this.

MARION [*Shouts in*]   I'm sure Miss Frost minds being asked leading questions.

DANGERFIELD   You don't, do you, Miss Frost.

MISS FROST   Oh, it's quite all right. I like to speak freely.

DANGERFIELD   Now, Miss Frost, you've seen the garden.

MISS FROST   Yes, Mrs. Dangerfield showed it to me.

DANGERFIELD   Now I don't want to tie you down technically, but would you say the garden out there was in good heart. Say capable of supporting one mouth absolutely, say forever, if one, of course, were to take a rather passionate interest in gardening. Now as a botanist would you say that was in the realm of possibility.

MISS FROST   Well, Mr. Dangerfield, I've never had to face a question quite like this before.

DANGERFIELD   Treat it carelessly.

MISS FROST   Well—

DANGERFIELD   And I think I'd rather concentrate on one wholesome vegetable. Something I could eat raw.

MISS FROST   It is rather hard to say. Limited to a single vegetable, eaten raw.

DANGERFIELD   Say it took a little cooking.

MISS FROST   An interesting question, but the more I think of it the more difficult it is to answer.

DANGERFIELD   Well what about the old fashioned vegetable, the spud.

MARION [*Enters*]   Miss Frost, please don't feel you've got to be subjected to this cross examination. I'm sure you've got a lot of things to do, and there's a hot water bottle in your bed. I hope you'll be comfortable.

MISS FROST [*Getting up.* DANGERFIELD *standing*]   Thank you very much, Mrs. Dangerfield, I'm sure I've put you to a lot of bother. I suppose I ought to get things sorted. But I have enjoyed chatting with Mr. Dangerfield. This may be an agricultural country but unlike Mr. Dangerfield they look upon the soil for nothing else but the money it will get them. Mr. Dangerfield's approach to the soil is more natural.

[DANGERFIELD *bowing deeply*]

DANGERFIELD   Flattering of you, Miss Frost, to see it that way.

MARION   Yes, I suppose he has the natural approach.

MISS FROST   Well, I guess I'll get going and get some sleep and let you and Mr. Dangerfield enjoy your evening.

DANGERFIELD   Always, Miss Frost, feel free to join us. I rather like to have an air of freedom about the house.

MISS FROST   Well, thank you. Thank you very much, Mr. Dangerfield. Well, good night. Good night, Mrs. Dangerfield.

MARION   Good night, Miss Frost, I hope you'll have a comfortable night.

[DANGERFIELD *all nodding and smiles*]

MISS FROST [*Exits to her room*]   Good night.

[*Sound of her closing door*]

MARION   Soil lover—

DANGERFIELD   Jealous that Miss Frost recognizes in me a lover of nature. [*Two loud knocks on the front door.* DANGERFIELD *rigid*] What's that, Marion. Are we expecting anybody. Where's the main switch. Jesus, where is it, quick. If I know knocks that's the blood man Egbert, odious face, Skully who never rings a bell.

MARION   It's there. But what about Miss Frost. You can't.

DANGERFIELD [*Ripping down switch*]   Just say a fuse blew. I'll creep and tell her. Lie low, Marion. This ship is now in my command if we're not to founder disastrously. [*Whispering to* MISS FROST] Oh, Miss Frost, sorry, there's been an accident, fuse. Just lie low, I mean, sorry, just don't worry, I'll get it fixed. Somehow, take a few minutes.

MISS FROST   Of course, Mr. Dangerfield.

DANGERFIELD [*In dark room*]   He'll go away, Marion, no worry about that. He'll just do a bit of sneaky snooping and be gone. Promise you that.

MARION   I knew it couldn't last.

DANGERFIELD   Nothing, my good Marion, lasts.

MARION   Oh, dear. Will our lives ever be free.

DANGERFIELD   Cheer up, the worst's over.

MARION   Oh, shut up, we're back where we started.

DANGERFIELD   Not at all. At the end, Marion.

MARION   And you tell me how we're going to explain all this hiding and not answering the door and things to Miss Frost.

DANGERFIELD   You're forgetting Miss Frost is a Catholic. How do you think they survive in Ireland.

MARION   And what do you say when he's snooping about.

DANGERFIELD   I'll send him a note from the North Pole.

MARION   Your great genius, giving him the slip.

DANGERFIELD   I can only try, Marion. Any and every ruse. We must warn Miss Frost.

MARION   Don't for heaven's sake. She's just arrived. And she's already been plunged into darkness.

DANGERFIELD   We've got to.

MARION   Why.

DANGERFIELD   Christian thing to do. Suppose Skully comes around some evening, pulling at doors and rapping on the windows. We can't sit here and do nothing. Right now Skully's across the street seeing if he can see any sparks from the chimney. I'll just explain to Miss Frost that I met one of those people who go on outings from the institution, mad as a hatter, bought him a drink and he's been after me ever since. She'll understand. This city is full of them.

MARION   What a dreadful business it all is.

DANGERFIELD   Cheer up. Have heart. Leave it to me.

MARION   I've made that mistake before. Why did we have to sign that lease. We'll have to pay till the rent is up.

DANGERFIELD   Custom of the country. Just relax. Tell Miss Frost about this crazy man, the Catholics have great respect for the insane.

MARION   And tell her we have to keep the front of the house blacked out.

DANGERFIELD   Of course. She'll understand. The whole of Ireland lives that way. They all hide out from each other in the back room. It's the custom.

MARION   Oh God, we can't suggest such a thing.

[*Two knocks at back of house*]

DANGERFIELD   Why that crafty bastard, trying the back door. Just call me Mr. Precaution, I battened that back latch. Always must do that soon as the sun sinks. I'll build a mobile barricade at the side of the house so he can't get back there. Never been partial to threats from the rear. Now I'll deal with Miss Frost. A measure of rapport there.

MARION   So I've noticed.

DANGERFIELD   [*Another knock at front door*]   Now, Marion, watch this, use a little mental telepathy on him. [*Whispering loudly*] Egbert, I say, Egbert. Mr. Egbert Skully. Listen to me. This is Dangerfield. Sebastian Balfe Dangerfield. To be accurate. I have gone to Greece. I tell you, Dangerfield is playing a drum in Athens. Left a month ago on the Holyhead boat because he didn't want that tiresome trip to Liverpool. He's not behind these green curtains with the red blobs as you think he is, terrified and ready to cough up a few quids to get rid of you. Go away from this house and forget him. What's fifty quid anyway. [*Another knock*] You're well rid of this bastard Dangerfield. Skully, can't you hear me. I tell you, I'm in Greece.

MARION   Oh, shut up. He will hear you.

DANGERFIELD   Irish animal. No brain to receive the message. Boor.

Philistine most odious. If I had my walking stick and morning suit by God, I'd deal with him.

MARION   Yes, in pawn, aren't they.

DANGERFIELD [*Master mariner*]   Shut up while I'm skipper of this ship. [*Sound of front gate swinging shut*] Ah. Sound the all clear. Say, Marion, how about a little bit while we're here on the floor in the dark.

MARION   Get away.

DANGERFIELD   Don't you want a bit.

MARION   Get your hands off me.

DANGERFIELD   Like to get you right here.

MARION   Stop it.

DANGERFIELD   Weeeeeeee—

MARION   You're revolting and put on the light.

DANGERFIELD   This is the way to live. The light. [*Switches light on*] Bing. Let there be electricity. Let there be gas for continuous hot water and cooking. Let there be hot bedlam for those needing it. And French horns for those needing to blow. We've come a long way, Marion. A long way.

MARION   And you had nothing to do with it.

DANGERFIELD [*Closing on* MARION]   Let's lock bodies.

MARION   Get away.

DANGERFIELD [*Does awkward dog dance and sings*]   They call this an emerald garden in the sea. Oh they do, they do they do. [*Spots large envelope slipped under door*] Whoops. What's this. [*Opening it*] Heeeeeeee—short little reminder from Egbert. [*Reads*] Dear Mr. Dangerfield, I have tried without success, to get in touch with you. [*To* MARION] See, Marion, he's finding it tough getting in touch. Egbert has a rather nice flow of English.

MARION   Is that all.

DANGERFIELD   Oh, few little items here.

MARION   Read it.

DANGERFIELD   I spot untruths.

MARION   Read it.

DANGERFIELD [*Reading*]   My wife is not feeling too well since we had so much trouble dealing with this property. And when we went to see the house I was sorry to find it in such a condition as to make my wife feel sick to her stomach. I want you to know, Mr. Dangerfield, that I did not disturb anything nor look in anything that appeared to be your property. But I feel that you should know that there is a large frying pan and a boiling pot missing out of the kitchen. There is only one cup left of the four supplied and two dishes, one badly cracked and needing repair, of the four supplied. The sofa is needing repair and the old, antique chair with the round knobs is gone completely from the drawing room. The Axminster rug is covered in soup stains and other stains which my wife, thinking of your wife, wishes me not to disclose. I had the plumber in at considerable expense to see the lavatory and he claims the lead pipe was hacked apart with an object which may have been an axe, and found other holes of a suspicious nature.

MARION   So you axed the pipes.

DANGERFIELD   What a disgraceful accusation.

MARION Oh read on.

DANGERFIELD All lies. [*Reads*] My wife and I are still proud of the citizenship we acquired in that land across the seas, and it is not for me to advise concerning your living methods, Mr. Dangerfield but it causes my wife great grief that an American gentleman such as yourself should perhaps not keep up the standards we mutually know as Americans. Before closing I will mention that the ceiling in the bedroom has fallen down to a great extent which would be such a blow to my wife that I did not let her go upstairs in the house. The two mirrors are gone, one which was antique and hard to come by and a lace curtain from the front room and nine pieces of assorted cutlery. And before closing I would mention my wife has been making a number of visits to the doctor and I have been put in the way of a great deal of expense. Also I would be glad to overlook such minor things as stains on the rug and of grease on the stove if I got satisfaction soon in the way of some payment this week. I do not want to get in touch with my solicitor yet, as I feel you have just been a little busy with your baby and have happened to overlook the little debt now outstanding between us. My regards to your wife, who both my wife and I hope is enjoying her good health. Respectfully yours, Egbert Skully. [DANGERFIELD *looks up from letter toward heaven and intones*] Dear Mr. Skully, I have caught my neck in a mangle and will be indisposed for eternity. Yours in death, Sebastian Dangerfield.

MARION I wish you were. [*Exits*] I have to wash dishes. I leave it to you to explain to Miss Frost.

DANGERFIELD Oh, aye. (*Calling*) Miss Frost.

MISS FROST Yes.

DANGERFIELD I wonder, could I trouble you a minute.

MISS FROST I'm not in suitable attire, Mr. Dangerfield.

DANGERFIELD Forgive me.

MISS FROST   Oh, it's all right. If you don't mind my kimono from Japan.

DANGERFIELD   Charmed. [*Bowing as* MISS FROST *enters*] Ah, most becoming. Suits you.

MISS FROST   [*Shyly*] Thank you.

DANGERFIELD   Miss Frost, I have a rather weird thing to tell. Ridiculous really. I hope it won't upset you. But there's been a man about here. Harmless sort. But mad as a hatter. Foolish of me, but just accidentally one night I loaned this man a cigarette in a public house not realizing the implications. I found him rather an interesting sort. At first. However, I was taken aback by his eyes. It turned out that he had an afternoon off from the institution. From there the whole situation developed in a most fantastic way. This man has got it into his head that he was a former landlord of mine and that I owe him money.

MISS FROST   Isn't that the limit though, Mr. Dangerfield.

DANGERFIELD   It is rather. Especially since he's had the nerve to come here. Of course best just to ignore him. Lock the doors and things, pull the curtains. But I thought it wise to tell you. Nothing serious. But I wouldn't want you to have someone tapping on your window. But perfectly harmless. So just ignore him.

MISS FROST   Couldn't you tell the police, Mr. Dangerfield.

DANGERFIELD   Oh, I'd rather not, Miss Frost. Live and let live is my motto. If you happen to be outside and he starts on about this rent money just tell him I'm not at home and smile. Does the trick beautifully.

MISS FROST   Yes, of course. Thanks for telling me. I imagine I would be a bit frightened by a strange man, Mr. Dangerfield.

DANGERFIELD   I think we all are at times, Miss Frost.

MISS FROST   And thanks again, Mr. Dangerfield.

DANGERFIELD   Not at all.

MISS FROST [*Exits*] Good night.

DANGERFIELD [*Bows, with quick rubbing of the hands*]   Night, night,
Miss Frost. [*A satisfied and pleased* DANGERFIELD *pops on his bowler
and calls to* MARION *in kitchen*] Marion, I must immediately get my
nose into the law of contract. I therefore must pop—

MARION   Well, pop.

DANGERFIELD   I've satisfactorily explained the situation to Miss Frost.
I'm retiring to the reading room of Trinity College, Dublin, for an
evening perusement of various obscure statutes—

MARION   Of various pubs, you liar.

DANGERFIELD   I may stretch a few points here and there but I am not
a liar.

MARION   Anyway I don't care. [*Flops in chair*] I just don't care. I just
don't care. You won't find me here when you get back.

DANGERFIELD   Nonsense.

[*Curtain*]

SCENE 2

Eleven Golden Vale, The Geary. A week later. DANGERFIELD
*unsteadily entering. Bowler on head. Slowly waving arms in
front of face.*

DANGERFIELD [*Goes to mantelpiece, takes up handful of letters, looks
at them*] Don't tell me anything unpleasant, will you now, nothing
unpleasant. Just nice things. I think I am going to go bye bye.
Marion. Marion, where are you. Blue blood from geek, wife and
washer. Slave to all me dirty little wants, where are you. [*Stands stony,
feeling the loneliness, touching the little pieces of air, gathering it in
little roundnesses in his hands*] Air, you're alone. And I'm alone.
All alone in this house. And you might give me that last and final chill,
the one to be avoided at all costs. I think this world has caused me
much distress and indignity. I'm broken hearted and frightened.
[*Slumps in chair. Pulling himself up slowly again*] Dangerfield. Don't
pack up, dry up or waste away. Mustn't allow my command to falter.
Climb up to the bridge of the ship. Issue the commands. [DANGERFIELD
at helm] Where are my calling cards. [*Goes to desk*] Where. [*Tugs at
top*] Where are my calling cards. Open I say. Open up. By God.
[*Grabs poker and pries open desk*] Ah, cards, calling cards. [*Throws
cards in air*] Control, must control. Make tea. Want warm moist winds
from Atlantic. Tropical plants in profusion. Marion, where are you.
I've sprinkled nitric acid on Skully's Axminster rug. [*Shouting*] Lower
the lifeboats. Launch them I say. You incredible oafs I'm skipper of
this ship, hear me.

[DANGERFIELD *staring at floor, looking over side of ship*]

MISS FROST [*Enters by front door. Stops*] Oh, Mr. Dangerfield.

DANGERFIELD   Excuse me, Miss Frost. Just a little lifeboat drill.

MISS FROST   Oh.

DANGERFIELD   I'm sorry for all this mess, Miss Frost.

MISS FROST   That's all right, Mr. Dangerfield.

DANGERFIELD   I hate to ask for such a thing, Miss Frost, but I wonder, could you ever let me have a cigarette.

MISS FROST   Certainly, Mr. Dangerfield, I'd be glad to. Here. [*She offers a little box*]

DANGERFIELD   I really am very grateful, very grateful indeed.

MISS FROST   I don't know how to say this, Mr. Dangerfield but Mrs. Dangerfield told me to tell you that she's not coming back.

DANGERFIELD   From where.

MISS FROST   From where she's gone. She left without saying exactly, although I understood she was taking the Liverpool boat.

DANGERFIELD   Rash.

MISS FROST   She was disturbed.

DANGERFIELD   More's the pity. Misunderstanding. Rash.

MISS FROST   I'll clean up a little here, Mr. Dangerfield.

DANGERFIELD   Oh, don't bother, Miss Frost. Leave it to me. I'll take care of it. Little accident.

MISS FROST   You look so tired, Mr. Dangerfield. I'll do it. It will only take a minute. I bought some bread and sausages. I think there are

some tomatoes. Would you like to share them with me, Mr. Dangerfield. You must be very hungry.

DANGERFIELD   I couldn't, Miss Frost, it's not fair.

MISS FROST   Oh it's nothing at all, really. [*Going toward kitchen*] Pre-
cooked, all ready.

DANGERFIELD   Ah. [*Raising up clenched fists*] God damn bitch.

MISS FROST [*Turning at kitchen entrance*]   Is something the matter, Mr.
Dangerfield.

DANGERFIELD   Oh no, Miss Frost. My vocal cords act up on me sometimes. [*Taking blanket*] Would you mind, Miss Frost, if I wrapped up
for dinner.

[DANGERFIELD, *the American Indian*]

MISS FROST   Not at all, Mr. Dangerfield.

[*Goes into kitchen*]

DANGERFIELD [*Grievously muttering*]   Put them back down. Get out.
Leave. Come back and my gamekeepers will drive you out. Out. Away.
Out.

MISS FROST [*Runs in*]   Is there anything wrong, Mr. Dangerfield.

DANGERFIELD   Just weariness.

MISS FROST   Oh. [*Comes with food and puts it on the table*] Whenever
you're ready, Mr. Dangerfield.

DANGERFIELD   Thank you, Miss Frost. [*In blanket, laying back, a little
opening through which his prayerful hands get at food*] This is cer-

tainly very good of you, although I don't think it's really fair to let you do it, Miss Frost.

MISS FROST It's nothing really, Mr. Dangerfield. I enjoy preparing food for someone.

DANGERFIELD But after a hard day. I think it's asking too much.

MISS FROST It's not, really. [*Eats and suddenly remembers*] Oh, Mr. Dangerfield, there was a man this morning. I don't know if it's the man you spoke about. I smiled as you instructed. But he told me he had a job as a cook in Roundwood and that he would be around to-night to see you.

DANGERFIELD Oh, just another one from the asylum. If he's been telling his friends, I may have the whole asylum here.

MISS FROST Ha ha. He did look rather mad.

DANGERFIELD [*Checking security around the windows*] Oh, we're ready for him. But the mad must be avoided, Miss Frost. At all costs. [*Smiles. A quick rubbing of hands approaching table*] Ah. [*Sniffing. Sitting. Taking a nip of sausage*] These sausages are delicious. I don't believe I've had them before, Miss Frost.

MISS FROST I get them on Pembroke Road. A shop just past the bridge. Homemade.

DANGERFIELD It just goes to show, doesn't it, Miss Frost, that there's no beating the homemade.

MISS FROST I agree so much, Mr. Dangerfield.

DANGERFIELD How was work, Miss Frost.

MISS FROST It's always the same, I'm afraid. In the shop I enjoy it because I see a lot of different people.

DANGERFIELD   And how is business.

MISS FROST   Tapers off about this time of year. Early potatoes are being ordered now and I think it's a good time to put down fruit trees. Can be boring.

DANGERFIELD   Sounds jolly interesting.

MISS FROST   I'm tired of working for other people. I'd like to be in business for myself. But it's so hard to get started.

DANGERFIELD   Things are a little difficult these days, Miss Frost, not what they used to be, of course.

MISS FROST   It's so true, Mr. Dangerfield. All sorts of people garden these days. So difficult to tell who is who.

DANGERFIELD   Extraordinary. Quite extraordinary.

MISS FROST   Do have those two sausages, Mr. Dangerfield.

DANGERFIELD   Oh I couldn't, Miss Frost, I've had much more than my share. Indeed, won't you.

MISS FROST   I've had a sufficiency.

DANGERFIELD   I insist you have at least one of them, Miss Frost.

MISS FROST   No, really. Here, let me help you.

DANGERFIELD   Well. Must say, I am a little hungry. I'm usually very careful about my diet. Tell me, Miss Frost, do you like Ireland.

MISS FROST   Well, Mr. Dangerfield, it's my home. I like it well enough. The people are good.

DANGERFIELD   I should say the Erse were a very fine race. Now Wexford is your county. Would you say Wexford had a better class of people.

MISS FROST [*Gurgling tiny laughter*] Oh, I don't know, Mr. Dangerfield, but they are industrious.

DANGERFIELD A great characteristic.

MISS FROST You mean work.

DANGERFIELD Very necessary thing. For most people. [*He leans across, eyes settling upon an item of eats*] I think I'll try this little morsel.

MISS FROST Oh, do. [*Tendering of plate*]

DANGERFIELD Thank you. [*Popping into the mouth*] Now, Miss Frost, I don't want to be personal, but if you had your choice what would you do in this world.

MISS FROST I guess just run my own business. What would you like, Mr. Dangerfield.

DANGERFIELD I think I tend toward the private income. Or own a stout ship. I should like, too, to inherit a large fortune.

MISS FROST Ha ha, we would all like that, Mr. Dangerfield.

DANGERFIELD Ha ha, quite.

MISS FROST But that isn't easy, ha ha.

DANGERFIELD Heh heh. No. I'm afraid it isn't, Miss Frost. To be sure. Ha ha.

MISS FROST Ha ha.

DANGERFIELD Miss Frost, come out and have a drink with me.

MISS FROST   Well.

DANGERFIELD   Come along now, you've had a hard day. And I think you deserve something after this extremely pleasant meal. Do you good to have a little walk. I know of a very interesting house, The Three Eyes.

MISS FROST   Oh, it makes me so upset. I know there's no harm in it. But I don't want to give the wrong impression, Mr. Dangerfield. You know the way people talk.

DANGERFIELD   Be all right. It's dark and rainy, won't see a soul.

MISS FROST   All right, then.

DANGERFIELD   Oh, just a little thing. I wonder, Miss Frost, could you do me just one little favor. I wonder could you let me have this week's rent, I'm a little short.

MISS FROST   I've already paid it to Mrs. Dangerfield. [Dealing with dishes]

DANGERFIELD   Oh, I see, that's a little difficult. Now I don't want to inconvenience you any, Miss Frost. This is entirely up to you and I don't want you to feel obliged in any way. But could you let me have a pound of next week's rent in advance. Now don't feel any obligation whatever. I certainly would never dare think of asking such a thing save for the circumstances. You understand.

MISS FROST   No, I understand but Mrs. Dangerfield took next month's rent. In advance.

DANGERFIELD   That dirty bitch. I beg your pardon, Miss Frost. I do beg your pardon. I get a little confused at times.

MISS FROST   That's all right, Mr. Dangerfield. [Goes to her bag on a chair and takes out a pound] Here, Mr. Dangerfield, please. Take this.

DANGERFIELD [*Taking it*]   Miss Frost, if I may say so, this is, indeed, most kind of you.

MISS FROST [*Clearing table*]   It's nothing at all.

DANGERFIELD   I do hate making these requests, Miss Frost but could you ever lend me a scarf. I'm afraid the one I'm wearing is most unsatisfactory. Disconcertingly feels like a rope.

MISS FROST [*Taking her silk scarf from top of bag on chair*]   Will this do.

DANGERFIELD [*Reaching*]   Miss Frost, how can I thank you—[*Loud knocking on door,* DANGERFIELD *crouching*]   Action stations. [*He beckons* MISS FROST *to crouch*]

MISS FROST   Is something wrong, Mr. Dangerfield.

DANGERFIELD   I rather think it's a citizen from the asylum.

MISS FROST   Oh, isn't it unfortunate. The one who was here this morning.

O'KEEFE [*Shouting from outside*]   God damn it, Dangerfield, I'll break this door down, I figured on this.

DANGERFIELD [*To* MISS FROST]   Oh, I think this one's all right, suffers from a rather harmless sexual deprivation, if it's all right with you, I'll let him in.

MISS FROST [*Hand flat upon her bosom*]   Well, if you feel it's safe, Mr. Dangerfield.

DANGERFIELD   I'll protect you, Miss Frost.

MISS FROST [*Retreating*]   I'll just do these dishes.

o'KEEFE [*Shouting from outside*]   You going to let me in. [MISS FROST *stepping quickly to kitchen*] Open up. [DANGERFIELD *opening door*] Boy, you're miserable.

DANGERFIELD   Dear Kenneth, what a surprise, come in, please. I thought you were in France. I had no idea it was you. How are you.

o'KEEFE   Where's that ten pounds. [DANGERFIELD *averting the eyes*] Just as I expected.

DANGERFIELD   Such a surprise, Kenneth. Let me welcome you back to this green garden in the sea. Take a seat. [o'KEEFE *wary*] Come, my dear Kenneth, put down this animal caution. [*Lifts a pointing arm*] Outside there, in this ancient Danish seaport is commerce. Barrels and barrels, steel girders and fine beasts fresh in off the grass ready to be cut to size.

o'KEEFE   I'm back here because I've got a job. I almost starved in France. I had a tin of peas, eating six a day. And no money arriving from you. Now I come back.

DANGERFIELD   Cheer up. Get you a tomato.

o'KEEFE [*Waves arms*]   Nothing. I've decided that I am destined to love beautiful women and to inspire in them a desire to lay for someone else. I'm thinking of joining the Jews to fight the Arabs or the Arabs to fight the Jews. What the hell, I'm sick of it all.

DANGERFIELD   Better days ahead, Kenneth.

o'KEEFE   I see a Lady Eclair tomorrow. She wants a French chef. That's me. Have to pose as a frog. And you've not got a penny of that money, have you.

DANGERFIELD   Must admit I'm a little short, Kenneth. Only temporary.

o'KEEFE   Everything goes wrong. I go out there now at the conversational mercy of this Eclair. People who eat three times a day have a big advantage.

DANGERFIELD   I think we'll admit that to evidence.

O'KEEFE   I want to impress her with my knowledge of antiques. Maybe meet some of Eclair's rich guests after they've feasted on the food from my well run kitchen. What the hell, if things go wrong I can always suggest Lady Eclair sail a nate in a sauceboat. And that's another thing. Eclair answers the ad I put in the paper in the third person. Lady Eclair would like to know if Kenneth O'Keefe is Protestant or Catholic. I wrote back that Kenneth O'Keefe is neither and will not require to be delivered to church on Sundays. She writes back, Lady Eclair feels that Kenneth O'Keefe should have some religion because everyone needs a church for the development of their immortal soul. So I said that Kenneth O'Keefe's immortal soul is already well developed and therefore did not find churches useful. Next letter she says, Lady Eclair would like to quote from Proverbs, "Poverty and shame shall be to him that refuseth instruction." I answered that Kenneth O'Keefe has already suffered much poverty and shame while a member of the Church of Rome and that, "The simple believeth every word but the prudent man looketh well to his going."

DANGERFIELD   Weeeee. And you're hired.

O'KEEFE   So far. This religion business will present a problem. I'm suspicious about people interested in saving other people's souls. [*Looking around*] Say, what's the deal. Pretty rosy. You got a toilet and running water.

DANGERFIELD   Wooden floors. Gas. Kitchen. Everything.

O'KEEFE   Where's Marion.

DANGERFIELD   Away. Taking the air.

O'KEEFE   What's wrong with the air here. And you're alone. [DANGERFIELD's *finger to lips*] What's going on, you're not alone.

DANGERFIELD   Not entirely.

O'KEEFE   Who's living with you.

DANGERFIELD   Not with, Kenneth. In the house. Miss Frost, a boarder, a charming young lady from Wexford.

O'KEEFE   Marion pregnant.

DANGERFIELD   I hope not.

O'KEEFE   Doesn't Marion mind you being in the house alone with Miss Frost. [DANGERFIELD's *fingers to lips*] Who's in there. This dame I saw this morning on the stoop. She looked at me as if I were crazy. Kept trying to shut the door. I kept putting my foot in it because I thought you were hiding under the rug. [*Lowering voice*] What's going on here. You screwing her.

DANGERFIELD   I beg your pardon, Kenneth. Miss Frost is a very good Catholic. Quite aboveboard. No fear, no scandal, Kenneth. A most interesting person.

O'KEEFE   [*Hunched* O'KEEFE]   I'm just an utterly defeated bastard. This God damn country. Drink is the curse of this country. Come back to this place starved, with no sex life, nothing and this is what I have to face. You haven't a cent. Not a cent.

DANGERFIELD   Kenneth, you're upset. Now don't be upset. I know you've had a hard time of it and I want to see you enjoy your return.

O'KEEFE   Jesus, shut up. Look, Dangerfield. At every meal there were seven pairs of hands reaching for a pile of spaghetti. Fights and yapping. Yap, yap, yap. I'm here because I want to get out of that forever and there's one thing that will get me out and that's money. I don't give a damn what you do, drink yourself to death, screw whoever you want, murder Marion, but me, I've had all I want. What have

I got to show for two years over here. This sack has everything I own in the world.

DANGERFIELD I'd like to cheer you up, Kenneth.

O'KEEFE Well, you're not. You're sucking me down. I don't want you on my back.

DANGERFIELD You don't mean that, Kenneth.

O'KEEFE I mean it. I don't care if I never see you again as long as I live. You could be dying in the gutter, I don't care. All I want is my money and you can go and drink yourself to death.

DANGERFIELD Hard words.

O'KEEFE The Irish are the same wherever they go. Faces compressed into masks of suffering. Complaining and excuses, rasping voices, squabbling and bickering. I'm sick of it. I hate it. I thought you got places when you learned to be an electrician. Good steady job. Good money. Have kids. I don't want kids. I don't want to be sucked down. And listen to some priested mick, saying this is the second Sunday after Pentecost, there will be a communion breakfast next Sunday so don't screw on Saturday and put a dollar in the collection basket.

DANGERFIELD You're distraught, Kenneth. Now calm. And remember poverty is sacred. Don't strain to get out of it. All these other things will come. A great pity the world hasn't more faith.

O'KEEFE I've no sympathy for the grief it's causing you.

DANGERFIELD Hate to see you this way, Kenneth. Bereft of faith. Bereft of—

O'KEEFE Money.

DANGERFIELD   That too, perhaps. But you mustn't let it make you hard. I know you want that thing they do in the dark very badly. But don't give up, a mate will come.

O'KEEFE   I don't want a mate, I want someone who is corrupted with the joy of screwing and wants me for me.

DANGERFIELD   Alas Kenneth, women lay down their virtue for bread-winners.

O'KEEFE   You're just a son of a bitch. You'd see me without a cent. [*Making move to go*] Tomorrow I see Lady Eclair. And I'm getting the eleven thirty bus to Roundwood. I want nothing to screw this deal.

DANGERFIELD   Don't leave.

O'KEEFE   I just get distressed with you.

DANGERFIELD   [*Smiling*]   Now, Kenneth, you're a man who speaks fluent Greek and Latin, a man of much useless knowledge, schooled in culture, who knows what Plato said to his boys. Where do you think this harshness is going to get you. I'm going to report you to the Legion of Mary. Come on.

O'KEEFE   [*Scenting scandal*]   What's going on here.

DANGERFIELD   Not a thing.

O'KEEFE   Yeah.

DANGERFIELD   Absolutely.

O'KEEFE   All looks fishy to me.

DANGERFIELD   The name Dangerfield has never and will never be touched with such.

O'KEEFE You're up to monkey business.

DANGERFIELD These are strange times, Kenneth. Very strange. There's a world out there with people with eyes and mouths. The eyes see these things and the mouths want the things the eyes see. Oh but they can't have them. That's the way things are arranged. Got to have things unequal or nothing would happen. Men like yourself who want to have carnal knowledge of the female nates and boob si boobs and the other thing they have.

O'KEEFE I'll get it.

DANGERFIELD And I hope you do. But if you get put down without it, don't be bitter, Kenneth. Those things are for a reason. Saints and things. You're a man equipped for old age. Don't waste your time on this sexual appetite. I think we are natural aristocrats of the race. Come before our time. Born to be abused by them out there with the eyes and the mouths. But there's no bitterness in me. Only love. I want to show them the way and I expect only taunts and jeers. But there are the few who listen. Worth it all. I put this to you, Kenneth. Go back. Go back to this church of yours. Put down these things of making money and living in a fine big house with nice comfortable chairs and an Irish maid putting logs on the fire and bringing in the tea. Get these tweed suitings out of your mind and trousers lined with satin and put down the desires of the flesh, nipple nuttiness, nate needy, boob bothered. You don't want an M.G. and a man servant, shallowness and deceit, or lawns to the lake and garden seats where one sits thinking of making more money.

O'KEEFE I'm listening.

DANGERFIELD For me, Kenneth, all I want out of this life is my rightful place and for others to keep theirs. The common people back down where they belong.

O'KEEFE So you don't have to work for a living.

DANGERFIELD   More, more. More of same. Kenneth, tell me, how do I pass these exams.

O'KEEFE   Study.

DANGERFIELD   My mind's a blank.

O'KEEFE   What the hell is the matter with you.

DANGERFIELD   Kenneth, I'm beaten, I'll never pass. Must dine with my tutor but I can't appear wearing a blanket with hunger written around the eyes.

O'KEEFE   [Hands in air, wagging on the ends of his arms]   God damn it, I love this country.

DANGERFIELD   Kenneth, you're off your jump completely.

O'KEEFE   This country can be so damn exasperating but just to be in Dublin sort of gets me all excited. I tingle in all my bones. And with nothing but four pence for a cup of coffee in Bewley's. I used to lie awake dreaming about coming back. Didn't take long. But if I could open up a restaurant with the money saved from this job, I'd be set.

DANGERFIELD   All you would need would be a place, chairs, tables, knives, forks and lots of rancid grease. But if one stays in the land of the crut too long, Kenneth, it gets a bit tight around the various glands. Need sun and the dance. And the song. [Calling to the kitchen] Miss Frost, would you come in here a minute.

O'KEEFE   I'm going.

DANGERFIELD   Stay and meet Miss Frost, she's so nice. [MISS FROST enters] Miss Frost, I'd like you to meet Kenneth O'Keefe.

MISS FROST   Hello again.

O'KEEFE I'm esteemed again.

MISS FROST Sorry if I was a bit hasty at the door this morning.

O'KEEFE That's all right. I had my foot in it. But I must be going. So long.

DANGERFIELD All luck tomorrow, Kenneth.

O'KEEFE Yeah.

[*He exits*]

DANGERFIELD Oh, I'm a friend of all kinds. And animals too so long as they don't get rough. Some of them have to be put in cages but oh aye, they deserve it. Everything is always fair and square in the end. Part of the rules. To The Three Eyes, eh, Miss Frost.

MISS FROST I'd so like to but I think it's a little late for me now.

DANGERFIELD It's never, if I may say so, too late for The Three Eyes. I must confess I'm dying for a little nip of something. [*Huddling shoulders*] Damp chill in the air.

MISS FROST If you've a chill coming on, Mr. Dangerfield, I've got some brandy if that might help you.

DANGERFIELD Miss Frost ah. How extremely kind. As a matter of fact I do feel a distinct chill coming on. But really, I mustn't impose.

MISS FROST It's no imposition, Mr. Dangerfield. It will just go to waste if someone doesn't drink it.

DANGERFIELD If you're absolutely sure, Miss Frost. But I must insist you join me.

MISS FROST Certainly, I'll get it. [*She goes to her room*]

DANGERFIELD [MISS FROST *returns with bottle and two glasses, hands them to* DANGERFIELD] Ah. Would you like me, Miss Frost, to do the honors.

MISS FROST Please do, Mr. Dangerfield.

DANGERFIELD This is most cordial. [*Pouring*] Just pop it in like that. That's the trick. [*Drinks*] Kills the chill. Would it be terrible if I were to make certain this chill's down for the count, Miss Frost.

MISS FROST Not at all, Mr. Dangerfield.

DANGERFIELD [*Having another*] You're so kind, Miss Frost. So kind. I like that gray sweater you're wearing.

MISS FROST It's nothing, Mr. Dangerfield.

DANGERFIELD I think it suits you. Really suits you. [MISS FROST *sits shyly on the arm of a chair*] Miss Frost, you have a lovely nape of neck.

MISS FROST Oh, Mr. Dangerfield.

DANGERFIELD Ah, I feel quite refreshed. Sporting in fact. Give me the facts Miss Frost and to hell with the fiction. I want the facts. What was your first ambition, Miss Frost.

MISS FROST I wanted to be a nurse. But I was for a bit and I didn't like it much. I didn't get along with the other girls.

DANGERFIELD Ah.

MISS FROST I worked for an assurance company but there was a man in the office I didn't fancy much. He thought a great deal of himself.

DANGERFIELD And you left.

MISS FROST I wasn't going to give him the satisfaction.

DANGERFIELD Quite rightly. Now tell me, Miss Frost, how old are you.

MISS FROST Oh, Mr. Dangerfield, I can't tell you that.

DANGERFIELD Oh yes you can, Miss Frost.

MISS FROST Oh, I couldn't tell you. I just couldn't.

DANGERFIELD Miss Frost, I'm your friend. Remember that. Friend. You can tell me anything, anything at all. Least of these, your age. Now how old are you. [Reaching to place a comforting hand on her wrist]

MISS FROST Oh, dear, Mr. Dangerfield, I'm thirty four.

DANGERFIELD Ah. [Offering bottle, pouring] Allow me.

MISS FROST That's heaps, Mr. Dangerfield.

DANGERFIELD Must always allow for sudden chills, Miss Frost. Be prepared. Thirty four is an excellent age. Best.

MISS FROST How do you know.

DANGERFIELD Miss Frost. Sometimes I feel fifty three. Seldom but at times I feel twenty. Recently I've been seventy. But I remember thirty four as a fine age. Do you mind, Miss Frost, if I have another quickly.

MISS FROST Oh no, do.

DANGERFIELD Now, Miss Frost, let's get down to business. What do you want. What do you want out of life anyway.

MISS FROST Dear me, what a question.

DANGERFIELD Answer me now, truthfully, Miss Frost.

MISS FROST Well, your question covers so much ground. There are a great number of things I want out of life. Of course, as I've said, my own shop.

DANGERFIELD   Ah, you want money, Miss Frost. Money is what you're after.

MISS FROST   I'd hardly put it that way.

DANGERFIELD   But that's what you'd like, isn't it.

MISS FROST   Doesn't one work toward saving one's soul, too, Mr. Dangerfield.

DANGERFIELD   Lot of people think God can do something for them, Miss Frost. He told me himself personally that he abhors these types.

MISS FROST [*Chuckling*]   Oh dear.

DANGERFIELD   Miss Frost, do you know, you would make someone a very fine wife.

MISS FROST   Oh Mr. Dangerfield.

DANGERFIELD   You would. And it's a great comfort to have you here. [MISS FROST's *head turning shyly away*] I really mean that, Miss Frost.

MISS FROST   I like being here.

DANGERFIELD   I must apologize for subjecting you to all this upset.

MISS FROST   I don't mind.

DANGERFIELD   I'd hate for you to be unhappy.

MISS FROST   I'm happy. I really am, Mr. Dangerfield. I think it's the nicest house I've been in yet. It's so free and easy.

DANGERFIELD   It's that Miss Frost, it's certainly that.

MISS FROST   I like things to be free and easy.

DANGERFIELD   I agree, a good way. Free and easy. Easy and free, it's the way things ought to be. Miss Frost, none of these binding things. They rust up the soul.

MISS FROST   Yes I think so too.

DANGERFIELD   I like you, Miss Frost.

MISS FROST   I like you too.

DANGERFIELD   I'm glad. Oh yes eyes. No eyes. What things they see. Some say happiness, others misery. Oh aye the eyes. Miss Frost.

MISS FROST   Yes.

DANGERFIELD   I'm going to be quite honest, as I know I can be with you without being misunderstood.

MISS FROST   Yes, Mr. Dangerfield.

DANGERFIELD   Miss Frost, may I sleep near you tonight. For both our sakes. In case of a visit from the citizen from the asylum. [MISS FROST's *eyes on her hands which join tightly in her lap*] I don't want you to misunderstand me, Miss Frost. Just bring our mattresses out here, neutral territory. It's rather a peculiar thing with me. Having had so much upset I don't think I could bear to sleep alone. Would you mind awfully. I know it must seem irregular, but dash it all, I may as well be honest.

MISS FROST   Oh, no, Mr. Dangerfield, it's not irregular at all. I know how you must feel. I don't mind. I understand what you mean.

DANGERFIELD   It's really very kind of you, Miss Frost, to take it like this. I sincerely hope I'm not imposing.

MISS FROST   You're not imposing, Mr. Dangerfield.

DANGERFIELD   I'm glad. Been such a pleasant evening and I think pleasures should be extended. Good of you to be so broad minded.

MISS FROST   I'd rather be that way, Mr. Dangerfield. I know people look down on it.

DANGERFIELD   Old fashioned, Miss Frost.

MISS FROST   I agree.

DANGERFIELD   I'll just drag in the mattresses. [DANGERFIELD *with two mattresses and sundry covers in tow*] I hope I'm not too early for you, Miss Frost.

MISS FROST   I'm ready to retire, Mr. Dangerfield.

DANGERFIELD   And leave those dishes. I like to have something to face in the morning. I'll douse the lights and light a candle. [DANGERFIELD *puts match to candle on mantel*] A pity they ever found out about this thing electricity. [*General movements of blankets and the reclining of two weary bodies*] Miss Frost.

MISS FROST   Yes.

DANGERFIELD   May I hold your hand.

MISS FROST   Yes.

DANGERFIELD   [*Wind blows up outside, the laurel leaves shake, the shutters clatter. Sound of* MISS FROST *weeping*] Miss Frost, bring me a glass of water. Now now, this is no way to behave.

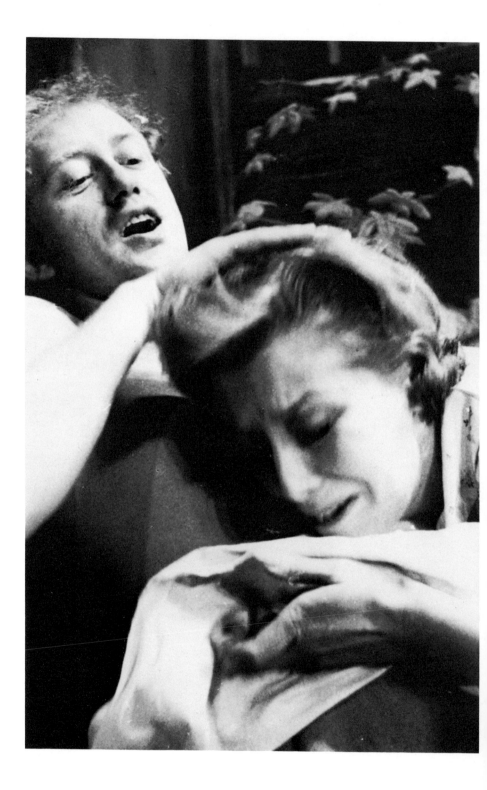

MISS FROST I shouldn't have done it.

DANGERFIELD Now, now, it's all right.

MISS FROST It isn't. Oh God, I shouldn't have let you. Put your mattress next to mine.

DANGERFIELD Through charity.

MISS FROST It wasn't. It was wrong. Oh dear. God forgive me.

DANGERFIELD Don't take it like this.

MISS FROST It's a mortal sin. And you made me, Mr. Dangerfield.

DANGERFIELD You made yourself, Miss Frost.

MISS FROST Oh God, I didn't. It wasn't my fault. I could never confess it. Why did you.

DANGERFIELD Why did you. Takes two to congress.

MISS FROST Please don't make it worse.

DANGERFIELD I'm not making it worse Miss Frost. You're being very childish about this.

MISS FROST I beg of you.

DANGERFIELD You're saved if you say the act of contrition.

MISS FROST I've got to tell it.

DANGERFIELD God's in the room. Tell it.

MISS FROST Don't say that. We could be struck dead.

DANGERFIELD Relax Miss Frost.

MISS FROST I didn't want to do this. I know I didn't want to.

DANGERFIELD Yes you did.

MISS FROST I didn't, please, I didn't. [*Weeping*]

DANGERFIELD Miss Frost, God is all merciful.

MISS FROST But it's a mortal sin which I have to confess to the priest and it's adultery as well.

DANGERFIELD Please, now, Miss Frost. Let me pop on a little more light, see matters more clearly.

MISS FROST No.

DANGERFIELD Just a dim one. [*A dim lamp lit by* DANGERFIELD] This won't do you any good.

MISS FROST It's adultery.

DANGERFIELD One mortal sin is the same as another.

MISS FROST It isn't. I'm damned. Right to hell.

DANGERFIELD I'll go with you.

MISS FROST You won't, you're a pagan.

DANGERFIELD Don't cry. God's not going to condemn you. I'm no pagan. You're a good person. God's only after people who are out and out habitual sinners. You must be sensible.

MISS FROST I'll have to give your name.

DANGERFIELD [*Up out of covers*] You what.

MISS FROST Your name. I'll have to tell the priest.

DANGERFIELD What makes you think that. Nonsense.

MISS FROST   He'll ask me.

DANGERFIELD   Not at all.

MISS FROST   He will. And they'll send the priest to my mother.

DANGERFIELD   Ridiculous. The priest's only there to forgive sins.

MISS FROST   No.

DANGERFIELD   Miss Frost, this has happened before.

MISS FROST   Please don't.

DANGERFIELD   Hasn't it.

MISS FROST   [Shaking head]   Yes.

DANGERFIELD   And they sent the priest to your mother.

MISS FROST   [Shaking head]   Yes.

DANGERFIELD   And they asked the name of the man.

MISS FROST   Yes. Please don't ask me any more.

DANGERFIELD   Come come, Miss Frost. Better to have these things out in the light, what there is of it. Who was this man.

MISS FROST   A man who worked for us. And they sent me to a convent in Dublin to do penance. The priest said he wouldn't give me absolution till I gave up his name. And you're a married man.

DANGERFIELD   Fear not. There's a special church on the Quays where you confess these things. I'll find out for you.

MISS FROST   God, I couldn't. Don't. I wouldn't be seen there. It's not respectable.

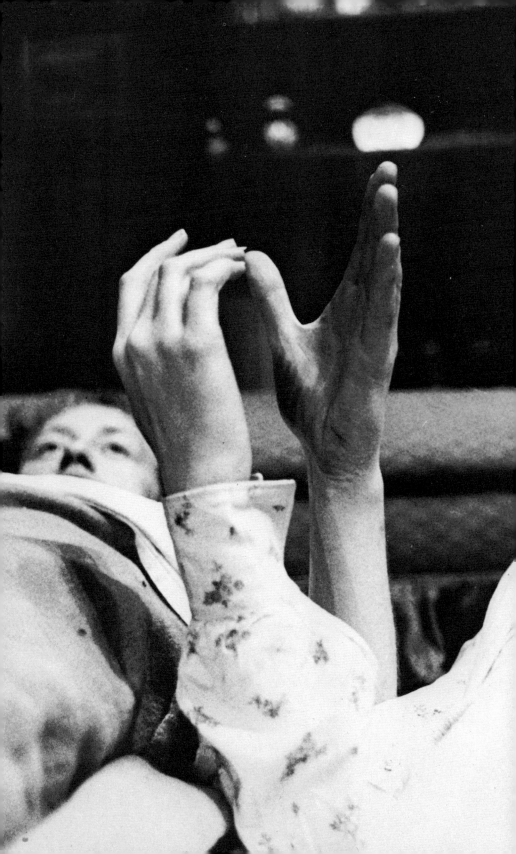

DANGERFIELD   Sin, Miss Frost, is never respectable. Now just relax a little and everything's going to be all right.

MISS FROST   I don't know what to do.

DANGERFIELD   Hell's the worst thing that can happen. I'll bring my fire extinguisher.

MISS FROST   Please, please. If word ever gets around. They'll drive me out of my job.

DANGERFIELD   Now, now. [*Pats her shoulders, gives her a bit of sheet*] Here, have a bit of sheet, have a good blow. That's it. [MISS FROST *blows nose*] Now easy. God's our friend. You've got a nice little salary, nothing to worry about. You must give up this right and wrong. We can even plant the garden back there if the worst comes to the worst. God made us do it. And if he didn't, we may as well get as much as we can in this world and confess it all at once. A lot of steps to heaven. And Ireland is closest of all. Tell me, Miss Frost, don't you think it's a fine instrument that God made for the poor likes of us to enjoy. [MISS FROST *gurgling laughter*] Why, Miss Frost, you're giggling. That's the way.

[*Curtain*]

SCENE 3

A dark afternoon, a week later in the Eleven Golden Vale, The Geary. Outside a gentle rain. Inside, DANGERFIELD in the supine chair, watching the ceiling. A candle burns on the mantel.

DANGERFIELD [*Quietly singing*] O Lord, I forgive you for all thy faults. [MISS FROST *enters.* DANGERFIELD *gives a shudder. Looks*] Ah, Miss Frost. How are you, tell me, how are you.

MISS FROST Oh, I'm all right. A little tired. I was in the shop all morning.

DANGERFIELD On your feet.

MISS FROST Yes.

DANGERFIELD Miss Frost, come give me a kiss.

MISS FROST Oh, Mr. Dangerfield.

DANGERFIELD [*Getting up*] Miss Frost, I've told you, you have a lovely nape of neck. Chew your ears. Ever chew ears. Miss Frost, chewing ears is the thing, down on the lobes. Especially the lobes. Get down on those soft things of flesh.

MISS FROST Oh, Mr. Dangerfield, you'll bite them off.

DANGERFIELD Tender.

MISS FROST You like them that way.

DANGERFIELD Mixed with eyes.

MISS FROST Hee hee.

DANGERFIELD Eyes.

MISS FROST You go on.

DANGERFIELD Little bite of the mouth along the shoulders. You'll take this off later like a good girl. Miss Frost, later. Yes.

MISS FROST [*With a parcel*]   I brought you some meat.

DANGERFIELD   Do you know, Miss Frost, you're a very fine person.

MISS FROST   You've had a few. [*Points to bottle*]

DANGERFIELD   Empty. Cross my little ticker. [*Two fingers crossed on heart*] Although never let it be said that I took to the highway or even byway without fewl for me little heart. Hear it in there. Go ahead, feel it. [*Takes her hand*] Here. Little feeble now. But going. Press a tip of warm nose in your white cool ear. Miss Frost, I've a declaration to make. I love you.

MISS FROST   You're just going on.

DANGERFIELD   Let me repeat. I love you.

MISS FROST   I don't believe it.

DANGERFIELD   I mean it, Miss Frost and there's not many or none I can say it to. I only feel that it's better to be in this world with a few polite possessions than without. [*Hand rubbing*] We'll cook meat tonight. Put ten years on our lives. Need a little garlic. Chew it all up with the redness.

MISS FROST   Oh, no, Mr. Dangerfield. Garlic.

DANGERFIELD   Of course, garlic, Miss Frost, of course. With the red meat.

MISS FROST   But it smells.

DANGERFIELD   That's what we want, Miss Frost. We want that smell. Oh I'm going to see some times yet. Going to buy a new large cup. Going to be a few changes made. A lot of changes. And Miss Frost, can I rely on you not to spill a bean or utter a word. Can I. Even

though they take the hook to you and other Irish instruments as well.
Yes.

MISS FROST Yes.

DANGERFIELD Miss Frost, this is top secret, an affair of state the like of
which would finish Ireland were it ever to get out, and me as well. Tomorrow night I go to London.

MISS FROST You're not.

DANGERFIELD I am.

MISS FROST What will you do.

DANGERFIELD Take a dinner at the Inns of Court which will last me a
week. Need a little rest from tension. General clearance. Few matters
need cleaning up, tiny grains of sand in the Vaseline. Miss Frost, I
like you very much. Do you know that.

MISS FROST What will I do. And about all that's happened.

DANGERFIELD Ah, arrangements are made with the landlords. Nice
elderly spinsters.

MISS FROST I mean between us and things. [Head bowed]

DANGERFIELD Come, tell me.

MISS FROST I don't know. Sometimes I feel I'm right and then I don't
know what's going to become of me. In my church it's a mortal sin.
God forgive me, I wish it weren't true and that it was all a pack of
lies. And they watch me in the shop. If it's ever found out. I think
I'm going to die and with this sin I'd be doomed forever to hell.
[Wringing hands] A country like this has nothing for a girl like me. I
won't be able to get married until I'm too old and they want so much
money and a farm and anything they can lay their hands on. That's

all they ever look for is the money. You're one of the first people I've ever met for whom money doesn't mean anything.

DANGERFIELD   Well, I don't know really, I wouldn't say that was entirely true, Miss Frost.

MISS FROST   This isn't a country for women.

DANGERFIELD   I would say that was true.

MISS FROST   I've had horrible dreams. They frighten me. I'll never do it again. I wish I could go away, too. I know they are talking about me at work.

DANGERFIELD   Now, Miss Frost, you'll do it again. Don't let these things upset you. Don't let them do that.

MISS FROST   But it's more than that.

DANGERFIELD   Nothing is more than that.

MISS FROST   If someone gets word that I've lived alone with you in this house without Mrs. Dangerfield here, it would be the end of me. And they find out, they don't miss a thing. They would go to the priest and he would be down here in a minute.

DANGERFIELD   So long as there's a drink, we're right for him, Miss Frost. Take it from me.

MISS FROST   I've seen people watching.

DANGERFIELD   Strollers.

MISS FROST   From across the street.

DANGERFIELD   Strollers. Out for a breath of—[Hand raised]

MISS FROST   But this is a cul de sac, Mr. Dangerfield. I know they're spies.

DANGERFIELD   Now, now. We'll have the meat tonight. Everything is going to be all right, Miss Frost. Not a thing to worry about, good days ahead. Beep. Beep. Days of richness.

MISS FROST   Mr. Dangerfield, why don't you believe in hell and things like that.

DANGERFIELD   Too many other problems.

MISS FROST   You're interesting.

DANGERFIELD   Miss Frost, I think I am a man with a future. What do you think. Do you think I have a future.

MISS FROST   Oh yes, I think you have a good future. You'll be in law.

DANGERFIELD   And the jigs and jail and incognito. All those.

MISS FROST   I think you would do well in almost anything, Mr. Dangerfield. I think business would especially suit you.

DANGERFIELD   [Pointing up]   Thank God up there for the codes, Miss Frost. Get down there now on your knees and thank him. And for the meat as well. All down on our knees. But never hit a man when he is down. Wait to see if he tries to get up and then by God, let him have it. Faith is killing me. I want to chop this house down. And you're just a little girl, Miss Frost. That's what you are. You need to be held, that's all. Come let me hold you in my own little forest. [Beckons, smiles] Into the big doors of my house. Big and thick and bronze for weight. Brass hinges. Big S.D. on it. Doors because you don't want people. Trust none of them.

MISS FROST   I don't believe a word you're saying.

DANGERFIELD   And a garden. Walls forty feet high. Three feet thick for strength. Hundred acres of it. Boxwood mazes. Monkey trees. Magnolias. My heart is mended and splendid under the yew tree. Then there will be lots of bells. And bells are balls. All balls bells. Big ones, little ones, hanging all over. Ring them. Ring them out like mad. Me, the mystic maniac. Want to be baked in a loaf of bread. Will you bake me, Miss Frost. [MISS FROST's *slow silent smile*] No one wants to do a decent day's work any more.

MISS FROST   You're so strange to be with, Mr. Dangerfield.

DANGERFIELD   You can't mean that, Miss Frost.

MISS FROST   You're not like other people.

DANGERFIELD   Well geek geek and all that, perhaps there is some truth in what you say.

MISS FROST   Mr. Dangerfield, why do you water that little plant in the front with an eye dropper.

DANGERFIELD   Miss Frost, you've been spying on me. On me in my secret moments.

MISS FROST   Oh, I haven't. But why do you do such a funny thing.

DANGERFIELD   I'm poisoning the plant.

MISS FROST   Lord save us.

DANGERFIELD   It's something in me, Miss Frost. I thought to myself why don't I slip this plant something to kill it. [*Smiles warmly*] Miss Frost, I feel sad. Strange things. I'm frightened. Need someone near me to be nice to me. You're nice. I don't like to be lonely. I want a home. I feel all my homes are behind me. Pawned everything [*Smiles at MISS FROST*] and everybody but you. One day some years ago I got out of a green upholstered tram. And there was the university. First day, new suit, white shirt, black tie. All dressed up for failure. Miss Frost, those green squares, trees, little bell ringing, the students. I failed because it was so beautiful.

MISS FROST   Oh, no you haven't, Mr. Dangerfield.

DANGERFIELD   Oh but I have Miss Frost, the rest of my natural life without a degree. All I looked for that first morning was for some other people like me who would also fail. That's when the white angels should have come. Taken me up to heaven. Cold morning in October. My tutor shook me by the hand, said, Dangerfield, delighted, delighted absolutely you're with us. I smiled so pleasantly, willing to please. Miss Frost, if there were music all the time. You know the cross they've got down there on the Mohammed Road to mark the end of the pale. I just lived outside. Now I go east, always east, forced to, away from where the sun sets.

MISS FROST   Please, Mr. Dangerfield, please don't say these things. You'll go west one day, I know you will.

DANGERFIELD [*Smiles*]   I fear I will, Miss Frost.

MISS FROST   I don't mean that, I mean you won't always have to be going east, won't you be able to stop and not go east or west.

DANGERFIELD   That's been my ambition. Be only north and south then. But alas. I guess, Miss Frost, that the spies that watch this house would never know the despair and yelling for love that goes on inside.

MISS FROST   You're so tired, Mr. Dangerfield. You look so tired.

DANGERFIELD   Yes, I am.

MISS FROST   Let me get you some hot chocolate.

DANGERFIELD   Miss Frost.

MISS FROST   Yes.

DANGERFIELD   Miss Frost, you're kind.

MISS FROST   No.

DANGERFIELD   What will you do when I'm gone.

MISS FROST   I don't know.

DANGERFIELD   Move somewhere else.

MISS FROST   I guess so.

DANGERFIELD   Leave Ireland.

MISS FROST   I don't know.

DANGERFIELD   Leave.

MISS FROST   It's a bit of an undertaking.

DANGERFIELD   Come with me.

MISS FROST   You don't want me.

DANGERFIELD   Don't say that. Don't say that. Listen, a little poem.
>   If
>   There's a bell
>   In Dingle
>   And you want to say
>   How sorry you are
>   I'm gone
>   Ring it
>   And make it go
>   Ding Dong.

MISS FROST [*Facing away, moves toward the kitchen*] I'll make the chocolate.

DANGERFIELD Miss Frost—[FROST *exits*] Ah, me. [DANGERFIELD *folds up in silence. A loud crash from bedroom.* DANGERFIELD *stoic. A figure appears at bedroom door. Bottle held up in a hand. Deerstalker, eye patch, high laced boots of* KENNETH O'KEEFE, *Duke of Serutan.*] Ah, Kenneth. Why didn't you use my door.

O'KEEFE You see an utterly broken man. I'm going to drink this till I'm stinko.

DANGERFIELD Wisest words you've ever spoken.

O'KEEFE [*Holding bottle high*] I'm finished.

DANGERFIELD Sad words, untrue words.

O'KEEFE I gave myself up. Went to the consulate and told them to ship me back.

DANGERFIELD Not the high seas, surely not that, Kenneth.

O'KEEFE Ship sails tomorrow night. It's in Alexander Basin right now. Sick man and I'm taking his place, Lady Eclair was a dead loss. As soon as I got out there I knew it was no go. Could feel it in my bones. Too good to be true. She took one look at me and almost had a fit.

DANGERFIELD Not unnaturally.

O'KEEFE My foreign accent went all to pieces. I sounded just like I got off the boat from U.S.A. No point prolonging the misery, I said just give me thirty shillings for my expenses coming out and I'll leave. I left and bought the first bottle of drink I've ever bought in my life.

DANGERFIELD An historic moment. [*Claps hands*] Glasses.

O'KEEFE [*Pointing to kitchen*] Someone's in there.

DANGERFIELD Miss Frost. [O'KEEFE's *evil eye looking for evil*] She must join us. [*Calling*] Miss Frost, don't bother with the chocolate for the moment. Mr. O'Keefe has just arrived with refreshment. Do join us.

MISS FROST [*Slowly coming out, speaks shyly to* O'KEEFE] Hello.

O'KEEFE Hi ya. [O'KEEFE *takes three glasses from mantel and pours.* MISS FROST *sits sedately aside*] And I was depressed before I got out to Lady Eclair. Someone tried to commit suicide in Dublin. First one for five years, but it was bungled.

DANGERFIELD The grand inefficiency of the race.

O'KEEFE A few days ago I was so hit up about it. Conjuring up wonderful dreams of zinc table tops, pans, dishes, scullery maids, then bang, when it comes time to do my stuff—kaboo, just one look at Eclair. So soon as I got off the bus on the Quays I went straight for the consulate. Went in and said deport me. A nice guy, five minutes and he had a ship. [*Taking a deep drink*] On my way back to the States, a beaten and finished man.

DANGERFIELD Don't let it get you down, Kenneth.

O'KEEFE I've never felt so damned screwed in all my life. My last day on the ould sod. As tough as this country is I hate to leave it, but if I don't I'll die. What are you going to do.

DANGERFIELD Direction east. Mail boat. Tomorrow, too.

MISS FROST It's a shame you're both going. I don't know you awfully well, Mr. O'Keefe, but I feel Ireland is losing two really interesting people and I'm sorry you're leaving.

O'KEEFE You know, I really appreciate that. Thanks.

MISS FROST [*Finishing her drink, standing up*]   I'm pleased you do. And it has been an experience just making your acquaintance. Now I've got to go and do some things. But, Mr. O'Keefe, I do wish you every good luck with all you do in the future.

O'KEEFE   Thanks. I'll remember that.

MISS FROST   Goodbye.

DANGERFIELD   Stay. Please, Miss Frost. Stay with us.

MISS FROST   I really must get on, Mr. Dangerfield. I've so much to do. [*Smiles goodbye to* O'KEEFE *and exits*]

O'KEEFE   She's pleasant.

DANGERFIELD   Very.

O'KEEFE   Your affairs are fishy.

DANGERFIELD   My life is an open book.

O'KEEFE   You're not fooling me. I leave this setup at dinner time, doesn't make a bit of difference to me because tomorrow that ship will be moving out of Dublin so who cares how you screw yourself up. But let me tell you one thing. Women, drink and the general chaos will ruin you. You'll end up in the institution. It's all over Dublin that you've been dancing in the streets.

DANGERFIELD [*Smiles*]   Off to the land of the big rich. The monstrous rich. [*Points west*] Over there the quids.

O'KEEFE   I'm not interested. This morning I got up early and walked down Fitzwilliam Street. It was still dark. I heard a clip clop coming along and the milkman singing. With that funny light on the streets. And the air was country air. Jesus, I don't want to go back.

DANGERFIELD   A fine great place of opportunity. Oh, maybe a little bit of unhappiness and people whoops out the windows. May even find a woman to love you.

O'KEEFE   If I can't do it here, I'll never do it there.

DANGERFIELD   I don't think I'm exaggerating when I say bodies over there are beautiful. How will you bear it being waved in your face.

O'KEEFE   I can wait. [*Slugs back drink*] Jesus, even when I marched with these guys to take the North by force. Everyone was going to shoot a policeman, couldn't hold them back, going to declare the North under the tricolor. Everybody's pockets filled with homemade bombs, hand grenades and gelignite. We finally get over the border, forty of us and one policeman walks up to us and says, 'ere 'ere, this 'ere is King's land, now behave yourselves or I'll have to lock up the whole lot of ye. Everybody gets long faces, rolls up the tricolor, puts away the bombs, and we all go into the first pub and get drunk, the policeman with us as well. Do you know, I think the North ought to take over the South.

DANGERFIELD   A sound suggestion.

O'KEEFE   What about these women of yours you got planted around Dublin when you go to London. [*Beckons with thumb*] And her.

DANGERFIELD   Do you think I keep a harem, Kenneth. I lead a life of 'spartan self denial. Miss Frost is one of the finest people I know. She leads a gainful respectable life.

O'KEEFE   [*Lowering voice*]   I heard the neighborhood was in disgrace over this affair.

DANGERFIELD   Miss Frost and I would never stoop. Or set upon one another lasciviously. Within the bounds of good taste and dignity. Furthermore, I would like to point out that Miss Frost is joining the nuns.

O'KEEFE You awful bastard.

DANGERFIELD Have you ever known me to involve myself in anything not above board or on boards or anything? I say, out with it, O'Keefe. Geek. You're so starved for it, Kenneth, that you're imagining things. You think I sin. Not me.

O'KEEFE [*Pointing the evil finger*] You're socked in there like a banana in the peel.

DANGERFIELD Absolutely outrageous. Miss Frost tiptoes through the tulips.

O'KEEFE [*Raising bottle*] Look at me. Drink. You. [*Points*] Drink.

DANGERFIELD [*Mock Irish accent*] And sure it's only the sociability that makes me drink.

O'KEEFE And you know what my ambition is. I'm going to come back and when I do. To move into the Shelbourne Hotel. Strut in through the front door and tell the porter will you garage my Daimler for me, please.

DANGERFIELD No, Kenneth. Would you garage my car.

O'KEEFE You're right. That's it. My car. And into the Shelbourne rooms for a drink. You'll come and meet me. [*Standing up*] I'll say, ah, Dangerfield, you souse, have an anchovy with me. [*A smiled pause*] Do you know, Dangerfield, if it weren't for the British this place would be so many wild savages.

DANGERFIELD Kenneth, I'm glad you've come to see it that way.

O'KEEFE The Irish feel that children are brought down upon them by the wrath of God for screwing. All you hear is that if it weren't for you kids, life would be rosy and we could have a good time. But we worked and slaved ourselves to the bone to give you a little more than we had and now look at you, won't bring a penny into the house. No good loafer wasting your time with these books when there are good jobs on the railroad.

DANGERFIELD   Geek.

o'KEEFE [Pulling at his sock]   My socks are soaking. Everything wet and gray.

DANGERFIELD   Anyway, Kenneth, it is fitting indeed that we should have the comfort of this friendly bottle on our last day. Think you should take a young woman with you. One willing to put the shoulder to the wheel in the new world. And push.

o'KEEFE   My sexual life depends on the nuances of wealth. I want to satisfy my carnal appetites with Lady O'Keefe. Discussing our estate and horses. Coffee and a bottle of Hennessy in the library. We go separately to our adjoining rooms. I notice the door between us is slightly ajar. [o'KEEFE tiptoeing, peeking] I wait a discreet ten minutes, tiptoe over, give a delicate knock, may I come in, dear. Yes, dear, do. Ha ha.

DANGERFIELD   Eeeeeee. Kenneth, if you're ever rich it will be an anti-climax.

o'KEEFE   Yeah.

DANGERFIELD [Brimming glass in his loose fingers, sucking back hand-somely]   One day, oh we'll see it. The white stiff collars. The striped blue suits. The mountains of mushrooms, carrots and peas. The raw meat. See it, I say. [Rubbing of the hands] Rich. Fogs outside our dark stone mansions. We'll be smiling. [Points to windows] They're out there. Out there. Watching us. That is our last night audience, Kenneth.

o'KEEFE   Yeah.

DANGERFIELD   After this, the curtain goes down.

O'KEEFE   Yeah.

DANGERFIELD   When you come back, Kenneth, I'll walk naked wearing a green bowler to greet you at the boat. With a donkey cart flying green streamers and shamrocks imported from Czechoslovakia and a band of girl pipers blowing like mad.

O'KEEFE   Yeah.

DANGERFIELD   Look to it. Got to fight, Kenneth. Must resist or go down in the pile. There'll be a little richness for one of us soon. And when you're out there on that high sea, I want you to remember to have faith. Because I'll be in that city of Londinium and the "dinium" is groaning with lust. What do you think of that.

O'KEEFE   Nothing. I hate the place. What the hell. Maybe you'll make out. [O'KEEFE *putting on hat*]

DANGERFIELD   Kenneth, don't give up. Must fight. And Kenneth, there are good books that tell us we must. And also about animals who gave up the ghost. No fight. They put a little word at the bottom of the page to tell you something. Extinct. To be avoided.

O'KEEFE   Here's where I leave you.

DANGERFIELD   Kenneth, I never thought this would happen to us.

O'KEEFE   I did. Anyway, although I think it's unlikely, I hope to see you on your arse in the Old Bailey.

DANGERFIELD   Count on it. I'll see justice gets done. Gray for rain. Pink for poodles. Colors for everything. Green for work. Brown for lust. Blue for deads. Kenneth, listen.

Take deads

Away

Play music
Please.

O'KEEFE   So long.

[*He goes*]

DANGERFIELD [*Up to window, parts curtains, knocks on glass, grins, waves. Back to chair, pours a drink, looks at it against the light.* MISS FROST *appears.* DANGERFIELD *looks at her. She stands*] I'm going to call you Lilly. [MISS FROST *looks down*] I think it's time I called you Lilly. Lilly. Only hours left. Last day. Miss Frost, my Lilly.

MISS FROST   Please, Mr. Dangerfield.

DANGERFIELD   Got our bodies mixed up on the bed.

MISS FROST   Please, Mr. Dangerfield.

DANGERFIELD   This is all a pitiful life. I want to settle somewhere. Somewhere to call my own, Lilly. That's what we all need. Don't need this lust, all it can do is get you to bed. Come closer.

MISS FROST   I can't, Mr. Dangerfield.

DANGERFIELD   You've been good to me. Like none of the others. Kept me company in loneliness. I could have gone mad, as it is [*Holds out trembling hands*] I've only got a few shakes here and there in the various limbs. Call me Sebastian, on this last night. Lilly.

MISS FROST   I can't. I just can't. Please don't make me.

DANGERFIELD   There just hasn't been enough money. O'Keefe off on the high seas. I must join the Trinity College dining club in London, they say it renews old friendships and keeps one in touch with the life of the University.

MISS FROST It's been a great experience knowing you, Mr. Dangerfield, even though I don't agree with all the things you say. But inside I think you are a good person.

DANGERFIELD [*Holds out hand*] Come here. Lilly.

MISS FROST I've made an oath, not to, again. Please.

DANGERFIELD No harm.

MISS FROST [*Moves toward* DANGERFIELD] Just on the cheek because I can't stop you once you get going.

DANGERFIELD And a little kiss in the ear. Never hurt. Just the one. Lilly, you're wearing perfume.

MISS FROST I beg of you, Mr. Dangerfield, please don't make me feel awful.

DANGERFIELD Our last night together.

MISS FROST Please.

DANGERFIELD Lilly, there are tears.

MISS FROST I hope you've liked me, even just a little.

DANGERFIELD All's going to be all right.

MISS FROST We won't ever see each other again.

DANGERFIELD Don't say that.

MISS FROST I'm packed to go.

DANGERFIELD The sadness.

MISS FROST You don't have to worry about me, Mr. Dangerfield. I'll take care of myself. You know I thought, even though it's none of my business, that you and Mrs. Dangerfield were so right for each other.

DANGERFIELD A little confusion.

MISS FROST And the house, Mr. Dangerfield.

DANGERFIELD The house.

MISS FROST Can I do anything.

DANGERFIELD It's all right. Come closer. Last night together.

MISS FROST Mr. Dangerfield, I'm leaving right now.

DANGERFIELD [*Taking* MISS FROST'S *hand*] There now, easy.

MISS FROST [*Head bent*] I've got to go.

DANGERFIELD Near it now, Lilly. As near as ever could be. Peace. Sacred silence. I've lived by the rules and regulations. Perhaps made up a special few of my own.

MISS FROST You're a gentleman, Mr. Dangerfield, I know you are.

DANGERFIELD [*Patting of her hand*] It's all right, Lilly, I know they've called me other things. Boarder bedded down with the landlord.

MISS FROST Oh God.

DANGERFIELD We were both in need. [MISS FROST *bends her head*] The little talks we had. God is on our side.

MISS FROST Don't bring God into it.

DANGERFIELD He's tender hearted.

MISS FROST   There are no tender hearts.

DANGERFIELD   Oh, aye. Lilly I thought you and I would go to work in the garden out back. Dig it all up, lace it liberally with lime and phosphates, mounds of kelp and ould bones.

MISS FROST   You're well away. Off on the boat. They'll be talking.

DANGERFIELD   Lill, forget ould talk and tongues.

MISS FROST   They'll sack me. I hate to be alive. I hate this country. [*Putting on her coat and cloche hat*] You think it's all a cod.

DANGERFIELD   Very nearly.

MISS FROST   You don't know Ireland. [*Getting her bag*]

DANGERFIELD   I know Ireland.

MISS FROST [*Standing with her bag*]   What am I going to do.

DANGERFIELD   The most fantastic collection of fan mail in the world comes to me and the houses I live in. Hired detectives to trail me around Dublin city and environs, posting children at street corners to watch me. Lilly, you see, talk is the least of it.

MISS FROST   Mrs. Dangerfield said you were a waster.

DANGERFIELD   I want only peace, Lilly, not ownership or even women and I hope not men. Just don't want to be watched and trailed. I'm a naval man. I've sailed dreamboats in my time. But waster, no. I've tried [*Pointing finger*] to pawn that plant out there. And it got so upset it started to die. Gave it medicine at first but went into decline and I changed to poison out of pity. Cheer up, Lilly. [MISS FROST *picks up her bag and* DANGERFIELD *moves after her and she runs*] What's the matter, Lilly. [MISS FROST *goes away and* DANGERFIELD *goes to the window to look*] A nice leg on Miss Frost. [*Picking up a pile of letters.*

Stands in the middle of the room and slowly tears them up] No, little daughter. Dada, Mommie says you're a cad. Easy, child, don't talk to Dada like that. Dada's a good daddy. He big, good man. Mommie says you pawned all the dishes and pram. Nonsense, child, Dada big, good man. Oh, it might be worse. Worse than that. [*Loud knocking on door.* DANGERFIELD *quick to attention with a click of heels. Shouting*] All hands on deck. Prepare to lower lifeboats at the signal. [*Tiptoes to window*] Ah. Egbert. Just in time for the leave taking. You're wearing a nice white starched collar, see you've got on the blue striped shirt O'Keefe says is fashionable with the brown tie. Black hat and black shoes. Aren't you getting a little wet. [*Shouting*] All right, all hands. Abandon ship. [DANGERFIELD *to kitchen and slamming back door, comes back and waits smiling, listening to the feet run around the house*] Egbert, don't hurt yourself, careful over the back fences, you scoundrel. Tomorrow, Egbert, you'll wait outside the house for weeks waiting for me to slip the white flag out between the curtains. And I won't. And maybe you think I hate you, but I don't. Only trying to get your own little pile of pounds. My dream was all lament. I think I'm weary of my terrifying heart. But not let the cold get it now because I must keep it hot for hours yet. But I need a change. The burial boat. Over the water and far away. [*Lights fade*] Travel east. Under the sea gulls. Or on my back in Ireland looking up out of the world. Set sail on this crucifixion Friday. Out between the lighthouses. And then feel the water. Come here till I tell you. Where is the sea high and the winds soft and moist and warm, sometimes stained with sun, with peace so wild for wishing, where all is told and telling. On a winter night I heard horses on a country road, beating sparks out of the stones. I knew they were running away and would be crossing the fields where the pounding would come up into my ears. And I said they are running out to death which is with some soul and their eyes are mad and teeth out.

God's mercy
On the wild
Ginger Man.

[*Curtain*]

Fairy Tales
of New York

FAIRY TALES OF NEW YORK *was first presented by Spur Productions, Ltd., and the Pembroke Theatre, Ltd., at the Pembroke Theatre, Croydon, Surrey, England, on December 6, 1960. It was then transferred to London and presented by Spur Productions, Ltd., and New Watergate Presentations, Ltd., in association with Jack Waller, Ltd., at the Comedy Theatre, on January 24, 1961, with the following cast:*

CORNELIUS CHRISTIAN	*Barry Foster*
1ST STEVEDORE	*Robert Ayres*
CUSTOMS MAN	
CHARLIE (ACT I)	
NORMAN VINE	
STEPHEN MOTT	
ADMIRAL	
FRITZ	
2ND STEVEDORE	*Harry Taub*
3RD STEVEDORE	
HOWARD HOW	
MIKE O'ROURKE	
CHARLIE (ACT IV)	
ELAINE MUSK	*Susan Hampshire*
MISS KELLY	
GERTRUDE GENTLE	
CHARLOTTE GRAVES	

Directed by Philip Wiseman
Settings by Assheton Gorton

ACT ONE

Helen

SCENE 1. THE PIER

Three o'clock cold February afternoon, a pier West 57th Street, New York City. Blasts of ships' whistles in the North River. Grinding winches, chatter of greeting people. Rumble of luggage laden handcarts and clinking chains. Next to two bags CORNELIUS CHRISTIAN *stands apostate under the letter C.*

FIRST STEVEDORE'S VOICE [*From behind mountainous crates*] Hey, Marty, what's in this box, somebody dead. Maybe we ought to be respectful and take off our hats.

SECOND STEVEDORE'S VOICE Don't be crazy, nobody's dead.

FIRST STEVEDORE'S VOICE Yeah. Feel the weight of it. Hey, I heard about this. See that guy over there watching. That's the husband. Wife's in here.

SECOND STEVEDORE'S VOICE Honest.

FIRST STEVEDORE'S VOICE   Yeah, honest.

SECOND STEVEDORE'S VOICE   Holy mackerel.

FIRST STEVEDORE'S VOICE   So move that trolley. Easy. Boy, you—you need glasses. This is a guy's wife, don't drop it.

SECOND STEVEDORE'S VOICE   I should live so long.

FIRST STEVEDORE'S VOICE   Shut up, maybe you won't. There, what did I tell you. Over there, see, customs is going over to him.

LOUDSPEAKER   Now hear this. All passengers are asked to remain under their letters until customs has examined their baggage, please. This will help clear pier. Thank you.

CUSTOMS MAN [*Crossing to* CHRISTIAN *and gently touching his shoulder*] I'm sorry sir, about this. I know it isn't a time you want to be annoyed by a lot of questions but if you could just give me some information I'll try to get this over as quickly as possible. It's just a formality. [*Raising clip board, writing*] I understand this happened aboard ship.

CHRISTIAN   Yes.

CUSTOMS   And your wife was English and you're American.

CHRISTIAN   Yes.

CUSTOMS   And you intend burial here.

CHRISTIAN   Yes.

CUSTOMS   It's just that we've got to make sure of these things because it can save a lot of trouble later on. Don't want to burden you with anything unnecessary. Do you have any children traveling.

CHRISTIAN   Just my wife and myself.

CUSTOMS I understand. And are all your other possessions your own property, all personal effects. No fine art, antiques. You're not importing anything.

CHRISTIAN No.

CUSTOMS Just sign here. Won't be anything else and if you have any trouble at all don't hesitate to get in touch with me right away. [*Taking out a card*] Here's my name and I'll straighten out any difficulty. Just Steve Kelly, customs'll get me. Vine Funeral Home phoned here just awhile ago. I told him everything was all right and they say you can go see them at their office or phone any time this afternoon or tonight.

CHRISTIAN Thanks very much.

CUSTOMS Have you got a porter.

CHRISTIAN No.

CUSTOMS Look. See the stevedore there. Guy with fur jacket. I'll send him over. He'll take care of you. OK. Don't worry about anything. [*He puts his hands on* CHRISTIAN's *shoulder*]

CHRISTIAN Thanks.

[CUSTOMS *exits*]

THIRD STEVEDORE [*Walking up to* CHRISTIAN] Excuse me. Steve Kelly, the customs guy. You want some help. This yours here.

LOUDSPEAKER Now hear this. Please load away from entrance. Please keep the entrance clear for passengers. Please.

CHRISTIAN Yes. This is mine.

THIRD STEVEDORE OK. You in a hurry.

CHRISTIAN No.

THIRD STEVEDORE OK. You don't mind if we wait a few minutes. Until some of these eager beavers get off this pier. Then you won't have to get crushed and get your bags broken in the rush. They come off this ship like a bunch of starving animals.

CHRISTIAN [*Taking out his wallet, tendering a dollar*] Here.

THIRD STEVEDORE I don't want any money. This is strictly a favor. I don't take money for a favor. You'll do the same for somebody. That way it goes round the world.

CHRISTIAN Thanks.

THIRD STEVEDORE Forget it. Where do you have to go.

CHRISTIAN I don't know. Have to think of somewhere.

THIRD STEVEDORE A million hotels.

CHRISTIAN I think I better look for a boarding house.

THIRD STEVEDORE A boarding house for a guy like you. You don't look the kind of guy stays in a boarding house, don't sound it either. You come all the way here without having a place to go. None of my business. OK. Maybe you got no friends. Takes all sorts of people to make a world. Keep telling my wife that, she don't believe me. Thinks everybody's like her. Across there long.

CHRISTIAN Went to college.

THIRD STEVEDORE Good education over there. Don't you feel lonely.

CHRISTIAN No, don't mind being alone.

THIRD STEVEDORE That right. Guy's got a right to feel that way if he wants. Free country. But hear the noise out there. [*The sound of traffic and hawkers*] It's going to explode any minute. Place full of dangerous maniacs. [*Looking around*] You know on this pier. Boy. If you even sneeze at the wrong time. What a life. You keep going, keep going. Like clock springs. They just wind you right up. I used to have a pet shop. I love animals. Yeah. Tell a relative about it. Gets big ideas how to make a lot of money. And I lose the whole thing. And I'm on the pier pushing a cart where every guy's after a fast buck and they kick in your teeth and pull them out of your mouth and your life isn't worth a dime. [*A stevedore passing with a hand cart*] Hey, Charlie, can I borrow that a second.

CHARLIE   Drop dead.

THIRD STEVEDORE [*To* CHRISTIAN]   See. Friendship. Means a lot around here. [*Looks at tag on* CHRISTIAN'S BAG] That's a funny name, Christian. You got a bit of a funny voice too, you English. Learn to speak at college.

CHRISTIAN   Just a bit.

THIRD STEVEDORE   That ain't the accent you were born with. Sounds OK anyway. People born speaking like that.

CHRISTIAN   I don't know.

THIRD STEVEDORE   Maybe I'm asking personal questions. But you're the kind of guy I would have been proud to walk into my pet shop. Those animals, I really loved them. They have personalities. All the little funny things they do. [*Distant siren*] Hear that. Guy just murdered his mother for a dollar. And I got to drink milk all day, live like a baby. Just because I don't want to hurt people. Is that bad that I don't want to hurt people. And that I love animals. Now my wife's relatives want me to go into air conditioning. Be a millionaire. Just like with the pet shop. They said all you have to do is feed these dumb animals. Get them a big farm. And they get babies like mad. I get the farm for the animals to have the babies. They smell my relatives around the place and they don't want to have any babies. How do you like that. And I go broke. Hey, what am I doing telling you my life's history. You're young; you got life ahead of you. [*Takes a long look at* CHRISTIAN, *and in sudden silence looks around*] Hey, pier's clear. Let's go. [*Picks up bags. Exits.*]

[*Curtain*]

SCENE 2. THE FUNERAL PARLOR

CORNELIUS CHRISTIAN *sitting, waiting, hands folded, head gently bent, coat collar up.*

CHRISTIAN Come all the way to a funeral parlor, after all these years. So tired. All I've got left of Helen are just her bag of clothes. I mustn't cry. No one to be with her. And I was so full of dying myself. How much is it going to cost. Only thing to do is wait wait wait. Helen could never pack things. I told her she was sloppy, why don't you fold things up. [*Takes out wallet*] What's his name. Norman Vine, funeral director. What do I say to him. Do I have to give him a tip or cigar. Might think I'm not sorry enough and can't concentrate on the death. [*Roar of elevated train*] I could have stepped right under a train. Just let it roar right over me. I'd be electrocuted. How would they know to take me here and put me with Helen. Ought to write it in my wallet. In case of death, take me to Vine funeral home and bury me with Helen. So slaughtered you could put me round her in the same casket. [*Hand to brow and eyes*] I just can't bear for you to be cold and you said last thing of all to put you in the ground. Always wore a green shadow around your eyes. And when you came near me in your silk rustling dress you sounded hollow inside. Shout at you and my voice would come back in echoes. The first day at sea, listening with her eyes and I didn't want to spend the two dollars for a deck chair. And I'd let her have it. I'd let her have anything now. Helen, you could have got two deck chairs or three and I'd have said nothing because I wouldn't be so lonely for you now. It wasn't the money. I just didn't want you to get cold because you looked so ill you'd freeze up there and no one knew how sick you were. We fought over a towel. I pulled it right out of your hands when you said you'd spend the two dollars. It wasn't the money, I'd tear up two dollars right here in this room. [CHRISTIAN's *head slumps forward, raises slowly*] God, it was the money. I've lost you. Two rotten bucks.

VINE [*Entering room*] Good evening, I'm Mr. Vine. Sorry to keep you waiting. You're Mr. Christian, aren't you. [*Offering hand*]

CHRISTIAN [*Slowly raising his head*] Yes.

VINE Are you all right.

CHRISTIAN Yes. I'm all right. Dusty city. Guess it's blown in my eyes.

VINE Make yourself comfortable.

CHRISTIAN Thanks.

VINE There are only a few little things here, a couple of documents. Customs man who dealt with you telephoned after you left the pier. Very nice of him, and I'll certainly do everything I can, Mr. Christian. [*Offering papers*] Only these to sign.

CHRISTIAN Thanks. [*Looks down, through and away from forms*]

VINE [*Gently holds pen out to* CHRISTIAN] Here.

CHRISTIAN [*Coming back from miles away*] Thanks.

VINE I'm not just an ordinary man in this business. It means a great deal to me and if there is any special help I can give anyone I'm really glad to do it. So understand that. If there's anything you want to tell me. Just talk. That helps.

CHRISTIAN   That's nice of you.

VINE   We can only do our best, Mr. Christian. Just the best. We understand sorrow. I've arranged burial at Greenlawn. Do you know New York.

CHRISTIAN   Yes, I was born here.

VINE   Then you may not be without knowledge of Greenlawn. One of the most beautiful cemeteries in the world, and it's always a pleasure to visit. Out there where there is much grass and trees the grind of the city is left behind. My wife's buried there as well and I know it's a place of great peace. We realize sorrow, Mr. Christian. I'll take care of all the immediate details for you and you can have a chat with them later on. All under my personal direction. Arranged as soon as you wish.

CHRISTIAN   Could it be arranged for tomorrow morning.

VINE   Yes. Will it give mourners time. The notice will only be in tomorrow's Daily News, only give anybody couple hours to get here.

CHRISTIAN   I'll be the only mourner.

VINE   I see.

CHRISTIAN   No one knew we were coming to New York.

VINE   We'll use this, [Hand out] the Emerald suit.

CHRISTIAN   I want to keep it very short.

VINE   I understand. In the way of flowers.

CHRISTIAN I'd like something simple. Perhaps a wreath with My Helen.

VINE Of course. Something simple. I'll see to it myself. We try to make friends with sorrow, Mr. Christian. That way we come to know it. You'd like us to use glass. For permanence.

CHRISTIAN That's all right.

VINE And where are you located.

CHRISTIAN Near the Museum of Natural History.

VINE I'm pleased you're near there. There's much to reflect upon in that building. We'll send our car for you.

CHRISTIAN Is that anything extra.

VINE Included, Mr. Christian. Shall I make it nine thirty, ten. Whenever you wish.

CHRISTIAN Nine thirty is fine.

VINE Mr. Christian, would you like now to have a little drink before you go. Some Scotch or Irish.

CHRISTIAN Well, thank you, I would. Are you Irish, Mr. Vine.

VINE [Crossing to a cabinet] My mother was. My father's German. [Returning with glasses] Soda.

CHRISTIAN Please.

VINE Now the way you said that. Just one word. I can tell by your voice that you're an educated man, Mr. Christian. I also like your name. I never had very much in the way of education. I was a wildcatter in Texas and then became manager of an oil field. Wouldn't think it to look at me, would you. I left school when I was nine years old. And I've always wanted to be in this business. But I was thirty before I got a chance to do a high school course. Did it in the Navy and then I went to morticians school when I came out. It makes you feel closer to people. It's dignified. And art. When you see what you can do for someone who comes to you helpless. To recreate them just as they were in life. Makes you able to soften things. You're a man I can talk to. You're a person who's got a proper mental attitude. I can always tell. There are some of them who make you sick. It's the only thing I don't like about the business are the phonies and I get my share of them. Here, [*Offering drink, a sparkling tinkling replenishment*] have another, do you good.

CHRISTIAN   Thanks.

VINE   Some people think I'm outspoken but I've given a lot of satisfaction and people put their whole families in my hands, even in a big city like this. I opened up another branch in the West Fifties. But I like it best here where I began. My two little girls are growing up into big women now. You meet people from all walks of life. I'm a bit of a philosopher and I feel anything you've got to learn you'll learn just through what you have to do with people, in that way I never miss an education. It's a fact, I never graduated. It's especially sad when I bury those who did. But everything is how a person conducts themselves. That's how I know all about you, customs man said over the phone you were a real gentleman. Would you like now for me to tell you something about the establishment. If you don't it's all right.

CHRISTIAN   I don't mind.

VINE   You'd like to feel that she was somewhere where she's really at home. We're empty now, there's just two reposings on at my other branch although it's a busy time of the year. [*Rising, expanding*] I never want to have an establishment of mine get so big you lose the personal touch. It must be warm and intimate to make people feel at home. I call the other branch a home, bit of an expense to change here because parlor is in the neon sign. I feel parlor is a word that

lets you down. Something poor people have. I like the word home.
I don't gloom at people, I smile. Death is a reunion. A pause in the
life of others. You understand me.

CHRISTIAN Yes.

VINE This suite here has its own private rest room. Which has been
of great success. I wouldn't say it to most people but certain functions
get stimulated at the passing of a cherished one. You've noticed how
I've used green light and how it glows from the walls, it's a special
kind of light that makes it do that. Only kind in New York. You
don't mind me talking.

CHRISTIAN No, it's all right.

VINE In a few years I'm opening a branch out in the country. For some
people the country signifies peace. You perhaps saw that picture out
in the hall. The Forest in the Winter Sun. Looking at that in my
spare time gave me the idea. It's not conducive to peace to come in off
the street to mourn. [Roar of train] You hear that elevated train out
there. Thinking of tearing it down. Won't be too soon for me. Shakes
the teeth out of your head. But I learned to accept it. And also I
have a chapel here. And it's round just like the world and again green
is my motif. I would like the whole establishment to have the air of
a studio.

CHRISTIAN It's all very nice.

VINE That makes me feel good. I'm pleased. And I hope you'll be satisfied you dealed with me. I always want people to feel that. You can
trust me and know I've got reverence for my work. To love your work
is happiness. It means I meet someone like you, too. I'm never wrong
about people. I know the real tears of death and they don't go down
the cheeks. And [Looking about in sentiment] this is the first room
I've ever used. One or two personages been here. Mr. Selk the manu-
facturer. I had that privilege. And we light a candle behind that green

glass when someone is reposing. I think it gives, or rather, let me say, lends a sacredness to the occasion.

CHRISTIAN   Yes, it does.

VINE [*Touching* CHRISTIAN's *elbow*]   You go home now. Put all bother out of your head. Get a good night's sleep. Remember it takes time. But time is a friend of ours. And I'm here, remember that, for any kind of request. Our car will be there in the morning. [*Light fading. Faintly, strains of Beethoven's* Fifth Piano Concerto, Second Part. *Handshake.* VINE *handing a catalog*] Take this. Good night, Mr. Christian.

CHRISTIAN [*Leaving*]   Good night.

[*Roaring of elevated train. Night comes. A long darkness. A light rises, a green fluttering glow around Helen's coffin. The profile of her white face.* ELAINE MUSK *enters, touches coffin, looks at Helen. She bends to the floral decoration, fixes a flower. She turns to a sound, looks at door.* CORNELIUS CHRISTIAN *enters*]

MUSK   Mr. Christian.

CHRISTIAN   Yes.

MUSK   I'm Elaine Musk, Mr. Vine's assistant. May I take your coat.

CHRISTIAN   I think I'll keep it on. For a moment.

MUSK   The music hasn't begun yet. But I'll tell Mr. Vine you're here.

[CHRISTIAN *turns to side of room. Takes off gloves.* MUSK *is watching.* CHRISTIAN *turns to her.* MUSK *softly withdraws.* CHRISTIAN *sits at side of room. Elbows slowly on knees. Head lowered and held between hands*]

CHRISTIAN   Helen, I wouldn't have brought you to a room like this.

Makes me feel I'm casting some poverty on her because this isn't the type of place she would ever be. Hers were fields and open meadows. All this shining junk. Like pies peaches or eggs. Helen's not a pie peaches or eggs. She's mine. And taking her away. Gone already. Where is she nearest to me. Asleep on top of my brain. Came with me all over the ship when I couldn't stand them staring at me everywhere I went and whispering. Our table out in the center of the dining room. They were all thinking of the day when they had the gala occasion with the paper hats and balloons and Helen just sat there at the table and wept, pink handkerchief tucked up your sleeve and pearls like tiny drops from your face and none of them ever saw you again. They even came up to my cabin door after you were dead to listen to hear if I was crying. And the steward who said they wouldn't do your washing. He stuck his brown face in the door and closed it quietly when he saw me prostrate on the bunk. And he slammed the door in your face. Both of us utterly helpless, could do nothing, could say nothing. I held the three dollars in my fist and watched his brown hand come up from his side and pull them out and leave quietly closing the door. The waiter who filled our plates with things we didn't want and came over the second day and said your wife don't eat no more and I said no. And lunch time he came back saying he was sorry he didn't know, the wine waiter just told him and he got me a plate covered in smoked salmon. He kept as far away as he could until the last meal when hovering for his tip he asked me if I was a refugee. Then I went out, from the ship's rails I looked at the strange flat shore with the fragile white fingers in the sky. In that cabin, Helen, where you left your soul and I've got to sit here helpless with and without you. [*Standing*] Shut that casket. Screw it down.

VINE   Is there something wrong, Mr. Christian.

CHRISTIAN [*Sitting, shaking head*]   No.

VINE [*First half minute, Beethoven's* Fifth Piano Concerto, *Second Part*] It's my favorite music I've chosen. She's very beautiful. [*Beckons to casket*] She's waiting for you. [*Offering hand to shake it.* CHRISTIAN *shakes it*] And just press the button there when you want me. All right.

[VINE *leaves*]

CHRISTIAN [*Looking at his hand*]   Almost broken my knuckles. Gone so dark. That green light flows and flickers all over the room. Even has my flowers lit up. He must rake in the money. I'm glad the casket's black. I'd die if it were green. [*Goes to kneel at casket*] So soft kneeling here and I can't look at you. See just the tips of your knuckles. You don't have to shake Vine's hand. If you'd move. You can't get up. Forgive me because I haven't got the courage to look at you. Because I'd see you dead forever. What happens to all the flesh and blood. No child. You leave nothing but the pain of missing you and because I didn't want the expense. A baby costs money. I wouldn't part with a penny. Only reason I had. I knew you were begging me and I'd always say let's wait. And we waited. Your casket's so smooth. Put my hand along the bottom to see if it's stuck with chewing gum. Vine would never allow that. And although he must be half crazy he's given me comfort because I don't feel you're laughed at or joked over dead. Got to keep my head down or I'll look by accident. Thought I would cry and I can't. Helen, I wish we were different from everybody else. Scream for some sort of thing that makes us you and me. Neither of us nothing. And on the ship you said you wanted to lie down in the cabin. Those first Americans you met just tired you out, Helen. And I was so proud of bringing you back to my country. I wanted you to like them. And even after you'd gone, you don't want anyone to come and touch you on the arm and say I'm sorry about it, about your wife, have courage or something, but you do want them. I wanted someone to show me something. Anything. But not a soul on that damn ship came near me except for money. Each second you get farther away from me. And now they dig the hole with the straight sides and before it gets dark you'll be covered up. And all the times I wished you were dead. So I could be free. But those were black thoughts of anger. But I thought them. Must get up. [*Stands, goes to window, pulls back the curtain*] Busy street. Izzies Best for Bargains. And Vine has a green handkerchief in his pocket. What has he got against the color green. Most of his life must be whispering, nodding, hand rubbing and the five words we'll take care of everything. Except the bill. Think pure. Thing straight. Be red blooded. Big hearted. Glad handed. Show them you can take it. And Vine will open up a country place called Green Beacon.

[VINE *entering quietly, slowly to the casket. Leans over with hand-kerchief*]

VINE   Must be a little condensation on the inside, Mr. Christian. But I hate anything to mar such a lovely face. Woman's lips are one of the most beautiful parts of her body. I can always tell a woman who looks at a man's lips when he talks instead of his eyes. Are you all right, Mr. Christian.

CHRISTIAN   Yes, I'm all right. Do you think we could leave now.

VINE   Yes, a few minutes. Our large reposing room is busy this morning. We never know in this business.

CHRISTIAN   Mr. Vine, I think maybe you're telling me too much about your business. I don't want to say anything but it's getting me down.

VINE   What's the matter.

CHRISTIAN   I don't want to know about the business. It's getting me down.

VINE   Don't get sore, Mr. Christian. I forget sometimes, I try to make everyone feel at home and not treat the funeral business as something strange. People ought to know about it. My own funeral is already arranged. I thought you'd take an interest. But don't get sore. When it happened to me and it was my wife I found I needed some sort of distraction and because I arranged the services myself it made me feel better. I thought you wanted to take an interest.

CHRISTIAN   This isn't distraction.

VINE Take it easy, son. Easy now. You're not alone in this, remember that. If I shot my mouth off I'm sorry. I don't want to do that with anybody but getting sore isn't going to bring her back. Beauty is the only thing you can remember. Try to remember beauty. Come on, I like you, be a sport.

CHRISTIAN My wife's dead.

VINE I know that.

CHRISTIAN Well, what the hell do you mean, sport.

VINE [*Slowly puts on his green tinted sunglasses*] I hope I understand you correctly, Mr. Christian, you would now rather I didn't conduct this any further. I can put you in the hands of my assistant, Miss Musk, if you prefer.

CHRISTIAN All right, all right. I'm not the kind of person who wants to start trouble. Leave everything as it is. I'm just worried about money and what I'm going to do.

VINE Look. Listen to me. I want to tell you straight. I don't cut cash out of nobody. I don't conduct this business on those lines. You've got as long as you want and longer. Understand me. And if that isn't long enough I'll think of something. If you hadn't come here alone from another country I wouldn't take all this trouble but you seem to be a nice guy. I even thought you were a type for this profession and that's a compliment as far as I'm concerned. How many of these slobs would think of wearing a green tie like you. You're a gentleman. And when it's over, if you want to come back and see me, I'd like that. There's a place for you here, remember that. And if you make that decision, I'd like that. If you want, we'll close it now, Mr. Christian. You're ready.

CHRISTIAN All right.

[VINE *presses the buzzer,* ELAINE MUSK *enters*]

VINE We're leaving now, Miss Musk.

MUSK Very good, Mr. Vine. [*She goes to* CHRISTIAN's *coat. Holds it for him to put on*]

VINE Mr. Christian, [CHRISTIAN *pulling on his white gloves*] since you've got no religious preference I might read just a few words of my own at the interment.

CHRISTIAN All right.

VINE And I'll be giving a few dollars to the grave diggers if that's all right. [CHRISTIAN *nods*] And perhaps now, you will wait with John, the chauffeur. We won't be a moment. [CHRISTIAN *exits*] Miss Musk, there's a boy we could use. He's a little upset. Inclined to be nervous. But that's good. He's got the touch. And that's all you need.

[*Curtain*]

ACT TWO

The Interview

SCENE 1. MOTT'S OFFICE

An April morning. STEPHEN MOTT *leans over and speaks into his desk interphone.*

MOTT   Send in Mr. Christian. [CORNELIUS CHRISTIAN *collegiately crosses to take* MOTT's *outstretched hand*] Well, if it isn't my boy Christian, isn't it.

CHRISTIAN   Yes, Mr. Mott, it is.

MOTT   Well sit down, delighted to see you, son. Have a smoke, my boy.

CHRISTIAN   No thanks.

MOTT   Well what can I do for you.

CHRISTIAN   Mr. Mott, I'd like to make money.

MOTT Ha ha. Well that's a pretty straightforward, you might say that it's a universal incentive. A word we use a lot around here, I mean incentive. Like that type of word, connotes purpose. Well now. How do you feel we can help. Got something to offer us.

CHRISTIAN Myself.

MOTT Well now, another pretty straightforward answer. I like that. It's Cornelius Christian, isn't it.

CHRISTIAN Yes.

MOTT Well now, I'll call you Cornelius. Well, Cornelius, so you'd like to make money. Come over here. [CHRISTIAN *to window behind* MOTT] Down there is the harbor of New York. Just look down there. What put us way up here.

CHRISTIAN Well, I guess the elevator.

MOTT Boy, I'm talking on a different level.

CHRISTIAN Oh.

MOTT Ingenuity. It's a word we use around here. Say it.

CHRISTIAN Ingenuity.

MOTT Come on, let's have some lung.

CHRISTIAN Ingenuity.

MOTT That's better, boy. I remember you. A party of my son's, wasn't it. Couple of months ago. Just back from Europe, weren't you. You had a bit of sadness with your wife. Which I was sorry about. I remember that party. The jukebox got short circuited in the rumpus room. Remember a couple comments you made caught my ear. Yeah.

CHRISTIAN   Yes, I was at the party.

MOTT   Look, tell you what. Bit rushed just now, excuse me a second. [*Into phone*] Miss Peep, get me personnel, Mr. How. [*Smiling large smiles of friendliness in the pause*] Ah. Hello, Howard. Got a young man here, friend of my boy's. He wants to make money. Want to talk to him and show him around. Thinks we can use him. Yes. Yes. [*Turning to* CHRISTIAN] Cornelius, you free right now.

CHRISTIAN   Certainly, yes.

MOTT   [*Into phone*]   All right, Howard, you take care of that. Kids, Howard, OK. Fine. Well, life will get less noisier as you get older, Howard, and the kids grow up. Great. Fine. Great. That's great. OK, Howard. Bye. [*Turning to* CHRISTIAN] Well, Cornelius, our Mr. How will show you around. See what we can do. And he'll talk it over with you. Maybe we can have a chat again. I like to talk to the young kids coming along. Now what's that word.

CHRISTIAN   Ingenuity.

MOTT   'At a boy, Christian.

CHRISTIAN   Thanks very much, Mr. Mott.

MOTT   Any time, Christian.

CHRISTIAN   And hope that spot's a little better. [MOTT *surprised*] You know the spot you had in front of your eyes, said you could follow it out the window like it was a bumble bee, only it would always come back again.

MOTT   You got some memory, boy. [*The long pause that does not refresh*] And memory makes money. Remember that utterance. Words are wonderful. Remember that, too.

CHRISTIAN   It's been extremely good of you, Mr. Mott.

MOTT   Anything any time for the young people. Keep in touch. Find Mr. How five floors down.

CHRISTIAN   Thanks again, Mr. Mott.

[MOTT *smiles.* CHRISTIAN *exits.* MOTT *stoneface*]

[*Curtain*]

SCENE 2. HOW'S OFFICE

HOWARD HOW *studiously at his desk.* CORNELIUS CHRISTIAN *entering.*

HOW   Mr. Christian.

CHRISTIAN   Yes.

[*Outstretched hand*]

HOW   I'm Howard How.

CHRISTIAN   Hello. I'm thinking of moving to the Bronx. [CHRISTIAN'S *hand goes to lib, my what an utterance*]

HOW   You're what.

CHRISTIAN   Oh, sorry, Mr. How. Guess I'm nervous. I've just strangely had something on my mind about the Bronx. Once it was meadow-land, I've been reading an old guidebook.

HOW Oh.

CHRISTIAN Yes, ha ha. Was thinking maybe some parts might still be meadowland.

HOW We manufacture spark plugs, Mr. Christian.

CHRISTIAN Of course, of course. I don't dispute that for a minute.

HOW And there are no meadows left in the Bronx.

CHRISTIAN I would never dispute that either.

HOW What do you dispute.

CHRISTIAN I don't dispute anything. Nothing at all. Oh there are some things I don't like all right. But I don't dispute anything. It was just that when I was looking out of the train [CHRISTIAN *upturns a left supplicant hand*] I just thought once [*Looking into hand*] there were real Indians running around here.

HOW Well, let's get back to the twentieth century now.

CHRISTIAN Sure.

HOW And you're interested in our using you.

CHRISTIAN I'd like it if you could.

HOW Point is, Mr. Christian, just what can we use you for. I note you have a rather English tone to your voice. Didn't by any chance pick that up in the Bronx.

CHRISTIAN As a matter of fact I learned it out of a book.

HOW Oh. Now look, I'm not trying to hurt your feelings. For what it's worth you might as well know Mr. Mott likes to have an English quality about the place. You've noticed the rural scenes of England in the halls. We know how to appreciate that kind of atmosphere here.

CHRISTIAN   Yes, nice and green. I mean, you know, rustic. I like it.

HOW   Glad. We feel it's a nice contrast to the product. Well, aesthetically we've made progress together. Arrived at a nice base to use as a springboard. Now. Well, what, Mr. Christian, are you exactly interested in doing. What are your qualifications, your degrees.

CHRISTIAN   Well, as a matter of fact, Mr. How—

HOW   Good. The facts. That's what we want, Christian, the facts.

CHRISTIAN   [Quickly out with the handkerchief to deal with sudden nose tickling] I just missed, I guess, by only a few subjects, of course, getting my degree. At that time I had a lot of things on my mind. You see I've always been deeply interested in human nature and I guess I got distracted.

HOW   Sorry, Mr. Christian, but I understand you don't have a degree.

CHRISTIAN   Well. Except of misery I guess. [The leaning forward. The careful agonization] But I almost made it.

HOW   Don't be alarmed, Christian, these notes I'm making are just a few facts. Note you got alacrity with words.

CHRISTIAN   But I almost made it, I really did.

HOW   Easy, boy. Easy. We make spark plugs. You want to make money. [CHRISTIAN's face is the setting sun of sincerity] You know, I can see you really do, don't you.

CHRISTIAN   Yes.

HOW   I'm glad your desire is sincere.

CHRISTIAN Thanks.

HOW We have progressed. You're a friend of Mr. Mott's son, I presume. Mr. Mott's a friendly but very busy man and this affair more or less, you understand me, rests in my hands if we're going to find something for you. Do you have any preference as regards production or management.

CHRISTIAN Well. I'd like to manage, if that can be arranged.

HOW Just give that pitcher of water a push in my direction, will you. Want some water.

CHRISTIAN Thanks a lot. [*The good things are free*]

HOW You got a faraway look in your eye.

CHRISTIAN Well, you see this water's got a history.

HOW Oh.

CHRISTIAN You'll think I'm crazy.

HOW I'm prepared to wait until conclusions are conclusive. Let's hear the water's history.

CHRISTIAN Well the water has got to come from the Catskills.

HOW That's fairly common knowledge.

CHRISTIAN From the Ashokan Reservoir.

HOW Maybe that fact is not common.

CHRISTIAN I read in a geography book, as a kid, what they had to do. Am I boring you.

HOW   Oh, no. I'm fascinated.

CHRISTIAN   Well, I know it's ridiculous but I just can't forget what it took to make this reservoir. Fifteen thousand acres. Seven villages sunk. Thirty two cemeteries with two thousand eight hundred bodies they had to dig up. [HOW *pushing his glass away*] And even an eighteen mile tunnel through the mountains which is one of the longest subterranean aqueducts in the world.

HOW   Boy, you're just full of facts.

CHRISTIAN   [*Raising glass*]   I guess we might be drinking somebody's soul. [HOW's *raised head to look toward sunnier thoughts*] I'm glad I've had this drink of water. Thanks.

HOW   Don't mention it. [HOW *licking of the lips*] We better reconstruct the relationship here. You're still looking for a job.

CHRISTIAN   Oh yes.

HOW   OK. We want men with ideas. Ideas more than anything. I may mention, along this line, that we prefer these ideas to be of a red blooded nature as opposed to weird. Can you type.

CHRISTIAN   Well. My parents gave me one of those little typewriters when I was a kid but I don't expect that would qualify me as a typist at the moment, but it's something I could pick up. I pick most things up rather easily.

HOW   Like your degree, for instance.

CHRISTIAN   Look, Mr. How, I'm after a job. I don't want to misrepresent myself or give a false impression, but as I said I'm interested in human nature.

HOW   You said that.

CHRISTIAN I don't have a degree. OK. Maybe I was too distracted by human nature in college. I got disappointed in human nature as well and gave it up because I found it too much like my own.

HOW Wow, Christian. You're some candidate.

CHRISTIAN But I wasn't stupid, you know.

HOW Look. Mr. Christian. You don't mind if we don't bother seeing things today. I mean you'll understand that until we know what you can do there isn't really much point in my showing you our setup at the moment. I know Mr. Mott's one of the friendliest men you could ever want to meet and I know he wants to help you, but it is rather a question, in the end, can you help us.

CHRISTIAN Yes, I understand.

HOW You're a very presentable person and, of course, well spoken and by the way, I like the way you tie your knots, that's a nice tie, always be sure of a man in this business if he wears a knitted tie. Just want us both to face the facts. And that suit, too. Just the facts, Christian. Just the facts.

CHRISTIAN OK.

HOW Got an opening for a courier representative. [At papers] Dispatch and deliver various important papers. Expenses, taxi and all the rest.

CHRISTIAN I'm almost thirty years old. You mean I deliver papers. Like a messenger boy.

HOW Not in so many words, Mr. Christian. Not in so many words. It's of the nature of a confidential dispatch agent and you would, of course, hold the title of executive courier.

CHRISTIAN What are the friends I've known all my life going to say. They'd be overjoyed. Never stop laughing. I went to college you know.

HOW   A lot, an awful lot of people go to college, Mr. Christian. Mr. Mott never went to college and he controls a business extending to twenty nine states, we just added Texas yesterday.

CHRISTIAN   Well, I've had a job before.

HOW   I'm keeping an open mind. I'm perfectly reasonable you know, Mr. Christian. What sort of work did you do. You see I'm not here to bring about a stalemate with applicants. I'm here to hire the right man for the right job. OK. Now what exactly are you experienced in?

CHRISTIAN   Does it matter.

HOW   That's up to you. I'm only trying to help. Just testing your qualifications. Want to know the sort of work you're best suited for. Where your interests truly lie. We're an outfit, you know, where, when it's expedient we take off our jackets, you understand me, and roll up our sleeves. And being a courier executive would allow your capabilities to rise to the surface. You see what I mean.

CHRISTIAN   To be frank. I've been, well, I'm experienced.

HOW   OK. But frank with the facts, Christian. How were you used.

CHRISTIAN   They used me, I guess, as a sort of representative as you might say. A specialist in human relations. As I've said I could count myself as a former student of human nature.

HOW   Yes, I know, you've said that three times now. You were in public relations then.

CHRISTIAN   [An *abhorrer of relations in public*]   Well, yes, sort of, I guess. I wasn't too clear at the time because I had a lot of things on my mind.

HOW   What firm was this.

CHRISTIAN   As a matter of fact—

HOW   That's right, the facts, Christian—

CHRISTIAN   It was called the Stars of the Forest, I guess, Incorporated.

HOW   How's that, boy.

CHRISTIAN   Stars of the Forest.

HOW   Don't mind telling me their product. Briefly.

CHRISTIAN   Death.

HOW   How's that, boy.

CHRISTIAN   Death.

HOW   What.

CHRISTIAN   What I'm telling you, death. One word.

HOW   You mean an undertaker.

CHRISTIAN   Since we're down to one word, yes, an undertaker. A Mr. Vine, director of Stars of the Forest, said I excelled in that professional capacity.

HOW   Well you know, God help me, Christian, I honestly don't know what to make of you. Get that chair over there and sit down. It's not been in my experience previous to this to consider anybody in the light, or, forgive me, darkness, of these circumstances. How long did you undertake.

CHRISTIAN   I undertook for, well, not long. I'm begging for a chance to prove myself, Mr. How. Just one chance.

HOW   Easy. Take it easy. [*Lifting his hand to his brow*] Just got to think. What an interview. I am deeply involved in this disorientation. Just let me ask you a question, will you. Wait, excuse me a second. [*Speaking into desk interphone*] Miss Kelly, would you please play over to me the background music we've chosen for Friday's conference for our Chicago representatives.

KELLY'S VOICE   Yes, Mr. How.

HOW   [*Andante Cantabile for Strings*] Cornelius. Now look, tell me, Were you looking for this job. Don't have to answer that if you don't want.

CHRISTIAN   Someone close to me died.

HOW   Sorry to hear that. By the way, you like this music.

CHRISTIAN   It's nice.

HOW   Soothes, doesn't it. Guess it's been one of the most successful innovations Mr. Mott introduced into business practice, almost like the invention of the wheel. [CHRISTIAN *glum*] Come on, Cornelius, cheer up. Only thing is we got a problem here. Your job in the funeral parlor business is not going to cut much ice with Mr. Mott, in fact, the mere mention of it will throw a distinct chill into him. But I'll tell you something before we go any further, you know, I like you, I think you're OK.

CHRISTIAN   Thanks.

HOW   You know, most of the people sent along to me with pull with Mr. Mott aren't worth their weight in paper, strictly between us you understand. You strike me as a guy with imagination. I'm going to give you a chance. If I assign you to our idea department, do you suppose you could get some ideas. It'd be a trial, you understand.

CHRISTIAN   Ideas about what.

HOW Come on Cornelius, what am I letting myself in for. Quick. Ideas. We make spark plugs. Mr. Mott loves the use of words. Think of something. Quick.

CHRISTIAN My mind's a blank at the moment.

HOW [*Into desk interphone*] Miss Kelly, give us something faster, for a fast idea session of approximately forty five seconds starting ten seconds from now.

KELLY'S VOICE Coming ten seconds from now.

CHRISTIAN Gee I'm worried. My whole life depends upon what I might say.

HOW Wouldn't put it like that. Think. One sentence. One idea, a rhyme, anything, don't care what it is, so long as it underlines an inescapable fact.

CHRISTIAN But all my facts have escaped.

HOW [*Liszt's Hungarian Rhapsodies*] Go go, boy.

CHRISTIAN I can't go anywhere, Mr. How, I swear it. The facts have escaped.

HOW Go after them boy. I know you can do it. Think of something to do with a spark plug. Think of the money. Money, boy. Think of the money.

CHRISTIAN I am. Wait. If you've got a heart, you've got a spark that could be a heart by Mott. [HOW *a giant in success.* CHRISTIAN *a sigh, relaxing back*] When you said money, those words just came pouring into my mind.

HOW Don't be ashamed of that, boy. [*Into interphone*] Miss Kelly, good, it did the trick, neat selection, make a note of it.

KELLY'S VOICE   Glad it worked, Mr. How.

HOW   It was swell. And make a note, we've got a new man for our idea department starting right away.

KELLY'S VOICE   Yes indeed, Mr. How.

HOW   [*Standing, hand extended to* CHRISTIAN, *a glad hand.* CHRISTIAN'S *descent into deflation*]   Hey boy. Hey there.

CHRISTIAN   [*Comes to, jumps to take that glad hand*]   Oh.

HOW   You're in, boy.

CHRISTIAN   Mean I'm hired.

HOW   Of course.

CHRISTIAN   Just like that.

HOW   Just like that.

CHRISTIAN   Well, isn't it too quick. Isn't there something more. Can't I fill something out. I just don't feel it's me.

HOW   Cornelius, I think you've got what it takes. Yes. If you've got a heart, you've got a spark that could be a heart by Mott. Here, gee, have another drink of water. Yes. Ingenuity—

CHRISTIAN   [*Mouth coming up out of the water which displaced 2,800 dead bods*]   Makes industry.

HOW   [*Leaning over interphone*]   Miss Kelly, can you hear what's happening in here.

KELLY'S VOICE   Yes I can, Mr. How. It's wonderful.

HOW   Well get it down.

KELLY'S VOICE   Got it, Mr. How.

HOW   Flash those two things to Mr. Mott. He's got to hear about this right away. Ingenuity makes industry. A follow up to Mr. Mott's favorite word.

CHRISTIAN   But this is awful, I mean I feel overrated, just for a few words.

HOW   [*Looking down an index finger at the level of his eye*]   We find a guy, Cornelius, with words like that coming out of his head, we buy that head.

CHRISTIAN   Mr. How, I'm—I think I'd rather be a messenger boy.

HOW   [*Into desk interphone*]   Miss Kelly, I want you to shout back just what you think of Christian's word formations.

KELLY'S VOICE   They're really impressive.

HOW   Now boy, hear that.

CHRISTIAN   But I'll tell you the truth—[HOW *calmly waiting for truth*] No. Maybe I better not. [HOW *smiling warmly*] But I don't know a thing about spark plugs or industry. Except that there's money in it somewhere.

HOW   Isn't that enough, boy. Money is the moment of truth. Boy. You have saddened my life right now. [*Into desk interphone,* CHRISTIAN *sadder*] Miss Kelly, would you make a fresh statement. Just tell him. Exactly what you think.

KELLY'S VOICE   I think he's really spontaneous.

HOW   There you are, boy.

CHRISTIAN   I'm only just a reasonably normal person.

HOW [*The deep concerned*]   You're not normal, boy. I know it. [CHRIS-TIAN *coming alive*] Oh, wait. Hold it. Whoa. Let's reconstruct this relationship here. [*Into desk interphone*] Miss Kelly, would you see that Cornelius and myself are left undisturbed here for a few minutes and stop all calls. We just need a little talk.

KELLY'S VOICE   Certainly Mr. How, anything for background music.

HOW   Not for the moment, thanks. [*To* CHRISTIAN] Now look, Cornelius, let's sit over here. [*Side by side on leather sofa*] I'll give it to you straight. When Mr. Mott gets these messages he's going to want to see you right away. Now I'm going to risk my life. You know why. Because I like you. When you first came in here I just thought you were another snooty sophisticate out of the ivy leaves. But you know, you've got a real quality in you. Which goes deeper than a shirt and tie.

CHRISTIAN   My job in the funeral parlor I suppose. But it was the only thing I could get when I first got back from Europe.

HOW   That's what I want to talk about. It's Europe. That's the thing's given you this quality too. A sort of thing that's real. Breeding. But look. I've got absolute faith in you. You could dazzle this industry.

CHRISTIAN   Mr. How, thanks but I think you're making a mistake. I'm not like that at all. That's just the way I appear. Some of the things I really think and believe would revolt you. I'm almost a criminal type.

HOW   What a remark. You're just full of ideas, boy. Why you're not more of a criminal than I am—[CHRISTIAN *alive*] I mean, [HOW's *light smile of relief*] I just mean we're alike. But look. I'm maybe ten years older than you. Got wife, kids, nice home out in Long Island. The real things. Sure I've got some gripes. But I'll tell you something. See those binoculars. Want you to look out the window with them. Go ahead. [CHRISTIAN *to window with binoculars*] Toward the Statue of Liberty. Got it. Now a little to the left.

CHRISTIAN   Yes.

HOW   See those barges.

CHRISTIAN   I think so.

HOW   That's refuse. Happens every day, all day. Comes down the Hudson and out of the East River, filled with stuff that's no more use. They dump it. Christian, it's made an awful impression on me. See, dumped. Maybe not in a river, but you know what I mean.

CHRISTIAN   Mr. How, I've lost my ambition.

HOW   Boy, don't ever say a thing like that. Not good for you to say it and it's not good for me to hear. Boy and I've heard an earful.

CHRISTIAN   But I mean it, Mr. How.

HOW   Call me Howard. And Cornelius, as a personal favor I'm asking you right now to take this job. I know everything's going to click. Do it for me. You know, I've got to laugh, here I am begging you work for us and ten minutes ago I was wondering how I was politely going to discourage you.

CHRISTIAN   Dump.

HOW   Well yeah, but—no, no—

KELLY'S VOICE   Excuse me for interrupting, Mr. How but Mr. Mott wants you to come up to his private reception room right away.

HOW   [To CHRISTIAN] There, boy. [Into interphone] Thanks, Miss Kelly. Right. Now, Cornelius. I'm asking you now, please. I've got to go through with this now. Just be yourself. Just let your personality come out as it's done with me. Only just don't give any hint of your past employment. Mr. Mott's toleration for the suppression of facts is nil, but to me it's worth the risk. Just go in with the trace of a smile, that's all I'm asking you. [CHRISTIAN's *mumchance mummification*] But don't look like that.

CHRISTIAN   I'm OK, Mr. How. [*Beethoven music softly heard*] My memory's just working. [HOW *is touched. A long silence*]

HOW   Yeah. [*Sadness*] Anyway, just say that thing once more.

CHRISTIAN   You mean about industry.

HOW   Please. With conviction. Ingenuity makes—

CHRISTIAN   I think I've got something better. Ingenuity made Mott, Mott makes industry.

HOW   Miss Kelly, get something for my heart, it's missing beats and get this down, it's Christian again. Ingenuity made Mott, Mott makes industry.

KELLY'S VOICE   Shall I flash that to Mr. Mott.

HOW   No, no. He's got a weak heart, too.

[*Curtain*]

SCENE 3. MOTT'S PRIVATE RECEPTION ROOM

A large room. MOTT *sits in a low chair. Window behind. Table covered with phones at his elbow. Legs are crossed. Holding up his hand for* CHRISTIAN *to shake.* CHRISTIAN *walks across and takes it.*

MOTT Howard, you saw what I didn't see, at first sight, that is.

HOW [*Slight wringing of the hands*] It was nothing, Steve. Miss Kelly selected the background music.

MOTT Sit over there, Christian. [*Directing him to a distant seat on* MOTT's *right;* HOW *to a distant seat on* MOTT's *left*] Well, let's hear all these nice things.

HOW Steve, he's got something even better, didn't want to flash it.

MOTT Give us a flash now, Christian.

CHRISTIAN Ingenuity made Mott, Mott makes industry.

MOTT Very happy. Very happy indeed. Let's have that once more with lung. Lots of lung.

CHRISTIAN Ingenuity made Mott, Mott makes industry.

MOTT Not bad. It's good. Youth refreshes. Of course, you don't expect to be paid much for that.

CHRISTIAN No. But I think it's good.

MOTT Oh, it's good. Youth refreshes. Well you're not kidding us son, I can see that.

HOW He's not, Steve.

MOTT No. At the risk of sounding too full of myself which I do not want to sound. On the other hand I'd like to sketch in my general attitude. Toward the way I personally tackle things. Don't get the idea that I think of myself as a king or anything. But I like to acquire the evidences of man's creative impulse from outside my own orbit. But sadly, not many are blessed with the creative impulse but of course, there's the repulsive creative impulse, too. We won't go into that. But if there are bright brains I don't care what kind of head you got the brains in. [CHRISTIAN *putting a hand to head*] Your head's all right, Christian, don't get nervous. But a head, square, ten feet high or like a ping pong ball is all right so long as it works. But don't let me sound like a king. So I think you have a future, Christian. Now what about the past.

HOW   Steve, I've been through his past with him.

MOTT   Once more fast won't hurt.

HOW   Thought we could get around to it later. Past's fine.

MOTT   I'm interested. At that party back there, that night, Christian, you had a lot of pretty pertinent things to say with maybe a few impertinent. What have you been working at.

HOW   Steve.

MOTT   Howard will you give the boy a chance.

HOW   Steve do you think, with the pressure of time, that we should discuss this now.

MOTT   It has always been my habit to discuss things now. Because after now might be the hereafter, you get me. Christian's been out of college awhile.

HOW   But Christian here is a peculiar case.

MOTT   Why.

HOW   I think his creative qualities are rare.

MOTT   That so.

HOW   Well, [A *hand toward* CHRISTIAN] you've heard him yourself, Steve, a natural alacrity with words.

MOTT   Howard, press the button there for the curtain. [HOW *steps to wall, curtains swing open, a pair of binoculars hang*] I don't usually show people this. But I want you to look out there, Howard. See any barges out there, going past the Statue of Liberty. Know what they are.

HOW   I think I do, Steve.

MOTT   Well it's a private little object lesson of mine.

HOW   I understand completely, Steve.

MOTT   Here today, gone tomorrow.

HOW   I completely understand.

MOTT   So now that nobody is misunderstood let's hear about your past career. Not that I'm buying your past, just the future. Nevertheless, past gives indication of future.

CHRISTIAN   Mr. Mott, I was employed as the star receptionist for Stars of the Forest, Incorporated. A funeral parlor.

MOTT   [*Turning from* CHRISTIAN *to* HOW]   Howard.

HOW   Yes, Steve.

MOTT   Howard.

HOW   Yes, Steve.

MOTT   Howard, I'm talking to you.

HOW   I know, Steve.

MOTT   What about this.

CHRISTIAN   I was expelled from school for lying and cheating. Didn't get my degree from college. And since, I've been performing a job in which I conducted the arrangements for those finding their final resting place. And nothing unseemly ever marred proceedings. Except once.

HOW   In the nature of human relations, Steve.

MOTT   I've got my own eyes and ears, Howard. There are all kinds of relations. But let me utter three things. Life is for the living. A dime is a dime. And last and most, a dollar is a dollar. I am not being vulgar mentioning money. I change my shirt three times a day. I also yesterday was on a plane from Washington when the steward asks me was I any relation to the Motts who had a mausoleum at Throggs Neck. When I said yes he tells me his father takes care of it. This is the curiosity of life. But young Christian here tells me he's a liar and a cheat, degreeless and can smoothly conduct people to their final resting place. Run the Mott empire like a morgue. Now just what exactly do you take me for? Why aren't the facts laid bare in the first instance.

HOW   Don't let facts fool you, Steve.

MOTT   Don't you be too hasty, Howard.

HOW   I feel most recent facts take precedence over previous.

MOTT   I am of the opinion, not wanting to be a king about it, that past facts forecast future facts.

HOW   You're wrong.

MOTT   Come again, Howard.

HOW   You're not exactly right in judging personalities.

CHRISTIAN   [Standing up slowly]   I think I better go.

MOTT Stay Christian. We'll have this out.

CHRISTIAN [*Standing*] But I didn't think I'd be coming between two people. Breaking up a friendship. [*There are looks between* MOTT *and* HOW. MOTT *emits a small chuckle.* HOW *allows some of his front teeth to show*] I know this is a business empire but aren't you two people friends.

MOTT You have the habit of asking a lot of direct questions.

CHRISTIAN In the fact finding maybe I ought to find some, that's all.

MOTT Those don't sound like the words of a liar and a cheat. I just would like to know what the score is on you, go ahead, sit down. I don't want to be rude or hurt your feelings. But you know underneath this gentle innocent exterior of yours, you seem to throw your weight about. In fact, I distinctly feel I'm being pushed. That little remark about friendship and coming between two people. Yeah. And the night at my son's party. You remember my spot. And I remember overhearing a few remarks about my house as well—[*Oh the look of innocence of* CHRISTIAN] don't look so innocent, about the new rich vulgarity. And don't think I planned this either, getting you up here with Mr. How to give you a working over. I was impressed but don't think that you can push us all over.

CHRISTIAN What makes you think this—

HOW Steve, I've never met such a candid fellow as Christian.

MOTT Oh, you think a fellow is candid because he tells you to your face that he is a liar and a cheat. And sweated away in a funeral parlor guiding people to their final resting places. And with a little background music he starts to spout beautiful utterances. Howard, don't be so naïve. Christian here could dazzle you all night with slogans each one better than the last.

HOW Wouldn't it be sad then, Steve, to ignore this talent.

MOTT   It just so happens I know Christian's background.

HOW   Steve, please let me in on all of this.

MOTT   You're not surprised, Christian.

HOW   I thought he was an unknown quantity to you, Steve.

CHRISTIAN   Whatever you say, Mr. Mott. But I think I really ought to be going.

MOTT   Aren't you going to abuse us a little before you leave, Christian. Call us vulgar stuffed shirts.

CHRISTIAN   What makes you think you're in a position to say that, Mr. Mott. Because you think there is nothing I can do about it.

MOTT   Don't threaten me.

CHRISTIAN   I'm not threatening you.

HOW   Please, please, let me in on this.

MOTT   And I suppose you thought that if you used a frontal assault, I'd be afraid to go into this little background. What happened between yourself and your wife is your own business—

CHRISTIAN   Thanks.

MOTT   But what you do where I'm personally—

HOW   Steve, isn't there a sunny side to this situation. Christian didn't tell me he was married.

MOTT   He's not.

HOW   How does a wife come into it.

MOTT   She's out of it for keeps.

HOW   You mean she threw a seven.

MOTT   That's how Christian here got into the undertaking trade.

HOW   I hope I'm not disrespectful. This is way over my head.

CHRISTIAN   Mr. Mott wants to avoid unnecessary contact with ghouls and charlatans.

MOTT   That's enough.

CHRISTIAN   I came here genuinely looking for a job to make money.

MOTT   And thought I didn't have the guts to tell you to your face that I know the whole score on you and that I'd let you just drift into my organization and blackmail my emotional life.

CHRISTIAN   Preposterous rot.

MOTT   Don't go all British with me.

HOW   Can't we galvanize this into a new situation from which it might be possible to evolve a solution. I think, despite the terrible things that have been said here, that underneath it all, we're good hearted people. That there is still something that could be considered constructive determined from—

MOTT   Determined to be a solve it all, are you, How. With your hired honey.

HOW   Nobody has ever talked to me like that before, not in the three years I've been working here.

MOTT   All right, all right, Howard, this is an emotional moment.

CHRISTIAN   Meanwhile I've been insulted but Mr. Mott, thank you for speaking the truth.

HOW   Now there's something we can start with. If the truth was spoken, well don't we feel the better for it. Maybe. [*Good old* HOW, *the looks he gets as he looks from* CHRISTIAN *to* MOTT] Hasn't the air been cleared. Maybe. Just a little. Isn't it just a case where personal history has intruded needlessly, personal lives dragged in and personalities giving vent to feelings that have just become too emotional for words—

CHRISTIAN   I have never laid a hand on my wife. When she was deceased, Mr. Mott.

MOTT   Stop being candid and embarrassing.

CHRISTIAN   It's only right that you should know. My wife's death was a blow and a lot of peculiar things happened immediately following it—

HOW   I was really proud of the impression Cornelius made on me, Steve, and I know the things you've said were tempered by some fact that could just as easily be fiction.

MOTT   Why weren't the facts laid bare, that's all, Howard. Naturally what can you expect if you attempt to obscure the facts—

HOW   I'm sorry, Steve.

MOTT   Maybe I was a little sudden myself, sorry to drag in your personal background like that, Christian.

CHRISTIAN   Maybe I said some things I shouldn't have said.

MOTT   Well, I guess I know I did.

HOW   We all did.

CHRISTIAN   Well, I better be going.

[*Rising*]

MOTT There's a place for you here, Christian.

HOW Construction from confusion.

MOTT We can use you, Christian.

HOW Steve, I'm glad you said that.

MOTT I'm glad I was king enough to say it.

[*Curtain*]

ACT THREE

The Knockout

SCENE 1. THE BOXING ROOM

An arena where all is fair and square on the white mat within the crimson ropes. And on walls are pictures of fighters with muscles, others with smiles but all standing ready to punch. Smell the sweet sweat and fluffy warm towels. A black leather couch for rest and folded hairy legs. On this Thursday, five o'clock in this month of May, MIKE O'ROURKE *sits, his feet crossed on desk by the telephone reading a newspaper as* CORNELIUS CHRISTIAN *bounces in where, of course, some people fear to tread due to fists.*

O'ROURKE   Hey what do you know, Cornelius.

CHRISTIAN   Hello.

O'ROURKE   Haven't seen you for a week or two. What've you been doing.

CHRISTIAN Making word formations.

O'ROURKE That's good. For money.

CHRISTIAN For money.

O'ROURKE That's good. You think this is a free country.

CHRISTIAN Sure.

O'ROURKE That's good. Now let me ask you a question.

CHRISTIAN Sure.

O'ROURKE I was talking to my wife last night. You know how you get into these discussions when you can't sleep. This is pretty personal, this question. You don't mind if I ask you a pretty personal question. Now promise you won't laugh if it seems funny to you.

CHRISTIAN I won't laugh.

O'ROURKE Do you think a girl can get pregnant sitting in the bathtub. You know. By someone taking a bath in the same tub before them. Now take your time. I don't need an answer right away but I told my wife it can't be done. I said it was impossible. [CHRISTIAN *pulling on the pair of yellow bag gloves, taking time to think*] That question needs some thought, think it over, tell me in a few days. I'll live in ignorance for a while. [O'ROURKE *spreading out a newspaper, looking up and down the columns.* CHRISTIAN *rotating his arms*] Hey tell me, Cornelius, you got a girlfriend now. You know I sort of feel you might be lonely.

CHRISTIAN Yes.

O'ROURKE You mean you got one.

CHRISTIAN Yes.

O'ROURKE Oh, that's good. Good. Sort of serious question these days, all kidding aside, you need companionship in this city. You take her out and go places.

CHRISTIAN Once in a while.

O'ROURKE Good. You met her around town.

CHRISTIAN Used to know her as a kid before I went to Europe.

O'ROURKE Childhood sweetheart. My wife was my childhood sweetheart. I never got a chance to know anything else. [CHRISTIAN *with the quick arm flex, shakes his shoulders, bounces on his toes*] How's the shape.

CHRISTIAN Not bad.

O'ROURKE You look good. Hey you know you've created some thinking in this boxing room since you've been back. Been interesting. Every time you go out of here and the Admiral comes in, he says what's with that guy Christian, he wants to know if you've got some grudge. He says you should have stayed in Europe. I sort of told him what happened to you. But he says you're a threat to the United States. You think that's true, Cornelius.

CHRISTIAN Yes.

O'ROURKE [*Shouting*] What. You mean I'm in the presence of a criminal. Hey get out of here. But seriously, Cornelius. Now you tell me. What do you think about a thing like American girls.

CHRISTIAN Whores.

O'ROURKE Hey you can't say a thing like that.

CHRISTIAN Why not.

O'ROURKE Because it ain't true. My wife's American. You mean she's a whore. That's what you said to the Admiral, he had a fit. But you know what he says. He says you're right. But he says if he ever gets you in the ring he'll kill you for some of the other things you said. He gets really burned up. He says people like you are encouragement for the Jews and Niggers to take over.

CHRISTIAN Good.

O'ROURKE Hey, what do you mean good. [*The righteous hand on chest*] And push the Irish out. Hey. Who do you think keeps this city honest. Wait until I tell the Admiral on you. He'll be in in a few minutes. Going to have his nails manicured. You know, the Admiral's a pretty important guy. He controls the whole harbor of New York. Could be useful, this is some harbor. Nice friendly waterfront where they're putting holes in each other's heads. And what's the Admiral doing. He's in here getting his nails manicured. You think men should have their nails manicured, Cornelius? Maybe since you've been away you think we're all homosexuals in this country. [CHRISTIAN, *that roving philosopher, sinking a few deft punches into the body bag*] Hey, come on. Cornelius, you think we're all homosexuals in this country.

CHRISTIAN Yes.

O'ROURKE Hey you can't say a thing like that.

CHRISTIAN Why not.

O'ROURKE Well it ain't right. That's why. Now I'll tell you right away if I was homosexual how could I have the ten kids I got, now you figure that out. I don't have time to be a homosexual. You see what I mean. I go home, before I have a chance to sit down, the kids are on top of me driving me crazy. I don't even get time to be sexually normal. That's why I was wondering about this thing in the bath, getting pregnant. Now you're an intelligent guy, Cornelius, you answer me that.

CHRISTIAN By the laws of physics, it's possible.

o'rourke [*Shouting*] By the laws of what. Hey, don't hand me that laws of physics stuff, can she get pregnant or not. You got to tell me because I'm arguing all night with my wife and I can't get any sleep. She even wakes me up to tell me she knows someone who got pregnant sitting in the bath. I say for Christ's sake shut up, it isn't the iceman or the milkman, OK, so she got pregnant sitting in the bath, kid's already got a christening.

CHRISTIAN It's possible, that's all I can say.

o'rourke I'm disappointed in you, Cornelius. I told my wife if anybody could settle this matter you could. That you studied physics at college. About these little bugs and germs. [*The phone rings*, o'rourke *picking it up*] Bellevue Morgue, headkeeper O'Rourke speaking. No. Yeah. Yeah. O'Rourke. Speaking. The Admiral will be here any minute but you can't make this place into a beauty parlor. [*Shouting*] Women are forbidden. This is a man's domain. I'm the head boxing instructor. What do you think we are, sexually normal. That we want women around. Yeah. I'm just having a discussion here about it. You remember Cornelius Christian, who was over in Europe, all those years. Yeah, he's come back. Been telling us about the women over there. He says these English women have no morals at all, what about that. You don't have to marry them. They do it because they like it. What about that, huh. Sure, we'll go over there together. Sure, book on the boat. And next time you tell the Admiral that he can't bring women into this room no more, this is the last time. . . . We're he men up here. [*Turns to* CHRISTIAN] That right, Cornelius, that we're he men. [*To phone*] This is a men's club. For real men. [*To* CHRISTIAN] That's right, too, huh, Cornelius. [*To phone*] Yeah, we don't want any fairies around here. Yeah yeah, the Admiral's expected any time. You also tell the Admiral he's not kidding me when he has tea. I know what's in that pot. I asked him why he doesn't put milk in it. You're right, this city is a disgrace. [*He hangs up*] Hey, Cornelius, I got a great idea. You know, the Admiral sees himself as one of the fighting greats. He says with his corkscrew punch he's invincible with one of the most powerful punches around. [o'rourke *with the confidential crouch*] And you know I think the Admiral wants to make time with this manicurist. Now I got a good idea. You know you get his goat. You answer him back. He doesn't like it. He's never heard anybody answer him back for years. Now you know what'd be good. We'll fix it up so you have a round or two. What do you say. I'll even tell him you're Jewish but you're called Christian as a disguise. How about it.

CHRISTIAN [Doing the one-foot fancy skip with rope] I don't know. I'm masquerading enough as it is.

O'ROURKE Hey, it'll really be funny. Now I tell you. You fake it. Let him knock you out. It'll go over great with the manicurist. Great with the Admiral. And you've got a friend on the waterfront for life. Come on, now, how about it. Jesus, you'll be riding around with the Admiral in his yacht.

CHRISTIAN I've taken so many beatings in various walks of life, I don't know if I'm up to an artificial one.

O'ROURKE Come on, it'll be good. Look at it for the laughs.

CHRISTIAN I am. It's soul destroying.

O'ROURKE I'll be referee. You go in there, like as if you're going to kill him. A few straight lefts in the mouth, not too hard because you might put him down. Get him around the belly. Make him feel he's taking punishment and has got to pull the fight out of the bag.

CHRISTIAN Supposing he quits.

O'ROURKE He won't quit. Not in front of the manicurist.

CHRISTIAN I don't know, I'm against harmful acts.

O'ROURKE What's harmful. You call it harmful rejuvenating the Admiral. Hey, what do you want, he keeps the foreigners out of New York. Why is there so much honesty on the waterfront these days, it's the Admiral. You owe it to the country, Cornelius.

CHRISTIAN Thanks. You just said they were shooting each other in the head on the waterfront.

O'ROURKE But it's honest killing, can't you see the difference, the Admiral keeps it like that. [*Getting up to demonstrate*] Now. A straight left to the Admiral's jaw. Then a right on the belly. Leave yourself open. He throws a counterpunch and you go down. Let him hit you at the end of the round.

CHRISTIAN I think it's against my principles to make anyone a victim like that.

O'ROURKE Hey, what do you mean, victim. We're all victims. Hey, you used to be one of the toughest little fighters I ever saw around here before you went to Europe. What happened.

CHRISTIAN OK. I'll spar with the Admiral.

O'ROURKE Great. [O'ROURKE's *long surveying look at* CHRISTIAN] You know now, you've changed, Cornelius. You used to be a wild guy here. [CHRISTIAN *throwing a few fancy left and right uppercuts, with some dignity*] You think it's because there are no moral values in Europe. That maybe you had to struggle against it. You know, all you hear from people coming back is how they got cheated, robbed and gypped, even in these quaint little English villages. I try to tell them everybody is gypping you, only here they do it right in front of your face. [*Turning to open door.* ADMIRAL *entering, white bundle of bathrobe, towel around neck, the new boxing shoes, with a nice rim of white sweat sock over tops, pair of boxing gloves strung over arm*] Hey, it's the Admiral, how are you, Admiral. Come in and sit down Cornelius Christian's here.

ADMIRAL So I see.

O'ROURKE What's the matter, Admiral. Christian's not a bad guy. He's a little naughty with his freethinking or something he learned over in Europe.

ADMIRAL   Don't talk to me about Europe. I'm a taxpayer.

O'ROURKE   We're all taxpayers, Admiral.

ADMIRAL   [*Looking in* CHRISTIAN's *direction as he does shoulder rotation under robe and sits on arse*]   I don't want my tax money supporting people like him, coming in here. Criticizing this country.

O'ROURKE   He only said American women are whores.

ADMIRAL   And it makes me very sad to have to agree with him.

O'ROURKE   Hear that, Cornelius. What the Admiral says. You agree on something. Hey, wait a minute. Where do I come into it, hey, what about my wife. You calling my wife a whore. Hey, you can't say that. She's a mother of children.

ADMIRAL   I'm not talking about wives.

O'ROURKE   My wife's a woman.

[CHRISTIAN *curls a few hooks into the body bag*]

ADMIRAL   [*In* CHRISTIAN's *direction*] He ought to get married, knock some responsibility into him.

O'ROURKE   [*Finger quickly to lips, hand admonishing quiet to* ADMIRAL. O'ROURKE *changing subject*]   Admiral what's the idea of making this into a beauty saloon every afternoon.

ADMIRAL   It protects me from the evil atmosphere.

O'ROURKE   Come on, Admiral, don't be like that. We're just a big family. Enter into the free spirit here.

ADMIRAL   What free spirit.

O'ROURKE   None of this bitter talk this afternoon, Admiral. We all want to be happy here. You're trying to depress us because you can't adjust to life. Cornelius has a lot of interesting ideas.

[ADMIRAL *grunts*]

O'ROURKE   Now how can I talk with you like this. He's been telling me a lot of real fascinating things. Why right over there in London they've got whores all over the street and in the houses. Now would you let whores on the waterfront, Admiral, that's all we want to know today.

ADMIRAL   Don't talk rot.

O'ROURKE   That ain't rot. Don't you think it's better that we get physical enjoyment without having to spend the rest of our lives raising the results. We ought to let some of these English women over here. You control the immigration, Admiral. Let them in. Christian told me only a couple of weeks ago that American women don't even excite him. Only English girls excite him. Right, Cornelius.

ADMIRAL   Why doesn't he go back there. I already pay too much taxes keeping people on relief in this city.

CHRISTIAN   [*Punching bag*]   You deserve to pay more taxes.

ADMIRAL   Why God damn it, do you pay taxes.

CHRISTIAN   I live in Limbo.

ADMIRAL   That's the kind of smart talk they learn these days. I wouldn't mind having you on one of my ships.

CHRISTIAN   Lots of admirals have felt that way.

ADMIRAL   God damn freethinking. [*The disgruntled pause*] Free fornication.

O'ROURKE   Hey, what's this about free fornication. Watch that word in here. Don't you know bad language is forbidden.

ADMIRAL   Just a day on one of my ships.

O'ROURKE   Hey Cornelius's been in the Navy, Admiral.

ADMIRAL   Children's navy.

O'ROURKE   He had a stripe.

ADMIRAL   On his ass.

O'ROURKE   Hey. Even I had two stripes. You can't insult officers, Admiral.

ADMIRAL   Who gave you your stripes.

O'ROURKE   [*Snapping to attention and salute, a nice flourish of tatty silk robe*]   Aweigh all anchors. Full astern. Secure all bulkheads. Off to the beach, fighting Amphibians. [O'ROURKE's *nice rendition of* "Anchors Aweigh"] How's that, Admiral.

ADMIRAL   I come in here and have to listen to all this claptrap.

CHRISTIAN   Jews and Niggers I hear are taking all the seats on the subway. I suggest burning in oil.

ADMIRAL   That's the kind of thing I'd expect you to say.

O'ROURKE   Forward with the Irish.

ADMIRAL   God damn trash.

O'ROURKE Hey, watch that about the Irish.

ADMIRAL [*Leveling the authoritative finger at* CHRISTIAN] But you better understand that you can't say that kind of thing here.

CHRISTIAN I've said it.

[*My goodness, the silent fury of that* ADMIRAL]

O'ROURKE Now why don't you two be friends instead of wasting a lot of hot air on each other, use this room the way it's supposed to be used. [*Shouting*] For the manly sport. The art of self defense.

ADMIRAL I'm expecting my manicurist.

O'ROURKE Now, Admiral, how many times do I have to tell you to stop using this place like that.

ADMIRAL When you stop using it as a place of business I'll start using it for the manly sport.

O'ROURKE How am I going to sell my antiques if I don't keep in touch with my store. Got a great thing, I got them drilling holes in the picture frames to make it look like real worms been in the wood. Want to buy an old master, Admiral. Come on, for the dining room on your yacht. Cheap.

ADMIRAL Forgeries from some back room in the Bronx.

O'ROURKE Genuine. Out of real castles in Germany.

ADMIRAL What do I care, maybe you've got a back room in Brooklyn.

O'ROURKE You heard him, Cornelius, trying to discredit my business.

ADMIRAL Have you ever been in an art gallery.

O'ROURKE What for. I do all right. Got two guys with doctorates in the history of art. I always say if they got degrees it stops them stealing. [*Knock on door. Shouting*] Come in. To the nest of vipers.

GERTRUDE GENTLE [*Tray in hand, peeking in door*] Oh, I thought this was the boxing room, sorry.

O'ROURKE Hey, come back, it is. Can't you hear us fighting in here.

GENTLE I'm looking for Admiral Fuller.

O'ROURKE [*Pointing the accusing finger*] There he is.

ADMIRAL [GENTLE *enters shyly*] Don't listen to this man. Come in. [*Hesitating* GENTLE] I won't bite you. Come in. Put the tray over here.

GENTLE [*Apprehensive look from face to face*] Yes, sir.

ADMIRAL That's it. Right over here. Sit down. [O'ROURKE *making mock motions behind* ADMIRAL's *back to* CHRISTIAN] Make yourself comfortable. What's your name.

GENTLE Miss Gentle.

ADMIRAL Your first name.

GENTLE Gertrude.

ADMIRAL Good. Now I'll have some ot that tea, Gertrude. You don't mind my calling you Gertrude.

GENTLE No, sir.

ADMIRAL With just one lump of sugar.

GENTLE Yes, sir.

ADMIRAL I'm sick of being called sir, call me anything but sir. Makes me feel I'm some sort of freak.

GENTLE Yes. Of course. I mean, sorry. I mean—

ADMIRAL Forget it.

O'ROURKE Now Admiral, none of that. I know what you've got in that pot.

ADMIRAL I'm having a lump of sugar in it.

O'ROURKE Put milk in it, too.

ADMIRAL I don't like milk. Tell him, Gertrude, what this is. What did you ask for from the dining room.

O'ROURKE Bar.

ADMIRAL Didn't you say the Admiral's tea.

O'ROURKE Whiskey.

GENTLE Yes, I did.

ADMIRAL And isn't this what they gave you.

GENTLE Yes.

O'ROURKE Put milk in it.

ADMIRAL I have this young woman here to testify.

[GENTLE *pours this particularly strong tea*]

O'ROURKE Put milk in it.

ADMIRAL   I happen to prefer my tea plain.

O'ROURKE   A hundred proof. What about that, Cornelius. Isn't this a disgrace. This a temple of athletic achievement. What an example. I better go back to reading about today's murders.

GENTLE   I've got my things here sir, I mean, no sir, I mean Admiral. Shall I start on your free hand.

ADMIRAL   Just put back some of this tea first.

GENTLE   Of course.

[O'ROURKE *from his paper, points a mocking finger at the* ADMIRAL]

ADMIRAL   [*Quickly lowering back handsomely the tea tinted firewater*] Ah, that's better. Could do with a crumpet. [*To* GENTLE] Tell me, have you been long here at the club.

GENTLE   Just a week.

ADMIRAL   Thought I hadn't seen your face before. How would you like to get the Admiral's tea tomorrow, too. [*Toward* O'ROURKE] I'll be having it up at the squash courts.

O'ROURKE   Not good enough for you down here, Admiral. Hey, you watch him, Gertrude, don't let him get you in one of those lonely squash courts.

ADMIRAL   Don't mind him. Won't have to tolerate this talk upstairs where people have better manners.

GENTLE   I don't mind.

ADMIRAL   Well you should.

O'ROURKE   Hey Admiral, before you have your nails done why don't you have a little spar around the ring with Cornelius.

CHRISTIAN   [*That lonely, left out, shadow boxing man*]   I think I'd rather not.

O'ROURKE   Come on now, Cornelius, the Admiral won't hurt you. That's true, Admiral, you don't hold any grudge against Cornelius, do you. Even though he wants to string up a few of the dark-complexioned citizens. Sorry, Gertrude, just a little discussion we were having.

[ADMIRAL *grunts*]

GENTLE   I'll just get started.

[GERTRUDE *making preparations for the manicure*]

O'ROURKE   See, Cornelius, the Admiral promises not to use anything lethal. Now, Admiral, the corkscrew punch is illegal, now you understand that. I don't want anybody hurt while I'm running this boxing room.

ADMIRAL   It behooves me—

O'ROURKE   Behoove behoove behoove, what do you mean behoove. Big words are banned here, all I want is your solemn promise not to use the corkscrew punch, never mind the behoove business. [*To* CHRISTIAN] There now, Cornelius, got the Admiral's solemn promise.

CHRISTIAN   I think I'd rather not.

[*Doing the drill of the desultory left and right hooks, albeit neatly executed*]

O'ROURKE   Hey, come on, Cornelius. What more can you ask for than the Admiral's solemn promise not to touch you with the corkscrew, which I now ban for all time from this boxing room. Miss Gentle is a witness, aren't you, Miss Gentle, a witness. [*Shy nod of* GENTLE *head*] There now. And you also have the solemn oath of O'Rourke. [*Hand raised in Boy Scout's honor*] Now you're not going to use that corkscrew, [*Pointing finger*] Admiral.

ADMIRAL Don't be preposterous, when have I ever struck a man who couldn't defend himself.

O'ROURKE There you are, Cornelius. Go in there with the Admiral. You'll get some pointers. Come on, before he has his fingers done.

CHRISTIAN [*Using the sad slouch to the slaughter*] OK. All right.

ADMIRAL To me sport is give and take. I don't want to mix it with someone who can't defend himself.

O'ROURKE Cornelius is no cripple, Admiral. But if you hold the corkscrew in check, nobody is going to get hurt.

ADMIRAL I can never promise to keep the corkscrew in check.

O'ROURKE But you just promised.

ADMIRAL It's an instinctive punch with me. And comes out of nowhere. I don't even know how I do it myself.

O'ROURKE It's pretty obvious Admiral where it comes from, look at the way you're set up, like a kid of twenty.

ADMIRAL [*Running up ensign of health, little expansion of steel chest*] I keep myself in shape. Every ship that goes to sea under my command is in a rigorous state of health.

O'ROURKE You're telling me.

ADMIRAL I keep myself in shape.

O'ROURKE Miss Gentle, would you know by looking at him that the Admiral has one of the most lethal punches ever seen in the ring. [ADMIRAL's *agonizing modesty*] Naturally he doesn't like it talked about. But you can't deny it, Admiral.

ADMIRAL I don't deny it. I prefer it be known. Anyone entering the ring with me knows the risk he runs by doing so.

O'ROURKE [*The supplication*] I just finished, you heard me twice, Admiral, telling Cornelius you weren't going to use it. You wouldn't be that kind of sportsman. I mean we're sportsmen here, aren't we.

ADMIRAL Why don't you buy a new robe.

O'ROURKE Hey, what's the matter with my robe.

ADMIRAL This young lady here, I don't want her to think that we boxers have no sartorial elegance.

O'ROURKE Where do you get off with that word sartorial. Speak English. Cornelius there, he's got no elegance neither. He told me it was a cultured European touch to wear rags.

ADMIRAL That's what American womenhood have to look forward to with his type. What's this country coming to.

O'ROURKE [*Shouting*] Protect yourself, Cornelius. Don't let him talk to you like that. [CHRISTIAN *smiles*] Admiral, you going to box with Cornelius or aren't you.

ADMIRAL If he's prepared I'm prepared.

O'ROURKE OK. On with the gloves.

[O'ROURKE *to* CHRISTIAN *to help him on with his gloves*]

ADMIRAL Would you give me a hand with these, Gertrude. Tie them tight around the wrists, no flying laces.

O'ROURKE Now remember, no hitting on the break. No rabbit punches. I'm going to watch for any foul blows in this.

ADMIRAL Don't tell me the rules.

O'ROURKE I want a clean fight. Especially with a lady present. Now let's see. [*Looking up at clock*] Set the bell on the clock. [*Bell rings*] OK. At the next bell come out fighting. [ADMIRAL *derobing. Poor old* CHRISTIAN *a little roughshod underneath, but even in these hard times faces life with a flourish. The two preposterous contenders slip through the velvet ropes. Repair to respective corners and each make a visit to the rosin in the neutral corner like real pros. And they wait for the bell.* O'ROURKE *naturally is at the teapot on the couch next to* GENTLE] And now I'll pour myself a nice cup of tea if you don't mind, Admiral.

ADMIRAL Get away from that teapot.

O'ROURKE [*Pouring and sipping*] Well, what do you know, it is tea.

ADMIRAL You scoundrel.

O'ROURKE Well, I'll just help myself to a little tea. [*To* GENTLE] This is what the Admiral trains on, it's what gives him the corkscrew. We know where you got that corkscrew punch now, Admiral. Cornelius, you duck when it comes.

CHRISTIAN If the Admiral should like to use the corkscrew, it's quite all right with me.

O'ROURKE That's the way, Cornelius. We don't want any withholding.

But Admiral, if you use that corkscrew, make sure it's at half power. Now as the referee of this sparring match that's an order. Hey, wait a minute. [o'ROURKE *goes to the wall, and takes head protector*] Just get this on. We've all got the raging bull in us and Cornelius you've got your future ahead of you. It fit?

CORNELIUS   Thanks.

[*Bong, the gong*]

O'ROURKE   OK, now go to it and may the best man win.

GENTLE [GERTRUDE *that gentle, disconcerted*]   They're not going to hurt each other.

O'ROURKE [*The whisper*]   Just humoring the Admiral along, he couldn't break a spider's web.

GENTLE   Oh, this is just a joke.

O'ROURKE   Just a joke. That's it, Cornelius, keep well away from that right. Circle to your right. Now, Admiral, remember what I told you.

ADMIRAL   Shut up.

O'ROURKE   Hey, I got to tell my fighter what to do. Watch it, Cornelius, he's sizing up your style. [CORNELIUS CHRISTIAN *briefly turning and running. Outright*] Hey, Cornelius, take your beating like a man. Don't go yellow.

ADMIRAL   He's backing away. I can't hit him.

O'ROURKE   What do you expect if you're going to· use the corkscrew. Only fair evasion. Christian has some of the best footwork I've ever seen. Hard man to hit. Be careful of Christian's right, Admiral. He's handy with the under the heart punch.

ADMIRAL I'm not worried.

O'ROURKE Are you all right, Cornelius.

CHRISTIAN I'm fine. Just warming up.

O'ROURKE Keep your gloves up, that's it, take his left on your shoulder, circle to your right, keep out of the way of the Admiral's wine punch.

ADMIRAL Very funny.

O'ROURKE I don't want any unconscious bodies in this boxing room. I'm watching you, Admiral.

ADMIRAL Why don't you shut up.

O'ROURKE I'm responsible for all lives in here. This is just like a ship.

ADMIRAL He's doing all right. He doesn't need your shipboard advice. He's got a nice little punch. Just caught me. [To CHRISTIAN] Nice punch.

CHRISTIAN Thanks.

ADMIRAL Only tell me if I'm hurting you.

CHRISTIAN You're not hurting me.

O'ROURKE Don't start to become friends. Hit him, Cornelius.

ADMIRAL [To CHRISTIAN] Sure I'm not hurting you.

CHRISTIAN Not a bit.

ADMIRAL Good. I like to punch clean and crisp. I like a good fight. It does not behoove me to do permanent damage.

CHRISTIAN   That's OK.

ADMIRAL   Just tell me when you've had enough. I like a good workout, get up a sweat. Sorry, that was a low punch.

O'ROURKE   Now watch him, Cornelius, he's sneaky. Watch for the flexing of his right knee, only don't let him hit you one when you're looking. There he just gave you his feeler punch.

ADMIRAL   Enough out of you, O'Rourke.

O'ROURKE   [To teapot]   Just try a little more of your tea, skipper. [To MISS GENTLE] Two fine men out there, don't you think, Miss Gentle. Two real sportsmen.

GENTLE   Yes.

O'ROURKE   Truly the manly art. Have a little spot of tea, Miss Gentle, plenty of cups.

GENTLE   Thank you, but isn't it against club rules for me to have anything. I think so.

O'ROURKE   I rule here.

GENTLE   [The smile of GENTLE]   Oh.

O'ROURKE   [Pouring, shouting]   Hit him. Hit him. Right in the beer belly, Cornelius. That's it, you're doing fine. [To GENTLE] Sorry for the language, but you know how it is.

GENTLE   Oh, it's all right by me. [Tea to lips] Oh, my goodness.

[A slight ladylike spluttering out. If only all women were as nice as MISS GENTLE]

O'ROURKE   Oh, sorry, Miss Gentle.

[Wiping MISS GENTLE with towel]

GENTLE   It's all right. I really thought it was tea.

ADMIRAL   Ruffian.

[*In that arena, there is a general slowing down of huffing puffing contestants*]

O'ROURKE   Jew fight. Let's see some action. [*A pirouette to a moment of Boccherini minuet*] He's wide open, Cornelius, for a left to the nose. That's it, get him before he tries the corkscrew. Punish him around the body. Now a left. Hook him, hook him. Now. Watch it Cornelius, that stance he's using is deadly. Duck. [CHRISTIAN *ducking* ADMIRAL'S *punch passing over head.* O'ROURKE, *leaping to feet, shouting*] I saw it, I saw it, that was it, Admiral. I saw you use the corkscrew. At full power. I saw you. You know it's fatal at close quarters.

ADMIRAL   You stay out of this and stop drinking any more of my whiskey.

O'ROURKE   You admit it. Well, I saw you and don't tell me I didn't. I'm ashamed. If I hadn't told Cornelius to duck we'd be picking up his head from over there on Wall Street. [*To* CHRISTIAN] Weight well forward on the balls of the feet. Cornelius, that's the only adequate defense against the corkscrew. [*To* ADMIRAL] That's how you run the waterfront. [*To* GENTLE] See, miss. Men who have unlimited physical resources and who don't know their own strength ought to be stopped using it. Good mind to stop the fight.

GENTLE [*Getting to feet, hands to lips*]   Oh my goodness.

O'ROURKE   Hey, you hit him with the corkscrew. [CORNELIUS *flat, spread eagled on canvas*] Now don't say you didn't, you hit him with the corkscrew. I saw you do it.

GENTLE   Is he all right.

O'ROURKE [*Winking*]   Look at him, you've knocked him right out, I told you not to use the corkscrew. You don't know your own strength. I told you.

ADMIRAL [*That mountain of power, slayer of all women, taking off gloves, he crosses the ring with the slow swagger*]   Ahem.

   [*Throat cleared*]

O'ROURKE   What's the idea, Admiral, hey we've got to pick him up, just don't leave him like that.

GENTLE   Can I do something. Get something, some smelling salts. Medical attendant in the hall has some.

O'ROURKE [*To* ADMIRAL]   Hey he needs artificial respiration, Admiral.

ADMIRAL   It was merely a tap. Leave him there. He's had that coming for a long time. Knock some sense into him. [O'ROURKE *smiling to* GENTLE *from behind* ADMIRAL] Won't be coming into this boxing room again talking a lot of damn nonsense.

O'ROURKE   Well Admiral, let me shake your hand. Now don't give me the dynamite shake. Just let me shake. Didn't want to tell you, but you know that's the first time Cornelius Christian's ever hit the deck. Didn't want to say anything. But he was middle Atlantic champion before he went to Europe, seven straight knockouts. Seven straight.

ADMIRAL [*Robe on, patting himself both hands on ribs*]   He had me guessing. Just for a few seconds. I've often refrained from using the corkscrew even when I've seen an inviting opening. But that kid's too smart for his own good. Not enough red blood these days.

O'ROURKE   Yeah.

ADMIRAL   That's the trouble.

O'ROURKE   You bet, Admiral.

ADMIRAL When I took my first ship to sea I used to skip rope around the quarter deck for two hours before breakfast. That's how I got that stomach you call a beer barrel. Barrel of nails. Give it a punch. You, young girl. Try it. Go on. Don't be shy. There. See.

[GENTLE *punch*]

O'ROURKE Armor plating. Bet Christian knew he was hitting something when he tried a few on that.

ADMIRAL That's what a clean life does.

O'ROURKE Cleaned your teapot for you, Admiral.

ADMIRAL Miss Gentle, take no notice of him.

GENTLE Oh, I'm not. [*To* O'ROURKE, *looking at poor* CHRISTIAN *prostrate*] But he's all right, isn't he.

ADMIRAL [*Taking the* GENTLE *arm*] My girl, it's nice to see someone like you so concerned. Gives your eyes a nice look. But I assure you he'll come around and be all right in a few days. [*Rotation of head for the new fields to conquer*] Well, that was a good afternoon's exercise.

GENTLE [*Looking back*] I just thought I saw him twitch.

ADMIRAL Little corkscrew never does anybody any permanent harm. It's scientific. The glove rotates as the punch leaves and when it lands, quicker than the human eye can see, it gives extra penetrating force. I developed it after years of experiment based on the rifling of a gun barrel.

O'ROURKE Rename it the sixteen inch shell punch, Admiral.

ADMIRAL Had enough of your suggestions for one afternoon. Well, Miss Gentle, rather, Gertrude, [*Offering of arm that threw the corkscrew*] I think we'll proceed to the baths department, to a more salubrious atmosphere where we can get down to having these nails done. [*To* O'ROURKE] I think he's been there long enough, throw some water on him. [*Moving out*] I don't want to embarrass him by being around. Come along, Gertrude, we'll give this Christian some privacy to recover in.

GENTLE [*To* O'ROURKE]   Sure you don't want any smelling salts.

O'ROURKE   Wouldn't help. Felled like a tree. But Cornelius took it like a man. But you shouldn't have done it, Admiral.

ADMIRAL   Do him good. But no hard feelings. Tell him I'll be in the athlete's lounge later, buy him a drink. In the ring I may be a killer but outside I believe in behaving like a normal human being. Any born boxer would have done what I did when he saw his opening.

O'ROURKE   Your conscience is clear, Admiral. I can tell you mean what you say. I think maybe Cornelius did have it coming to him. Like a lot of guys who feel this country could do with changing. And that our wives are out to get us for alimony and sell themselves.

ADMIRAL   I think that kind of talk is out of turn with Gertrude present here.

GERTRUDE   But I like men who hate women.

O'ROURKE   Hey, get that, Admiral. If Christian was only conscious he would have liked that remark.

ADMIRAL   I think it's time to have my nails done, Miss Gentle. Down to the baths.

O'ROURKE [*At door*]   So long, Miss Gentle. Bye, Admiral, and watch that corkscrew, that's banned from now on. [*Turning now to the ring*] That was great, Cornelius. Why the Admiral will be inviting you down to his boat, get free rides all around the harbor. I have to laugh, that was really good acting, for a second I really thought it looked like he knocked you cold. [*Getting closer*] Hey, Cornelius, what's the matter. The Admiral's gone, get up. [*Touching head that rolls*] Hey, Cornelius. [*Shouting after* GENTLE *and* ADMIRAL] Hey, come back, bring the smelling salts.

[*Curtain*]

ACT FOUR

Peach Shoes

SCENE 1. THE RESTAURANT

This old but lavish eatery with its factory windows. A white covered table is in the sunken garden. In June and waiters go to and fro, high nosed and sniffing and brow lifting. CORNELIUS CHRISTIAN and CHARLOTTE GRAVES step down steps and a waiter, disdaining, points them to a table during this late high sunned afternoon. Pots of deep grass wave white and warm. They walk and sit at chairs, iron, white and filigree. CORNELIUS sad and silent and touches the silver salt and pepper things. CHARLOTTE bowed, her straw, wide hat on her haystack hair. The sad late afternoon begins.

CHRISTIAN [*A proffered hand half across the table*] But didn't you know, that peach is really the snazz.

GRAVES No, I didn't know.

CHRISTIAN I'm starting a fashion.

GRAVES [*Straw haired head up*] But they looked at us.

CHRISTIAN I thought you were so tickled pink to go out with me.

GRAVES I was. I am.

CHRISTIAN I feel smooth in these shoes. I walked along the highway this afternoon really feeling big time. Policemen were parked sitting in their car, in their nice blue uniforms waiting for speeders. They just looked at me from behind their sunglasses. Ha ha, you've never seen such bellies in blue. They saw my shoes. And I just looked back at them with that air, that I know somebody who knows somebody who's something and you better watch out. I made no impression but I wasn't arrested. I passed by, putting an extra inch on my chest and smiled. [*Shooting a shoe forward*] I am proud of these shoes.

GRAVES We're just sitting here. [*Her head down*] And nothing is happening. They're just ignoring us. [*The light gay music and laughter from another room*] And listen, all those other people in furs in the other room. The men all had black shoes and black ties and white shirts. They were all formal. And the waiters were hurrying around them. [*Waiter returning across the sunken garden room*] See.

CHRISTIAN [*Raising a hand, two delicate snaps of thumb and index. Ignored*] I see. [*A supplicant hand to foot*] My own toes are inside. Which I'm wiggling at the moment. This place was just a factory once. Way out in the woods. They had Alsatian dogs to nibble at the unruly. Also a policeman patrolling with a night stick, up and down between the tables.

GRAVES This is our big night out together. I'm dressed in the best I have. This belonged to my grandmother. She was married in it, it's an heirloom. [CHRISTIAN *mumchance*. CHARLOTTE GRAVES *reaches out for his hand*] Don't think, please, that I mind, it's only that we're here. And I don't want everyone just to notice us.

CHRISTIAN You're a kid, Charlotte.

GRAVES I'm not a kid. I feel awful. And I can't help it.

CHRISTIAN You shouldn't let these waiters scare you.

GRAVES We could have been taken into that other room where they have the music and dancing. And there's nothing in here. [CHRISTIAN *turns swiftly to the lurking waiter at the pantry door, who swiftly turns and goes into the kitchen beyond*] You see what they're doing to us. We don't even have menus.

CHRISTIAN [*Upturned palms*] Doubts about my taste are evident. Do you want me to hide my shoes.

GRAVES It's too late now. They won't come to us.

CHRISTIAN We'll wait. Smile.

GRAVES I can't.

CHRISTIAN You have such a real mouth. And such large teeth. And such a worried frown. Face my shoes. [GRAVES *with mumchance*] Remember the summer when we were kids. [CHRISTIAN *rubbing hands*] The Labor Day picnic and parade. I saw you coming out of your house, in a white silk blouse, and the same haystack hair. You gave me the biggest hello I've ever had in my life. [*He looks up in air*] I can still hear it. It made me even march in the parade, no, I'm lying. I skulked behind the trees, stealing ice cream while the citizens of my country marched. You're still such a kid. My shoes are in bad taste. [*Shouting*] My shoes are in bad taste.

GRAVES Please. [*Worried appearance of two waiters*] Please, I don't mind your pink shoes.

CHRISTIAN Peach.

GRAVES Peach. But should we go.

CHRISTIAN [*Fighter for freedom*] No.

GRAVES Can't we ask for something then.

CHRISTIAN   For them to forgive us. And me for my shoes that cost eighteen dollars.

GRAVES   Just so that they come and go from the table.

CHRISTIAN   Alas, I reckon I do lower the tone.

GRAVES   Cornelius—

CHRISTIAN   I've got such a beautiful name.

GRAVES   We come from the same background. Our backgrounds are medium and middle. We can't be sure we're right, that's all I'm saying. The better people are right.

CHRISTIAN   We're not the better people.

GRAVES   We may be better than some people. But we're not the best people, that's all I'm saying.

CHRISTIAN   You were so tan and lovely at the Labor Day parade.

GRAVES   I just don't want all the best people thinking we can't be just like them.

CHRISTIAN   I took you out on your first date. Bought you a soda after the movies. I remember distinctly my aplomb. As I said to the candy store man, two pineapple, please. I was his customer. He welcomed me.

GRAVES   Because you were nice.

CHRISTIAN   What am I now.

GRAVES   You're different. You're not the same Cornelius Christian I used to know.

CHRISTIAN   Who am I.

GRAVES You're just not the same as you were. Before you went to Europe. [CHRISTIAN *performing a close examination of his person*] And before you—

CHRISTIAN Got married.

GRAVES Please. [*Looking around*] They'll start to listen to us.

CHRISTIAN Good.

GRAVES You said I was so tan and lovely at the Labor Day parade. You don't think that now.

CHRISTIAN You're still an apple I'd love to eat.

GRAVES I haven't been swimming yet. I guess. Living in the city I don't get a chance. That's why tonight to come to the country and all.

CHRISTIAN [*Picking up the silver cellar, pounding it on the table, shouting*] Service, service.

GRAVES That's the last thing I want you to do.

CHRISTIAN I am merely asking for service. [*Shouting and pounding*] Service.

[*Peeking heads of waiters*]

GRAVES Now you have ruined the whole evening. No one has ever behaved in my presence like this before.

CHRISTIAN Do you want me to leave.

GRAVES You know I don't want you to leave.

CHRISTIAN Well that's just fine.

GRAVES No it isn't fine. You're being conceited.

CHRISTIAN   You do want me to leave. Do you. Tell me. Do you want me to leave.

GRAVES [Shouting]   Yes. Leave.

[CHRISTIAN, a movement of the lips, rising slowly, steps back, hesitates for reprieve. None. Gently pushing chair beneath the table. Proceeds slowly past headwaiter and waiter, who straighten backs to look down their high sniffing noses at the peach tootsies of CORNELIUS CHRISTIAN. Up the steps CHRISTIAN goes. Stopping at top to speak. Waiters gingerly into kitchen. And CHRISTIAN's eyes upon CHARLOTTE GRAVES, an anguished bent head. CHRISTIAN exits.
    WAITERS pop out. Wait and whisper. GRAVES looks up the empty stairs. Bites her lips. And with pinkly colored nail, she touches the table things one by one. Looks up again and around in this unfriendly world and the waiters turn ashamed away. They take trays held over shoulders toward that room where the gay and better people live and laugh in crowded lavishment. A tide of laughter and GRAVES turns, but it's not for her. She takes up her straw, wide hat and puts it back on her straw hair. A mouse alone. This open field. FRITZ, the headwaiter comes. Stands, a hovering hawk. She looks up the black shoes, trousers, to the white shirt and face]

FRITZ   Would madam like some service for herself. [GRAVES shakes head no] Isn't there anything I can get madam. Like water. [Shakes head no] An omelette. Crêpe suzette. Steak. [Shakes head no] Would madam then, like some explanation? [Shakes head yes] We have certain unwritten rules. Which it is understood people understand before they come here. We do not mind when persons come where this is not their natural habitat. We try to make them feel at home and not as if they don't belong. [GRAVES puts a hand to her forehead] Maybe madam would like to be seated in the other room. [Shakes head no] I don't want to hurt madam's feelings but should madam be interested in my advice I would say that he is not your kind. We expected him to leave. But we have a lot of experience in telling who is who. No gentleman would treat a lady the way he has treated you. He shouted for service.

GRAVES   Because you wouldn't give us any.

FRITZ   Oh no, nothing like that.

GRAVES   It was like that.

FRITZ   If madam will permit me, we get lots like him. We know his kind well. Distinctly from the other side of the tracks.

GRAVES   He's from my side.

FRITZ   Look, we know you feel you owe him some kind of loyalty, but boy I wouldn't like to have to count the trains on the tracks between you and him. Girl like you could meet people of top quality. And really frequent places like this.

GRAVES   I wouldn't want to.

FRITZ   You're a hard kid to please, you know that. You don't mind if I say one or two very personal things. You know, I can tell you're a girl who comes from real nice people. Only. Don't take what I'm going to tell you wrong. But that dress you're wearing looks like it belonged to your grandmother. [GRAVES *turns her head away*] I'm just trying to help you out. You don't want to misunderstand me. I'm just joking about the dress. OK, I think it suits you. But a kid with your looks wants to show them off. Guy with a lot of dough would like to be seen with you. I'm not saying you looked like you stepped out of an antique shop.

GRAVES   You are.

FRITZ   No, no. You got real good looks. And tone. Excuse me for saying it, but that guy was a greaseball. [GRAVES *bent*] Hey, I said something. Look, you're going to cry. Don't cry. I said something. I did, didn't I. Just tell me what I said. [*Motions to other waiter and* CHARLIE *comes. They stand, towels over arms*] Charlie, what am I going to do.

CHARLIE   Leave the kid alone. [*To* GRAVES] Here, kid. [*An offering of towel*] Help you mop up. [GRAVES *opens her bag for hanky*] Don't worry, kid, it's all right. Nobody's going to hurt you. [*To* FRITZ] What you do this to the kid for. She's crying.

FRITZ   It was that guy.

CHARLIE   So what. No need to make the kid cry.

FRITZ   I was trying to steer her straight.

CHARLIE   I suppose you know just how to straighten everybody out. [*A hand toward* GRAVES] What the hell, it's none of your business.

FRITZ   She came in here with a guy who was a phony. I could tell a mile off.

CHARLIE   So what. Everybody in this place is phony.

FRITZ   [*Apocryphal hand lifted*]   You call Mr. Van Hearse and his party in there phony.

CHARLIE   Yeah. I call them phony. What the hell is he but some guy who makes rubber goods.

FRITZ   Don't say that in front of women. Mr. Van Hearse is a public benefactor.

CHARLIE   Don't start giving him titles. He makes rubber goods.

FRITZ   You said that once, you don't have to say it again.

CHARLIE   I like the sound.

FRITZ   I'm busy. We better clear this table.

CHARLIE   Why don't you leave the kid.

FRITZ   We got to clear this table.

CHARLIE   Who's coming. We don't need this table.

FRITZ   Who gives the orders around here.

CHARLIE   I'm just telling you to give the kid a break.

FRITZ   And I'm giving you an order to clear the table. Understand English.

CHARLIE   Thought you were trying to help this kid.

FRITZ   She still thinks the guy who walked out on her is something. When he's a phony. A phony cheapskate.

CHARLIE   Look, cut it out, you're really hurting the kid's feelings.

FRITZ   Any kid go out with a guy like that deserves to have her feelings hurt.

CHARLIE   [*The pointing finger held high, punctuating*]   Look. I don't care if I've got to take orders from you. But you're not going to upset this kid any more. Because I'll slug you. That's English. Understand it.

FRITZ   You touch me and you're fired.

CHARLIE   And you say one more thing to this kid and I'll slug you right out the window up there.

FRITZ   Tough.

CHARLIE   About this. Yeah.

FRITZ   We'll see.

CHARLIE   You see.

FRITZ   I'll see. Don't worry.

CHARLIE Go ahead. I'm worried.

FRITZ You just clear that table like I said, that's all.

CHARLIE And you just leave this kid alone, that's all.

FRITZ Clear the table, that's all.

[*Leaving with the backward step*]

CHARLIE [*To* GRAVES] Sorry, kid, I got to do this. Don't worry. This happens to everybody, if not every day at least once in their life. Don't mind that guy, this joint's a dump, believe me. We just had to give your boyfriend the cold shoulder because the owner thinks he's going to make this dive into a toney establishment if he makes a few people think they're not wanted. [*A slow popping of the table's items onto his tray*] Some hope he's got. I know it's kind of late to say these things. But look, I didn't have anything personal against your boyfriend. [*Picking up tall glass vase, three roses, puts tray on table, snaps off a rose*] Here. Here's a rose.

GRAVES Thank you.

CHARLIE Look, I tell you what. Why don't me and you go somewhere. I'm quitting this job right now. I know of a swell place just a couple of miles down the highway. Nice floor show, take your mind off this. What about it, huh.

GRAVES Thanks, but—

[*She shakes head no*]

CHARLIE Look, believe me, he's gone. Your boyfriend's not coming back. He's run out on you and left you here. All alone. [*Picking up tray*] Come on. What have you got to lose. Think it over. We could go to a nice quiet place if you want. With soft lights. Then I'll take you back where you live. Take you right home. [GRAVES *shakes her head no*] So.

GRAVES I can't.

CHARLIE OK. [*Collecting the eating instruments*] OK. I've got to go and do my job. I've got to clear this table then. I'm going to even have to take the tablecloth, even the chairs, even the table. So no use waiting. That kind of guy just never comes back. What do you want to waste time waiting for. Come on. You going to go out with me. [GRAVES *shakes head no*] OK, sister, it's your life. I tell you, you're wasting your time waiting. [*Turning with his tray, stops, comes back*] Look, kid, say let me get you an apple. I don't want to see you just sitting here.

GRAVES I'm all right.

CHARLIE Have an apple. Free. [GRAVES *shakes her head no*] Have [*Reaching to breast pocket*] a piece of chewing gum. [GRAVES *shakes head no. He turns to kitchen with trayful,* FRITZ *comes out. To* FRITZ] She won't budge, see what you done.

FRITZ The table's got to be cleared, that's all.

CHARLIE [*Muttering*] Yeah, that's all, that's all.

FRITZ [*At* GRAVES' *table*] Look, miss, I've got my orders and I got to keep my job. Don't listen to this waiter. All he's looking for is some innocent kid who don't know what she's doing to go out with him. He's got three kids. I counted them myself. And his wife's so fat she can't walk. Can't even get near enough to kiss her. Just what he deserves. You see, you can't trust anybody. [*Lifting tablecloth from table*] Like I'm saying I've got to do my job. [GRAVES *taking her elbow from table as cloth comes up.* FRITZ *folding it*] Just like the waiter, give you a rose that don't belong to him. [FRITZ *takes cloth to the pantry, passing* CHARLIE] Baby snatcher.

CHARLIE What's the matter, jealous.

FRITZ [*Into pantry*] Some Romeo.

CHARLIE [*Comes, puts his hands on* CHRISTIAN's *chair*]   I've got to take this, honey, you're making this the saddest day of my life. [*Shaking head*] I feel it.

[*Faintly the humming chorus from* Madame Butterfly. CHARLIE *takes chair away.* FRITZ *comes out, lurks.* CHARLIE *comes out. They each take one pot of white waving grass away.*

Lights fade and they take the flowers from the walls. Waiters come back and FRITZ *gives* CHARLIE *a nod of command. Both to the table, one on each side,* GRAVES *lifts her elbows, puts clenched fists against her cheeks, and they carry the table away.* GRAVES *sits on the edge of her chair.* CHARLIE *and* FRITZ *come hesitant toward her.* FRITZ *nods to* CHARLIE, CHARLIE *hesitates. Then both take chair*]

FRITZ [*Hands on chair*]   Sorry, miss, but we can't help it, we've got to take your chair.

CHARLIE   Sorry, kid. [CHARLOTTE GRAVES *slides forward. They step back.* GRAVES *to her knees in front of empty chair.* FRITZ *and* CHARLIE *each hesitating to take it and both go to take it and lift it away.* CHARLOTTE GRAVES *alone, her clenched fists up over her eyes as she kneels and silently weeps. Outside an afternoon turned to night.* FRITZ *and* CHARLIE *pausing at pantry door, chair held between them, and look back over their shoulders at* CHARLOTTE GRAVES, *and then at each other*] You lousy rat.

FRITZ   You lousy rat.

[FRITZ *and* CHARLIE *enter pantry humming the latter part of the chorus. Momentarily at the high factory window the head and shoulders of* CORNELIUS CHRISTIAN *as he kneels, looking in on this sadness, the trembling lonely figure of* CHARLOTTE GRAVES. CHRISTIAN *enters this restaurant. Standing an admiral on his bridge at the top of the stairs, in gray topper, tails and white tie, evening cane tucked under his arm, as he waits in the sudden bright rising lights and the fading end of the humming chorus. Bare feet resplendent, a large sparkling diamond on each toe*]

CHARLIE [*Appearing at the pantry door. A gander at this scene*] Holy mackerel.

FRITZ [*Appearing behind* CHARLIE] What's this, somebody arrived. A personage.

CHARLIE I should live so long.

FRITZ Shut up, maybe you won't. Get out the table. [FRITZ *forward to receive this glistening guest. To take his hat and cane. And with an open arm welcome him to proceed*] Sir.

CHRISTIAN Thank you.

[CHRISTIAN, *pausing to give a general perusement of feet and the large sparkling diamonds, goes with the slow step, wearing the frozen smile of the potentate across his appearance and moves down into the midst of this preposterous eatery.* CHARLOTTE GRAVES *rises, goes forward to* CHRISTIAN. *Lays her head on his brave chest. And they stand, waiting and watching the feverish preparation of their table by tricky* CHARLIE *and* FRITZ. CHARLIE *placing the table. Rushes back and returning with cloth.* FRITZ *flattening the creases.* CHARLIE *out and back with vase of flowers, places them on table, hesitates*]

FRITZ [*Arranging flowers, turns to* CHARLIE *using the side whisper*] The condiments and cutlery, you fool, fast.

CHARLIE Oh. Yeah.

[*Off and back with tray, the condiments and eating instruments. The laying of instruments.* CHARLIE *picking up a plate, brief examination in light, a flash wipe of the sleeve. The wide eyes of good old* FRITZ]

FRITZ [*With large menus tucked under arm, beckoning to* CHRISTIAN] Sir. Madam. [*Eyelids are fluttering everywhere as* CHRISTIAN *steps high footed forward.* CHARLIE *at action station at* CHRISTIAN's *chair.* FRITZ *does for madam. And this couple are gently seated. A flourish of arms and* FRITZ *makes the presentation of menus*] Good evening, madam. Good evening, sir.

CHRISTIAN   Good evening. What's choice.

FRITZ   May I be so bold as to suggest the consommé en gelée.

CHRISTIAN   Ah. Charlotte.

[*She shakes head yes*]

FRITZ [*To* CHARLOTTE]   Might madam like some kind of fish to follow.

GRAVES   Shrimps.

FRITZ [*On his little pad*]   Crustaceans for madam.

CHRISTIAN   Smoked salmon.

FRITZ   Saumon fumé for sir. And to follow, sir. For madam.

GRAVES   Steak.

FRITZ   Mignon.

GRAVES   I guess so.

FRITZ   Rare?

GRAVES   Yes.

FRITZ   Garlic?

GRAVES [*To* CHRISTIAN]   Should I.

CHRISTIAN   Feel free.

GRAVES   Garlic.

FRITZ   Very good, madam. Vegetables? Madam?

GRAVES   Asparagus.

FRITZ   Sir?

CHRISTIAN   Asparagus.

FRITZ   Asparagus for two. Potatoes? Madam?

GRAVES   Boiled.

FRITZ   For sir.

CHRISTIAN   Fried.

[CHRISTIAN *with his silver cigarette case, which looks like platinum for this occasion. Offering* GRAVES *a cigarette. She takes it. An awkward putting in the mouth*]

FRITZ   [*Diving to assist. The striking of a match*]   Allow me, madam.

[*The sunset smile as madam blows out that first puff. And he then retreats, using the backward lilting step, head inclined for and toward* CHRISTIAN, *this present potentate*]

CHARLIE   [*With pitcher of water, pincers and lemon peel*]   Good evening sir.

CHRISTIAN   Good evening.

CHARLIE   Good evening, madam.

GRAVES   Hello.

CHARLIE   [*Pouring and poised with pincers*]   Will madam have some peel. [*Nod of yes*] And for sir.

CHRISTIAN Ah. I think so.

CHARLIE [A bow] I hope the water will be to your satisfaction.

[The backward retreat]

FRITZ [Waiting with high sniffing sneer as CHARLIE backs by him, FRITZ holds a satin stool aloof in his hands. CHARLIE looking at stool, backs into wall. FRITZ with dignity proceeds to table. To CHRISTIAN] Sir. May I. For your feet, sir.

CHRISTIAN Ah.

FRITZ [Placing it. CHRISTIAN crosses tootsies on satin stool] Make sir more comfortable.

CHRISTIAN Ah. Thank you.

FRITZ A pleasure, sir. And now perhaps sir would like something to drink. [Another menu handed over] A white wine to start, perhaps. With the poisson and madam's crustaceans. [A pointing finger] I can recommend this one.

CHRISTIAN Cordial.

FRITZ Very good, sir.

[Retreating with the backward step and genuflecting head]

GRAVES [A hand forward over CHRISTIAN's hand] I'm sorry.

CHRISTIAN [CHRISTIAN, that forgiver of all minor sins] That's all right. You see, [Presenting a foot] the color of this too is peach.

[Curtain]

[Applause]

A Singular Man

A SINGULAR MAN was first produced on October 6, 1964, at the Cambridge Arts Theatre. It opened in London, at the Comedy Theatre, on October 21, 1964, with the following cast:

FIRST ACTOR   *Bill Nagy*
GEORGE SMITH   *Ronald Fraser*
SALLY TOMSON   *Susannah York*
ANN MARTIN   *Annette Crosby*
SHIRL   *Thomasine Heiner*
MRS. MARTIN   *Moya O'Sullivan*

Directed by Philip Wiseman
Designed by Carl Toms

CONTESTANTS

FIRST ACTOR
(Old Friend, Waiter, Butler, Ralph, Herbert)

GEORGE SMITH

SALLY TOMSON

ANN MARTIN

SHIRL

MRS. MARTIN

NEW YORK CITY
MID TWENTIETH CENTURY
Do Choose a Year

ACT ONE

SCENE 1 GOLF STREET
An area of finance
Old Friend
George Smith

SCENE 2 THE OFFICE, GOLF STREET
Five minutes later
Sally Tomson
George Smith

SCENE 3 THE OFFICE, GOLF STREET
A curious week later
Sally Tomson
George Smith

SCENE 4 FLAT FOURTEEN, MERRY MANSIONS
Four windy hours later
Sally Tomson
George Smith

SCENE 5 THE OFFICE, GOLF STREET
A foolish Friday morning
Ann Martin
George Smith

SCENE 6 CLUB CAR, EVENING TRAIN
Four days later
George Smith
Waiter
Sally Tomson

SCENE 7 THE GOOSE GOES INN
Twenty four hours further on
George Smith
Shirl

ACT TWO

SCENE 1 CONSERVATORY, POMFRET MANOR
Three untoward months later
Sally Tomson
George Smith
Butler

SCENE 2 ROOM 604, DYNAMO HOUSE, OWL STREET
Forty hours have passed
George Smith
Ann Martin

SCENE 3 BAR AND BEER RESTAURANT
A chilly rainy April evening
Ralph
George Smith
Sally Tomson

SCENE 4 MISS MARTIN'S MOTHER'S APARTMENT
The wilds beyond Fartbrook
Ann Martin
George Smith
Mrs. Martin

SCENE 5 ROOM 604, DYNAMO HOUSE, OWL STREET
Four o'clock in the middle of May
Shirl
George Smith
Sally Tomson
Herbert

ACT ONE

SCENE 1. GOLF STREET

This crisp morning on the eleventh day till Christmas. On a sidewalk amid the babel of pedestrians, the darkly GEORGE *early morning noncommunicative* SMITH *emerges from the east behind his blue sunglasses on his knickerbockered legs as another folk emerges from the west to a slow motion confrontation. This particular folk, approaching* SMITH *in his prime, slowly lights up with the rays of recognition, raising a right hand as a possible sail for this renewal of friendship.* SMITH, *downcast eyes ready to spot any idle change lurking in the gutter, comes to a stop as this figure obstructs him in his forward motion at this ever critical time in his personal history.*

OLD FRIEND   I know you, hey, aren't you George Smith.

SMITH [*The low foghorn*]   Beep.

OLD FRIEND   Ha, you're George Smith all right.

SMITH [*A tenor tremor*] Beep.

OLD FRIEND What do you mean, beep for an old friend. We were prepsters together.

SMITH [*The abrupt, high, curt, I should like to be in a hurry beep*] Beep.

OLD FRIEND Variations. Ha ha, George. It is you. Greetings. No kidding. Well, how are you. I mean I heard you got an office right around here. Read your ad. Ha ha, like the phrasing. Ha ha, secretary wanted with a desirable demeanor. I mean that could be a play on words. Guess you can afford it. I mean you're a somebody.

SMITH [*Bass baritone*] Beep.

OLD FRIEND I mean I'm not doing badly. I'm doing all right. Got myself a little old partnership. But I mean how are you, all right.

SMITH [*High*] Beep [*Low*] beep.

OLD FRIEND Now wait a minute, George, ha ha. I know this is a funny situation. Well, ha ha, do you need first aid.

SMITH [*Automatic beeping buoy*] Beep.

OLD FRIEND But a joke's a joke. OK.

SMITH [*Medium*] Beep [*High*] beep.

OLD FRIEND Now hold it. Let's not make a meeting like this in the middle of Golf Street with all the congestion holding things up. I mean, you are located here, I mean for good. What do you say.

SMITH [*The low foghorn*] Beep.

OLD FRIEND Gee George, is there something wrong. Are they crowding you. This has kind of gone on too long to be comic. I can take a hint if that's it. What are you saying this beep to me for. If you don't want to recognize me say so.

SMITH [*Fast medium*] Beep beep.

OLD FRIEND What is it. Is this a method, something happened and you use this method. I mean are you nervous.

SMITH [*Low*] Beep.

OLD FRIEND It's a method.

SMITH [*Low*] Beep.

OLD FRIEND I see that's one beep. Oh I'm catching on, a voice lapse. It's one beep, maybe, for yes.

SMITH [*Medium high*] Beep.

OLD FRIEND And two for no.

SMITH [*High*] Beep.

OLD FRIEND I'm sorry, I didn't know anything about this, George. Is it permanent.

SMITH [*Low*] Beep.

OLD FRIEND Gee that's tough. Guess, ha ha, with this new silence you want a staff around of desirable demeanor.

SMITH [*The careless high of the easy come easy go acceptance of blood-curdling hardship*] Beep.

OLD FRIEND Would help with this kind of problem. You're under specialists.

SMITH [*Low*] Beep.

OLD FRIEND   New method like this must tax the mind. You must want to really say something once in a while. Like an opinion.

SMITH [*The careless high*]   Beep beep.

OLD FRIEND   Is that right. [*Taking a glance at the world to see if there were any stray witnesses to this remark*] If there's anything you need. I know you must be all right for money. But if you're bothered by a problem, staff or spiritual, you know. Why are you holding your hand to your ear. You're not deaf too.

SMITH [*Low*]   Beep.

OLD FRIEND   Oh, gee that's tough. You lip-read.

SMITH [*Low*]   Beep.

OLD FRIEND   That's why you're looking for new staff.

SMITH [*Medium high*]   Beep.

OLD FRIEND   You remember Alice. You know I married her.

SMITH [*The medium high of is that so*]   Beep beep.

OLD FRIEND   She only mentioned you the other day. [SMITH *raising a hand to his ear*] My Alice, yes, mentioned you. [*Raising his volume somewhat, leaning in a little to the* GEORGE SMITH *ear.* SMITH's *slight frown*] She mentioned you. [*Dropping the volume*] This is a really rotten world. Real rotten. [SMITH's *frown and inclining ear*, OLD FRIEND *raising the volume once more*] It's rotten. [*Lowering the volume, speaking in a southerly direction where the world is sunnier*] Guy's speech and hearing cut off in his prime. [SMITH *leaning in an ear to receive this latest message*, OLD FRIEND *raising volume once more into* SMITH's *ear*] I said in your prime. [*Lower volume*] It's a shame. But you can still see. [*Pointing to* SMITH's *dark blue sunglasses. Raising*

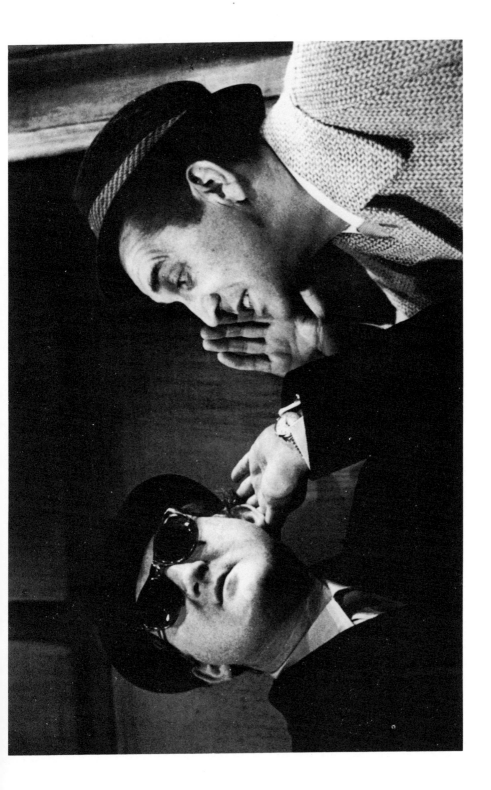

the volume once more] I said see, you can still see. To lip read. From
behind the glasses.

SMITH [*The oh yeah*]   Beep.

OLD FRIEND   Thank God for that. Can they do something for you. I
said, help you. [*Shouting*] Can they help you.

SMITH [*Low*]   Beep beep.

OLD FRIEND   It makes you sick, doesn't it. A disgrace. [SMITH *inclining
head.* FRIEND *raising volume*]   I said it was a disgrace.

SMITH [*The possibly is*]   Beep.

OLD FRIEND   Believe me I'm really sorry for what's happened to you.
I mean that sincerely. [*Raised volume*] I said, I'm sorry, sincerely.

SMITH [*The slight yessiness of* SMITH's *head*]   Beep beep beep.

OLD FRIEND   That's three. [*Smile of recognition*] I got it. For thanks.

SMITH [*Hey you won the prize*]   Beep.

OLD FRIEND   Only George, I'm in a sort of hurry. Like to hang on, talk
over old times. [*Spying out the space ahead, having to walk into it
backwards to let* SMITH *lip read*] Get together, won't we. I mean
sometime, old sport, when you're well again.

SMITH [*Low foghorn*]   Beep.

OLD FRIEND   You'll be all right. Thing is not to worry. [*Raising up a
conspicuous arm*] Looking at my watch. [*The smile*] Got to be dead
on time somewhere. [*Another smile*] An appointment. [*The slowly
raised hand of parting*] I wish you all of God's luck that someday
you may be well again. [*Increasing volume*] Hope your health comes
back, I mean that.

SMITH [*Machine gun*]   Beep beep beep.

OLD FRIEND   Sorry I got to rush. But if you can read my lips I'm saying the answer may be in prayer. George. Pray. So long.

SMITH [*High low high low*]   Beep beep beep beep.

OLD FRIEND   Ha ha, good bye. Good bye. [SMITH *watching* OLD FRIEND *go, retreating backwards away.* SMITH *turning into doorway to the tune of "Eine Kleine Nachtmusik"*]

SCENE 2. THE OFFICE, GOLF STREET

A *few minutes later on this crisp morning the eleventh day till Christmas. The lonely one flight up office at Thirty three Golf Street, past which a wandering tenor voice sings "Annie Laurie."* GEORGE SMITH *sitting darkly at his desk in his early thirties but looking older since running his own business and signing contracts. The door opens. A worried* MISS MARTIN *hesitantly delivering a letter to the desk of* SMITH. MISS MARTIN *lifting her eyebrows, lowering them, exits.* SMITH *slitting open the letter with a long skewer, holds the white paper between the pincers of each hand. Ship's bereft hoot from the river. Puts letter sadly down and looks up and out the window. A knock on the door.*

SALLY TOMSON [*Blond head peeking in door. This figure steps in. Tall, chilled and blue at the neck in a collarless black slim coat. A bare foot of arm between her sleeve and skimpy black gloved hand holding a folded newspaper. She brings a pointing naked stiff finger through the air*]   Are you Mr. Smith put this ad in.

GEORGE SMITH   Yes.

TOMSON   I want the job.

SMITH   Won't you sit down. [TOMSON *taking a leisurely view of room. Spying distant chair*]

TOMSON   Sure. [*Pressing a hand on seat. Little backward glancing smile for* SMITH]

SMITH   Well, Miss—

TOMSON   Tomson. Sally Tomson.

SMITH   Miss Tomson, I suppose you do all the usual things.

TOMSON   I can type. And I can work. Hard too. Even though I come from the south. I've got a brother who's a socialite. His picture gets in the paper if that's a help. I can do what you want me to do. With reservations, of course.

SMITH   Of course.

TOMSON   [*Pointing at her little circle on her newspaper*]   This pay isn't bad. I'd only do this work for this pay.

SMITH   I see.

TOMSON   Do you want me.

SMITH   You're the first applicant I've seen.

TOMSON   Do you want me.

SMITH   Can I have some time to think it over.

TOMSON   [*Standing and so full of understanding*]   Sure, I'll go outside for a minute.

SMITH   Look, Miss Tomson, before you do, would you mind answering me one question.

TOMSON   Sure, shoot.

SMITH   If I were to hire you, is the behavior I'm seeing now the natural, everyday behavior I can expect to get from you here in the office.

TOMSON   It'll vary. But I'll be an office girl. [*Making a long stride toward the door*] Whatever you hire me for.

SMITH   All right, no need to go outside for a minute. You're hired. I think you're a sympathetic person.

TOMSON   [*A gentle rise of chin from this elegant winsome skyscraper*] Don't get me wrong, I'm easy come easy go. But.

SMITH   [*Regathering his voice from a sudden guilty quiver*]   Hours ten to five. I don't like to rush the day. Hour for lunch. Your desk is the one just outside the door. And I'll introduce you to Miss Martin.

TOMSON   O yesh, I kinda barged by her. [*Languid wave of long tapering fingernails*]

SMITH   Don't mind my asking do you, are those fingernails real.

TOMSON   [*Spreading a hand in the morning light for a quick perusal*] Yesh. I grew them that way. And by the way I better tell you now I say y e s, yesh. Said it that way right from the time I started saying it. Some people get the idea I'm trying to be coy.

SMITH   OK Miss Tomson, it's all right with me. When can you start.

TOMSON   What's wrong with right now. You see I got a dog to support.

SMITH   I see.

TOMSON   You can have me on trial. So should we get going. [*Getting out of her coat*]

SMITH [*Suddenly searching for the tiller of this business ship*]   Perhaps you would file this letter for me. In the yellow cabinet file marked caution. [*Into desk intercom*] Miss Martin, will you please come in.

TOMSON [*Holding the letter, her coat, the newspaper*]   Hey. This is rich. [*Reading*] December thirteenth, you well know which year. [*Smile of discovery flashing at the mumchance* SMITH] Ha ha. Some date. [*Glancing down and up*] Some letter. Dear Sir, only for the moment are we saying nothing. Sorry. Maybe you don't like comments.

SMITH   Do feel free. [MISS MARTIN *entering in her gray wool dress and twenty sixth year*] Miss Martin, I'd like to introduce Miss Tomson who'll be with us starting today.

ANN MARTIN   How do you do.

TOMSON   Hi.

SMITH   Well. [*A general clearing of* SMITH's *throat*] Ahem. [*And look at his watch*] I must be going. Miss Martin, do please familiarize Miss Tomson with things. The green files for go, yellow for caution and red marked stop. I'm having an early workout at the club before lunch.

MARTIN   And your fencing lessons at four.

SMITH [*Rising*]   Gracious. Yes.

TOMSON [*Taking a pace back to make much room for her raised pointing arm*]   Hey. I mean, pardon me. But what century are you in.

SMITH [*Taking a view down at his lower anatomy*]   Sometimes one prefers a little ease about the lower leg.

TOMSON   Nice leg.

SMITH   Thank you. [*Taking his hat from stand*] If I don't get back this afternoon, hope you both have a nice weekend and see you Monday. [*"Eine Kleine Nachtmusik," as* SMITH *slips shyly past these two employees. Lights dim.* SMITH *opening door looks back with a faded little smile*]

SCENE 3. THE OFFICE, GOLF STREET

TOMSON   [*Offstage outside that frosted glass door*]   Good morning, Mr. Smith. [*Offstage a large canine growl, the lurchment of a desk, a snarl and growl.* GEORGE NIPPY SMITH *leaping into his office behind a slammed frosted glass door for a moment's refreshment of safety. Doffing the narrow brimmed recently purchased hat to fan the sudden panic from one's face as the low menacing growling continues.* SMITH *opening door a crack to attend to his untoward office situation*]

SMITH   Does it bark. [*Three thigh sized barks*] What does it eat, Miss Tomson. [*Whoosh. Clack. Those were the teeth.* SMITH *slamming door tight once more*] Miss Tomson. The dog.

TOMSON   [*Offstage*]   Yesh.

SMITH   Will we be seeing it [*Taking deep breath*] every morning.

TOMSON   Do you want to. Got a cute name. Goliath. He's like a lion.

SMITH   To be sure.

TOMSON   Sorry he tried to get you. But he doesn't know you yet. [*Low growls*] Goliath say a nice good morning to Mr. Smith. Right there, that shadow behind the glass, go on, Goli, Mr. Smith isn't going to bite you.

SMITH   Please. Don't show me to him.

TOMSON   [*Offstage*]   Mr. Smith, you didn't think I was going to bring Goli to work with me every morning, did you.

SMITH   Miss Tomson, I have a vivid imagination, likely to believe anything.

TOMSON   [*Offstage*]   Well why didn't you say so, Mr. Smith. Goli is just on his way to the boarding kennel. Didn't have room this morning. Raw steak is his dish. Rump. [SMITH *reaching behind to nervously collect a bit of his own haunch in each hand*] Thought you wouldn't mind. [SMITH *sniffing suspiciously in the air at a distinct odiferousness and* GOLI, *that enormous woof woof, gives a woof*] It's going to be your first time away from me, Goli, and you mustn't eat Mr. Smith. Our new boss.

SMITH   [*Looking slowly and regrettably down his person. Toward the footwear. Lifting one up toward the nostril*]   O my God.

TOMSON   [*Sticking her head in* SMITH's *office door*] Tomorrow he has his checkup at the animal medical center. [SMITH *doing the rigid straightening up*] It's so near the office here. [*Sniffing*] O my God. [*Exits. Offstage*] Naughty Goliath, naughty.

SMITH   [*Removing shoes and slipping same into his desk drawer. Into intercom*] Miss Tomson, do come in, please. [*Putting on his hat*]

TOMSON   [*Entering fanning herself under nose with a newly arrived letter. Sniffing*] Ah, the all clear. Hey, that hat. That's better.

SMITH   What do you mean, Miss Tomson.

TOMSON   That hat. It's a slight improvement. Don't ever wear that other thing again, it just doesn't suit you or anything you're trying to be.

SMITH   Oh.

TOMSON   Let me give you a tip. Don't wear that green tie with that green shirt. [*Standing back a pace to take a general view of* SMITH] But that's not bad what you're wearing, not bad.

SMITH   Thanks.

TOMSON   Sure.

SMITH   Would you like to see my underwear, Miss Tomson.

TOMSON   Ha ha. Sorry. Am I meddling in your affairs. [*Calm amusement*] I've taken an interest in you. I want to see you make it. But the shoes. [SMITH *twitching at his knee hole desk*] The color is definitely too light. [*Peering down*] Gee they've gone dark.

SMITH   [*Sneaking a peek at his stockinged feet*]   My socks.

TOMSON   Oh. [*Holding out the white sheet*] Anyway this letter. The guy's bluffing. Says you're infringing on his area of operations. I mean how·could you be infringing. [*Easy wave of the hand and* SMITH *holding out his hand to take the letter*] Look at this little setup. [SMITH *taking deep sigh as he briefly glances at letter*] By the way, you got a license for a gun. [SMITH *mumchance*] OK, you don't have to answer that.

SMITH   Miss Tomson.

TOMSON   Yesh.

SMITH   Miss Tomson, don't mind my asking you a question.

TOMSON   No.

SMITH   It's about you.

TOMSON   Sure, what about me.

SMITH   Why were you looking for a job when you came to me.

TOMSON   I got jilted.

SMITH   I don't want to pry into anything as personal as that.

TOMSON   Sure, pry if you want.

SMITH   Well, if I might perhaps ask, were you terribly hurt by this.

TOMSON   Let's say I was amazed by it.

SMITH   Oh. [*Taking off hat and laying it gently on side of desk*]

TOMSON   I was the cheapest thrill he was ever likely to get in his life. [*Picking up hat*]

SMITH   I'm surprised you were jilted.

TOMSON   Well I wasn't really. [*Turning hat around*] Some guy started writing me poems and I thought they were kinda cute. [*Deblocking hat with little punches.* SMITH *with wide eyes and ears*] So the guy I'm giving the cheapest thrill he was ever likely to get which was costing him a fortune I admit, hears of this and said get rid of this poetic curiosity and I said no. [*Inflicting some odd dents*] And then he asked for the gold key back.

SMITH   I take it, Miss Tomson, this gold key was to a nest somewhere.

TOMSON   Nice way to put it, Mr. Smith, but it didn't have a cozy quality. [*Deblocking hat once more*]

SMITH Pardon me for using your jiltor's reference, but what happened to the poetic curiosity.

TOMSON He beat it. After I used to feed him and drive him around in the car the jiltor gave me as a present. [*Slowly reblocking hat in a new image*] When I gave the jiltor the car back, the poetic curiosity took off south where he said it was warmer.

SMITH Although I don't want to suggest this if you think otherwise, the poetic curiosity was really the jiltor.

TOMSON Yesh, put it that way. But he used to give me laughs. [*Holding out hat to see if it will fly*]

SMITH I see.

TOMSON Do crazy things like taking an orange and tying it to the cat's tail. [*Final delicate little touches of reblocking*] He was full of deals too to make lots of money until he said he didn't have time to think if I wasn't able to support him. [*Returning hat to* SMITH's *desk*] He was like you in some ways, had no taste at all.

SMITH I see.

TOMSON [*Leaning toward and too shy to touch* SMITH] I hurt your feelings.

SMITH Not at all.

TOMSON Yes I did. You're vulnerable.

SMITH Miss Tomson, I'll let you know when I need the care of an institution.

TOMSON You do that. [*Offstage woof woof from a peckish* GOLIATH]

SMITH [*That busy executive taking the nervous glance at the timepiece*] I think I'm leaving for the club. I have a fencing lesson.

TOMSON How's your sword.

SMITH [*Momentary pause of disbelief at the possible indiscretion*] Fine, Miss.Tomson. Would you put this letter in the red file marked Stop. And are you free this evening.

TOMSON That's a Jew question, Mr. Smith.

SMITH I beg your pardon, Miss Tomson.

TOMSON You should ask if I can work overtime. Or are you asking me out to a nightclub. [SMITH *bowing head*] Sure. I'm free. [*Humming voices of "Annie Laurie"*]

SMITH Can you come to my apartment with paper and pencils tonight?

TOMSON Sure. What time.

SMITH I'm having food brought in. Perhaps you'd like to dine with me. Seven. [*Standing putting on hat. Freezes as* TOMSON *surveys him*]

TOMSON That's better. [SMITH *giving a smile to go with the new dash of the reblocked hat*] You know, you're a deceptive guy.

SMITH Thanks.

SCENE 4. FLAT FOURTEEN, MERRY MANSIONS

In a warmth and comfort cut off from winter. A table laid for dinner in this quiet, dim solitude. Fire glowing. Distant sirens to multiple murders everywhere. Wine bottles. SMITH, *hands*

entwined across midriff, silently viewing a table of delectabili-
ties. SMITH *reaching for a little tidbit. The blue light flashing*
the arrival of a guest. SMITH *pressing a button. Enter an open*
coated MISS TOMSON *upon whose chest quiver those two natural*
gems to which is added one extra shake, surveying SMITH's
chambers.

TOMSON   Not bad, not bad at all, strictly not what I expected. Real
cozy. [SMITH *taking* MISS TOMSON's *coat*] Your door's iron.

SMITH   Steel. [*Presents* MISS TOMSON *with one of his very best welcom-*
ing smiles] Take your coat. [MISS TOMSON *holding pad, pencil and*
letter]

TOMSON   Here. [*A large white envelope*] Your doorman gave me a letter
for you. [*Handing letter to* SMITH. MISS TOMSON *puts pencil and pad*
on table. SMITH *hanging coat in one of his invisible closets.* MISS TOM-
SON *pirouettes on one of her low heels. Puts hands out toward the red*
glow] Nice big logs. Pretty fancy apartment to afford out of your little operation. [*Viewing herself in front of the fire and with a low*
octave delivery] Would you take me for a campfire girl, Mr. Smith.

SMITH   [*Standing with the big white envelope and a nervous smile*]
Sherry, Miss Tomson.

TOMSON   Sure.

SMITH   [*Pouring two sherries*]   You look terribly well this evening, Miss
Tomson.

TOMSON   Thanks. [SMITH *opening letter, takes a glance, puts it in his*
pocket] I could get really stupid tonight. The girl living below my
apartment is driving me nuts. Always waiting to jump me with her
troubles. [*As she stares into the firelight glow*] Some troubles. She
hired a detective to watch her husband and catch him with the hussy.
But the detective catches him with a guy. [*A wave of arm as she con-*
fronts SMITH] How do you like that.

SMITH   Irregular certainly.

TOMSON   Crazy. Say, what's got you so nervous. That letter. [SMITH *taking a sigh*] Not again.

SMITH   I'm afraid so.

TOMSON   May I see it, Mr. Smith. [SMITH *fetching it from pocket. The reaching out of* MISS TOMSON's *long comforting fingers would save one from all the ancient deeps of fear, as* SMITH *longingly views that arm, so marvelously exposed this evening from her dazzling dress.* MISS TOMSON's *flick of talon across the paper. One blond lock falls forward as she reads*] This is a new one, Mr. Smith. This guy prides himself. Sees himself as a big important operator. Coming on with the dignity. Get this encroach crap. Big bark no bite.

SMITH   I'm not particularly anxious to be barked or growled at.

TOMSON   Old Goliath put the wind up you, didn't he, Mr. Smith. Ha ha. But got to admit this guy's approach is nicely sneaking in from the side.

SMITH   Precisely why I'm not underestimating him.

TOMSON   [*Handing back letter*]   But Mr. Smith, if you want to know the truth, you overestimate these things. And take it personally as well. [*A gentle symphonic ushering of her blond hand*] Sit down. [*Taking an anchovic tidbit from table*] You really look white. [*Handing anchovic tidbit to* SMITH] Sorry about the fingers.

SMITH   Thanks, Miss Tomson, I suppose it has got under my skin.

TOMSON   [*That light blue pillar of strength*]   Mr. Smith don't let it. Here's an olive.

SMITH   You're right, Miss Tomson. I shouldn't let it but it does.

TOMSON Ignore it. [*Taking a thoughtful sip of sherry*] And see what develops. Soon as you show you're worried that's when they've got you.

SMITH It's an imposition.

TOMSON What is.

SMITH Of the worst kind. To involve you like this in matters which quite frankly are extremely distasteful.

TOMSON You're kidding.

SMITH I'm not.

TOMSON Here, have another tidbit. It's life, Mr. Smith. I mean millions are trampling and struggling toward the top. [*Looking down around her*] It's so nice up here. [*Warm soft smile*] Anyway, you're not bad to work for. [SMITH *wearing a little hope on face*] I thought working was going to kill me. Besides it's not me they're after. It's you.

SMITH Alas.

TOMSON But whatever you do, don't let them shove you around. How was the fencing.

SMITH Think I kept the instructor on his toes. Some terrifying physical specimens around the club recently.

TOMSON Gee, tell me about them, Mr. Smith. I love hearing about these big tarzans, that's the way my brother's built, the one who gets his picture on the social page. [*Putting her drink on the table to take up her stance, her arms cutting a V with a whistle*] He goes right out under the arms. Shape of a V. [*Pulling in stomach, putting out chest.* SMITH *with great imperceptibility moistening lips*] No stomach at all. At home in our kitchen he'd come in without a stitch on and open up the icebox, take out the milk and drink a whole quart in one gulp. [*Throwing back head underneath the memory of this quart,*

SMITH *stiffening at the revelation of her jugular, a delicate blue tumescence*] His body is really magnificent. I used to see it a lot. [*Gathering herself in a quick jungle crouch*] Even big as he is, he moves like he was a panther. [SMITH, *that hero with pen and paper, showing alarmed but affirmative interest*] Mr. Smith, aren't you afraid of being killed by one of these guys. You just seem too frondlike for that kind of thing. Ha ha, I can just see it, you grappling with one of these tarzans. [SMITH *reflecting on his folded hands with lonely sadness*] Hey, come on, Mr. Smith, I hurt your feelings, didn't I. Come on now, I did.

SMITH Oh no, no.

TOMSON I have. But you're not just one of these big apes. I mean I can see you with your sword. [*This ennobling vision sinking upon* SMITH] You're no weakie, Mr. Smith, you've got things they haven't got.

SMITH What, Miss Tomson.

TOMSON Well even without a sword. I mean you can sign a contract.

SMITH Oh.

TOMSON You're not mentally weak, maybe that's what I'm saying. Like you're gentle. Got nice hands. You show consideration. Those things are something, Mr. Smith. [*Slow dawning smile across her countenance*] I just could never, but never, you know see [SMITH *standing to take the onslaught of the coming image*] You stark at the icebox under a bottle of milk, that would be just, just . . . [*Relenting look*]

SMITH Well, dinner, I suppose, is served.

TOMSON [*In her low octave down the sidelines*] I'll say. Just like to take a look out your window. You got poor people living across the street. [*With a deliberate exercising of the physique slowly crossing to window, hips swinging, those two handy melons fore and aft flash-*

ing back and forth under her dress. As she suddenly stops, swings back her head over her shoulder, catches poor old SMITH's *eyes glued*] You think I'm walking like I was compromised, Mr. Smith.

SMITH   I don't quite get you, Miss Tomson.

TOMSON   You know, Mr. Smith.

SMITH   I don't, Miss Tomson. Why are you shaking your head.

TOMSON   Because Mr. Smith, you're one of the most innocent guys. Ha ha, I think. Can't you see I'm walking as if I'm looking for it.

SMITH   For what.

TOMSON   For it. Don't force me to say it because I will. [*As this fast sea going cruiser turns and heads back*]

SMITH   [*Clearing throat, lifting the cover of the tureen*]   Miss Tomson, I hope you like asparagus. [*Subdued gentleman, moving to help* MISS TOMSON *with her chair*]

TOMSON   Hey, you're a gentleman. [SMITH *withdrawing slightly scalded hands*] Yesh, I love asparagus. [SMITH *sitting, a general adjustment of napkins.* MISS TOMSON *leaning aside to peer around flowers*] Well this is some business conference. [SMITH *handing little plate of asparagus around vase of flowers*] Thanks.

SMITH   May I cut you some bread, Miss Tomson, white or brown.

TOMSON   That brown looks good. Mr. Smith, you don't mind my gobbling up the asparagus with my fingers. Some people are touchy about using the dinner hooks.

SMITH   Of course not, Miss Tomson, I intend to use my hooks too. Much healthier that way.

TOMSON   Say you really go in for this health. [*Removing huge vase of flowers blocking her view of* SMITH. *Putting them on floor*] That's better.

SMITH   Just an interest in a certain robustness, Miss Tomson.

TOMSON   Aren't you a little long in the tooth for that. [SMITH *looks up, looks down, looks away*] Now. [*Her hand touching her brow*] I hurt your feelings again.

SMITH   I exercise to keep my figure.

TOMSON   [*Short burst of six bullets to* SMITH's *vital midsection*] After thirty you can't go back. [*This dazzling saleswoman*] What's a little pot. Real cute. I like it. No kidding. [SMITH *is not to be cheered,* MISS TOMSON *leaning in*] Why don't you try a corset, if you're worried. You know this office life is pretty unhealthy anyway. Why don't you some-time come to my apartment. We could go roller skating in my living room. [SMITH's *raised eyebrows,* MISS TOMSON's *smile*] Even got a type-writer there. To work, if you wanted.

SMITH   That's kind, Miss Tomson, [MISS TOMSON *as she peers out over her length of asparagus in her mouth*] but you've got your own per-sonal life to lead. I'm already imposing too much on your free time.

TOMSON   What free time. I go home now, especially while Goliath's at the medical center, just mess around, listen to music, make some clothes. I do nothing. Sometimes my brother comes around, crowds the apartment out with celebrities. [SMITH *ladling out the wine*] Bunch of stuffy stuck up deads. I used to be crazy for that kind of crowd. You know, tennis, squash, a really healthy looking bunch of people. Then one day just like that, [*Waving a piece of asparagus*] I took a look at this crowd. Just stood and listened. I was hearing them for the first time. And boy, were they saying nothing. And same day I'm standing on the court with my racquet, resting, when I get this poke in the back through the fence. It's a guy passing on the street. [*Peeking over her shoulder*] I turn around, I'm going to say who the fuck, sorry about that, but who the, and he hands me a piece of paper. It's my first sight of the poetic curiosity. There's a poem on the paper and his address on the back. Hey, am I talking like mad. Must be the wine.

SMITH [*That ever ready host pouring*]   A little more, Miss Tomson, I'm most interested to hear you talking.

TOMSON   You're not kidding.

SMITH   Certainly not.

TOMSON   Gee, [*Giving* SMITH *that on the level look*] I was kind of crazy then. Going up with that gold key to the nest, the elevator crammed with presents I'm buying with this guy's money. I said everybody get a load of this, some guy's handed me a note with a poem. I started to read it. I stopped right in the middle. I thought Christ, this guy might have meant this and the words are nice and they were about me too, that's why I stopped I guess. [*Taking nip of asparagus*] This is good asparagus. Funny, after that I was thinking what's this kind of life, what good is it. It was pretty good. But I was selling myself for peanuts. There I got all interested in the real things, you know deep things, and the poetic curiosity all the while is interested in the free meal ticket I am and the big time living up in the nest. Boy. [*Moisture in* MISS TOMSON's *eyes*]

SMITH   Miss Tomson, please don't say any more. Have a little sip of your wine.

TOMSON   You know, Mr. Smith, I do you injustice you don't deserve. You're a nice guy. As well as a strange one. Why some debutante didn't nab you I don't know. Weren't they swarming all over you.

SMITH   I regret to say Miss Tomson they weren't.

TOMSON [*Shifting in her seat*]   Just undoing this buckle a notch. I'm getting a pot too. I need more padding on me. [*Hands under bosoms*] Could use more right here.

SMITH   You're all right there, Miss Tomson. If I may suggest.

TOMSON   How do you know these are real.

SMITH   Come come, Miss Tomson.

TOMSON   Ha, ha, almost caught you guessing, didn't I, come on, admit it.

SMITH   For a moment perhaps. [*Serving more wine*]

TOMSON   I could get stinko. I keep forgetting I'm here to do some work. Come on, let's work. Get the letters out. I'm really all set. I got choice replies to all of them. Dear Buster, they're holding a big sale somewhere down town, full of kite bargains, you are invited. How's that, Mr. Smith.

SMITH   [*With a platter of meat*]   Have a cold cut, Miss Tomson.

TOMSON   Maybe you don't go for that one. Now this guy, J.J.J. who says he's aware of the nature of your business, how could he know when I don't even know. How about, Dear Jack, beat it, or we'll give you plenty perforations and pink carnations and a pair of cement shoes to walk across the river. Sorry, Mr. Smith, you figure that's the wrong approach.

SMITH   Sometimes silence is best.

TOMSON   [*Taking a long look at* SMITH]   Mr. Smith, I don't want to pry but why hasn't a guy like you got a wife and kids. [SMITH *looking up mumchance*] It's none of my business, forget I asked. [*Faintly from the street, scraggly children's voices singing,* "Noël, Noël, the angels did sing"] Hey, Mr. Smith, a choir of kids. Let's look. [*Over to window, peering down into the street*] Hey come here, Mr. Smith, look at this, isn't that a sweet group of urchins. They're singing. How do you get this window open. [*Waving down into street*]

SMITH   I'm afraid it's sealed.

TOMSON   I'd throw the kids out some money. Hey, they see me. Poor things singing out there all alone in the cold. Nobody around even to listen. Can't we do something for them. Maybe I could run down there with à platter of stuff. Some of the cold cuts and bread. Let's do that.

SMITH   Miss Tomson, I'd rather you didn't.

TOMSON   Hey why.

SMITH   You'll get chilled.

TOMSON   Not me, I'm as healthy as they make them.

SMITH   I still rather you didn't.

TOMSON   What's got into you, Mr. Smith. You mean you don't want me to give those poor kids sustenance. Is that what you're telling me.

SMITH   Miss Tomson, please, you're misunderstanding me.

TOMSON   [*Withdrawing from window to her full blond statuesque beauty*]   I wonder if I am. Cold and hungry down there. If I were a kid I'd wish someone would come out of a rich looking window like this and give me something, even though it was only food.

SMITH   I've got my reasons.

TOMSON   I guess you have. [*Children's voices fade*] I've got my pad if you want to dictate. [*To table taking up pad*]

SMITH   Miss Tomson.

TOMSON   I'm ready.

SMITH   Miss Tomson, [*Loading at crazy speedy random, cold cuts, remains of asparagus*] here. Take it down to them.

TOMSON   No, it's all right.

SMITH   Now please do. Put the pad down.

TOMSON   No, it doesn't matter.

SMITH   Miss Tomson, it does matter. It matters to me now. There's a silver platter.

TOMSON   It doesn't matter. I've got my pad ready and pencil poised.

SMITH   You're upset.

TOMSON   I'm just waiting for the dictation.

SMITH   Well I'm so upset I can't dictate.

TOMSON   Well maybe we better leave it till another time then. [*Pad and pencil at her sides*]

SMITH   Are you saying you'd like to go home now, Miss Tomson.

TOMSON   You could tell me where my coat is.

SMITH   Miss Tomson, I apologize for not letting you go out to those children.

TOMSON   Let's forget it. Where's my coat.

SMITH   Out there. [MISS TOMSON *moving toward hall. Faint strains of* "Annie Laurie"] Miss Tomson. [MISS TOMSON *hesitating at door. Turns to look at* SMITH. *Her eyes slowly drop*] Please don't go. [MISS TOMSON *exits,* SMITH *stands. Waits. Sound of steel door closing.* SMITH *turns to window looks down into street to strains of* "Annie Laurie," *legs astride at parade rest, two hands come slowly from his sides and join in each other behind his back*]

SCENE 5. THE OFFICE, GOLF STREET

Friday morning, fifth day till Christmas. SMITH *standing at his office window, looking down into street, legs astride at parade rest, his two hands joined behind his back. Tenor singer passing below singing "Annie Laurie."* MISS MARTIN *peeking in at the silent* SMITH, *and at the papers strewn over desk and floor.*

MARTIN   Mr. Smith, excuse me.

SMITH   Yes.

MARTIN [*Stepping in*]   Shall I parcel up Miss Tomson's things and send them to her.

SMITH   No one's to touch that desk; leave it just as it is. [*Head bowing at the window*] I'm sorry, Miss Martin.

MARTIN   You said if she didn't show up by Friday.

SMITH   I know. But leave everything.

MARTIN   There have been a few phone calls, you know when no one speaks on the other end. The breathing is awful. I switched the music in with the adaptor.

SMITH   The bagpipes record.

MARTIN   Yes. They hung up right away.

SMITH   Good.

MARTIN [*Hanging head, eyes looking down sadly at tips of toes. Perhaps a little tear falling. Turning slowly*] Is there anything else, Mr. Smith.

SMITH [*Turning from window. A long look at* MISS MARTIN] Miss Martin. What is it.

MARTIN Nothing.

SMITH There is.

MARTIN No.

SMITH Something I've done or said.

MARTIN It's nothing.

SMITH These letters and phone calls.

MARTIN I had a dream last night.

SMITH Oh.

MARTIN They got you.

SMITH [*Caught in the nervousness of this dream*] Please, come in, Miss Martin. [MISS MARTIN *stepping farther into room*] How many were there.

MARTIN I don't know, six.

SMITH I see.

MARTIN Maybe only four, or five. Mr. Smith, I don't want to ever let you down. But I'm scared.

SMITH Miss Martin, you mustn't take things so seriously. [*Taking out hanky*] Here have a good blow. [MISS MARTIN *taking hanky and clearing nostrils heroically*] That's it.

MARTIN   I'll wash and iron it.

SMITH   It's all right, Miss. Martin. You keep it now.

MARTIN   It has a nice smell. Your hanky.

SMITH   Lemon.

MARTIN   The whole world is horrible and mean.

SMITH   Now now.

MARTIN   I feel the innocent are cowering. [*Voice rising an octave*] And the guilty are closing in on them murderously. [SMITH *nodding an understanding head*]

SMITH   Certainly the world has gone commercial, Miss Martin. But we must keep calm.

MARTIN   Yes, Mr. Smith.

SMITH   I should never like for you to be unhappy here. I really mean that, Miss Martin. [MISS MARTIN's *eyes flicker down*] You've got nice eyes, Miss Martin. [*Hoot of a ship in the river*] A ship setting sail.

MARTIN   I'd love to go on a ship.

SMITH   Takes one away from a lot of things.

MARTIN   You say that so sadly. [SMITH's *sad smile, another hoot from the river*] Mr. Smith. [*Another hoot*] I'd like to ask you something.

SMITH   Yes.

MARTIN   You won't mind.

SMITH   No.

MARTIN [*Viewing strewn papers*] What do you want to be. [SMITH's *eyebrows up*] I mean not that you're not something. [*Bending to pick papers up*] I'll just pick these up. Sounds as if I don't think you're important but I do. [*Glance at a letter in her hand*] I mean something with a position and a name. Is there something you would like to be.

SMITH A great criminal.

MARTIN Ha ha, Mr. Smith. Really. What would you like to be.

SMITH That's it, Miss Martin.

MARTIN But you're crooked already. [SMITH's *steely Asian eyes. Muscles move down one octave on his face in this bleak silence*] Oh I don't mean that. You're not crooked. No. Mr. Smith I swear you're not crooked.

SMITH I am. When one proceeds straight in life there is always an obstruction.

MARTIN You're honest, Mr. Smith.

SMITH [*Moving off at a military pace at this information, stops at door, turns back to* MISS MARTIN *standing hands full of* SMITH's *untoward correspondence*] Can I ask you something, Miss Martin.

MARTIN [*Laying out papers on* SMITH's *desk*] Of course, Mr. Smith.

SMITH [*Standing as the little gears in his head whirr to build up the current to broadcast this next utterance*] Come with me to the country for a few days. [MISS MARTIN's *mouth opens and closes*] Just to sort of trample the flowers and shrubs.

MARTIN Oh.

SMITH We could walk through the snow. This is entirely up to you. You see, I must go to the country on Tuesday evening.

MARTIN   Christmas Eve.

SMITH   Yes. I have to be a Santa Claus with toys and I'd like to sort of get used to the country silence first. We could wander between trees and over outcrops of rock. Needless to say, you would have your own bedroom.

MARTIN   I'd have to tell my mother.

SMITH   Do.

MARTIN   A hotel.

SMITH   More or less.

MARTIN   [*Whiff of "Eine Kleine Nachtmusik"*]   Gee. [*Putting a hand out for support on* SMITH's *desk and flops back in his chair*]

SMITH   Gosh, Miss Martin.

MARTIN   Sort of sudden. [*Her hands spread on desk guiding her little ship*]

SMITH   [*Putting a tentative best foot forward*]   I just suddenly thought.

MARTIN   [SMITH *bringing second best foot forward to best first foot*]   My mother.

SMITH   [*Putting forth first best foot*]   Phone her. [MISS MARTIN *staring at phone*] Use mine.

MARTIN   Yes.

SMITH   [*Bringing second best foot forward*]   But you know how mothers are, Miss Martin. [*At desk*] It might be only politic to say you're housepartying fully chaperoned with other young people.

MARTIN   All right [*Dialing.* SMITH *turning his back, taking his military pace back to look out of window*] Hi, Mom. It's me. Look. [SMITH's *hands join and rotate once*] Mr. Smith has asked me to attend a house party. [*That little pause as* MRS. MARTIN *says* What the hell do you mean house party, what does he need you at a house party for.] To take some notes, of course. [SMITH *turning in some amazement from window*] In the country. Chaperoned. [SMITH *turning confidently back to window*] Over Saturday and Sunday. Yes. I told you Mom, chaperoned. [SMITH's *hands fold again behind his back*] Yes. Just a bunch of young kids. Games. Swimming. Indoor pool. Bunch of young kids. Tennis. Very rich important people. Mom [SMITH's *hands unfolding and falling to sides*], I'll never have another chance like this one. They'll loan me all the clothes I need, Mom. Please. Don't worry. Yes. [SMITH's *hands fold again behind back*] I'll ring you. You worry about nothing. You have to trust somebody. [SMITH's *hands unfolding and falling to sides*] Do you want me to die without any fun, Mom. All right. OK. I'll phone. Goodbye, Mom. I will. I promise. Goodbye. [*Puts down phone.* SMITH *slowly turning to view this efficient secretary*] Mr. Smith, guess you heard, that was my mother.

SMITH   Yes.

MARTIN   Mr. Smith. I don't know what to do.

SMITH   We'll call for a car. Get away from these gloomy financial streets.

MARTIN   Oh God. My mother will kill me. She'll ask me the name of the people. Then she'll try to look them up in the phone book. And try to telephone them and ask if I maybe left my gloves there or something. Mr. Smith, I'm scared.

SMITH   Now now.

MARTIN   I better not go.

SMITH   Fresh air. Away from the dirt and grime of the city. But if you feel in some way it will make you unhappy, I wouldn't want that.

MARTIN [*Turning ninety degrees away from* SMITH *in the swivel chair*] Oh boy.

SMITH Vouchsafe.

MARTIN [*Turning back ninety degrees*] What do you mean.

SMITH I don't know. I'm just saying the first thing that comes into my head. What can one say.

MARTIN I don't know I feel—

SMITH Feel what.

MARTIN [*Turning ninety degrees away from* SMITH *in the swivel chair*] Oh boy.

SMITH What, Miss Martin.

MARTIN [*Turning back ninety degrees*] That, maybe, you're an operator.

SMITH I beg your pardon.

MARTIN That there might be a whole string of girls. Like Miss Tomson you had back to your apartment. Or something like that.

SMITH Miss Martin. Do you know what you're saying.

MARTIN Yes.

SMITH [*Popping on his recent black chapeau*] Very well, Miss Martin. I can proceed alone.

MARTIN [*Making her reflective aside to her conscience*] A harmless trip to the country. [*Spinning around in* SMITH's *swivel chair, her back to* SMITH] Don't rush me.

SMITH [*Looking at his watch*] I must order the car.

MARTIN I'm not going.

SMITH Don't be silly.

MARTIN I'm not going.

SMITH But you have your mother's permission.

MARTIN [*Swiveling back in* SMITH's *chair, confronting* SMITH] Don't try to be funny.

SMITH Very well, Miss Martin, suit yourself. [*Moving for phone*] I'll phone for a car. And make other arrangements for myself. [*Dialing. His finger in the last number*]

MARTIN OK. I'll go.

SMITH [*A smile full of year's warmth*] Miss Martin. I'm glad you said that.

MARTIN Wish I was glad I said it.

SCENE 6. CLUB CAR, EVENING TRAIN

SMITH *reclining in one big blue armchair across from another and a small round cocktail table between. All blue and smoke, ice tinkling in the glasses.* SMITH *watching lamp posts and shadows flash by outside. Turns to take a read of his newspaper, long red underwear calmly showing from under a trouser leg. Wail of diesel whistle, train roaring through a station.* WAITER *passing in light blue, white towel over an arm.*

SMITH Waiter.

WAITER Sir.

SMITH A cocktail.

WAITER Of what variety or nature, sir.

SMITH [*Taken aback by this new sympathetic behavior he had not noticed before on trains*] I'd appreciate your suggestion in the matter.

WAITER You might try a derobe, popular with our evening travelers.

SMITH I beg your pardon, waiter.

WAITER Sir, derobe—

SMITH I certainly will not.

WAITER Sir, it happens to be the name of the drink if you don't mind.

SMITH In that case make it double strength. [*Lifting newspaper to read. A figure tall, blue and blond, gently hip swinging down the train. Past* SMITH. *Stops. Comes back, leans over to look*]

TOMSON Hey. [SMITH *turns to look speechless*] Hey.

SMITH [*Rising slowly to feet behind newspaper*] Sally, I mean Miss Tomson.

TOMSON Sally, why not.

SMITH Well. [*Brave uncertain smile*] Sit down, Miss Tomson.

TOMSON   You sit down. [SMITH *slowly detumescing into seat*] I only just got up to go to the ladies. This train rocking makes me want to go. See you on the way back. [SMITH *turning with his spiritual spotlight to slowly sadly watch her waltz away.* WAITER *taking up an observation position near, naturally to watch as well*]

WAITER   [*Putting drink in front of* SMITH *to bring him back to land of living*]   One derobe.

SMITH   Oh. [*Casual return to the problems of the present with a sophistication that one body is the same as another if you have known enough beautiful ones*] Pardon me, waiter, how did this rather fascinating name come about.

WAITER   Woman comes in one evening. Says she wants something really new that no one has ever had before so Franz concocts this. She sits down. Drinks it and next we're looking at her stark naked. So derobe.

SMITH   How refreshing.

WAITER   Took five attendants from the loony to hold her down. Lucky we were near the state hospital at the time.

SMITH   You don't say.

WAITER   And yours is double.

SMITH   Comforting.

WAITER   But I think she was crazy before she drank it.

SMITH   Thanks for the folklore.

WAITER   [MISS TOMSON *cruising up*]   Any time. [*Departing*]

TOMSON   [*Careless throwing out of an upturned palm*]   Hey anyway, Mr. Smith—

SMITH [*Instant jolting rise*] Miss Tomson, will you join me for a drink.

TOMSON [A *left handed thumb pointing up the train*] Can't. I'm with people. [*Her right hand tips of fingers flickering at* SMITH's *seat*] Gee, sit down.

SMITH [*Lowering down to his seat. This faint voice in the wilderness of this go ahead world*] Just one, Miss Tomson.

TOMSON [*Her blond tresses shaking*] Can't get over it, isn't it rich, you right here all the time and I didn't see you. No, I really can't.

SMITH You didn't collect your last pay check.

TOMSON Forget it, Mr. Smith. Donate it to orphans. [*Little pistol of her right hand shooting a first index finger out*] Hey, you're derobing. [SMITH, *alarmed, looking down at his person.* MISS TOMSON *pointing her pistol finger at the drink*]

SMITH Oh. Won't you join me, Miss Tomson.

TOMSON Ha ha, Smithy, since you put it like that, sure. [*Sitting in opposite chair, and with one large sweep crossing her legs, uncovering three inches of thigh as* SMITH *finds a need for a deep breath and swallow and a stretch of his legs to calm a trembling heart*] Always willing to take off my clothes. But I can't stay. See down there. [*Turning*] No you can't see. But see what you can see. The big blue shadow. That's my brother.

SMITH Amazing shadow.

TOMSON [WAITER *passing*] Yesh.

SMITH Waiter. Two derobers here.

WAITER You catch on fast, mister. [*Departing with a nod at this catcher on, and lingering look over his passing shoulders at the delectably healthy* MISS TOMSON]

SMITH [*Taking in the vision of* MISS TOMSON *along with another lungful of air*] Miss Tomson, I'm glad.

TOMSON What for, Mr. Smith.

SMITH I'm just glad.

TOMSON What are you doing on this train. On Christmas Eve.

SMITH Just glad I took it.

TOMSON You can't be on a train because you're glad. [*Straightening out an index finger at* SMITH's *tie*] Nice tie. Not bad, goes with the shirt.

SMITH What stop, Miss Tomson, are you for.

TOMSON The last. What's yours.

SMITH The Junction. I take the branch line.

TOMSON All by yourself like this. I can't get over it. Guess you're seeing friends.

SMITH Not exactly.

TOMSON You're a mystery.

SMITH What do you mean, Miss Tomson.

TOMSON Why don't you find yourself some nice girl.

SMITH Are you suggesting, Miss Tomson, I just find some nice girl just like that.

TOMSON   Sure, just like that. Crazy for a man living alone not getting any.

SMITH   Miss Tomson.

WAITER   [*Slipping in the drinks between these two conversationalists*] Two derobers. [SMITH *pulling out wallet from inside pocket*] That'll be three. [SMITH *handing over three notes then taking a little purse out of pocket*]

TOMSON   And you could get plenty if you got—[V*oice trailing off at* SMITH's *display of frugality as he chooses a coin to pop on* WAITER's *tray.* WAITER *looks at singular coin.* MISS TOMSON's *voice fades back*] If you were a little more open handed. [WAITER *retreating with that look, Say Bud what has the world done to you anyway*] I don't mean to sort of go into your personal life, but from my view [*Making binoculars with her hands over eyes at* SMITH] you're going to become one of these guys running around to museums collecting brass monkeys and that kind of thing. Your life's unnatural.

SMITH   What's natural Miss Tomson.

TOMSON   [*Hand to her pearls*]   These, anyway.

SMITH   I beg your pardon, Miss Tomson.

TOMSON   I mean the pearls. But these are natural too. Guess they should be hanging right down the cleavage. The pearls. Nature between nature. But it's a pretty cold night. [*Smile, and the airy rise of her eyebrows*] I just can't get over seeing you all by yourself on this train. And taking the branch line as well. Hey, come and meet my brother and his friends, why don't you. [SMITH's *heart looking for somewhere to hide*] Maybe you want to be alone. And I'm barging in. [W*hiff of* "*Annie Laurie*"] But you don't want to meet anybody, do you.

SMITH   Are you coming back.

TOMSON You mean the office, I don't know. I just honestly don't know. I've been laying in bed late just thinking of it. If I'm really built for a working life. I got a machine that wakes you up with music and pours out hot coffee. You ought to get one. What you need, Smith. Lacking a loving hand when you wake up.

SMITH Any machine I would get would spit and grumble.

TOMSON No it wouldn't. They're real magic.

SMITH Where did you buy your machine, Miss Tomson.

TOMSON It really was a present.

SMITH Oh.

TOMSON I couldn't refuse it. On the floor outside my apartment in the dark. Tripped over it and broke the glass on the clock. Couldn't sell it back to the store. From the guy I gave the cheapest thrill he ever got to. You know all the while I'm working for you he had me watched. How do you like that. The nerve. You know what I told him. [*Making a naughty movement of the hand*]

SMITH Yes.

TOMSON That's right. And he's been sending flowers ever since, my apartment's like a funeral parlor. I say to the boy, give them to your mother, sonny, or your girl friend. Know what he says. I laughed. He said I like men. [*Catching a glimpse out of train window*] Hey, look, the pond in front of the dam, they're skating down there. Isn't it beautiful, love to be on that.

SMITH You skate, Miss Tomson.

TOMSON On my ass mostly. Maybe you'll give me a lesson sometime. Smithy, I can't get over it running into you like this. [*Taking a large swig of her drink*] Just what I need, a good derobe. Say, where you going on the branch line.

SMITH   Last stop.

TOMSON   Just like us on the main line. But that ain't too far, last stop of the branch from the last stop on the main. We're right in the same neck of the woods. Why don't you drive over or we drive over to you. [*Click clack of the train, whistle wailing through the lonely stations and* SMITH's *silence*] What's the matter Smithy, you've gone all silent. You don't want us to drive over. Unless of course you're all tied up.

SMITH   Oh no, I'm not all tied up.

TOMSON   What's the matter, Smithy. [SMITH *twisting mixer in drink*] It's OK, you don't have to say anything. Just a wild suggestion. Just if you didn't have anything better to do you might enjoy a skate, that's all.

SMITH   Miss Tomson, I'm not really such good company.

TOMSON   You're swell company. Just a little stingy maybe. You'll be all right when you get into the big time. Come to our house party. Drop in. Goliath will be there. [*Opening and ogling of eyes*] Woof woof. [*As she bends a mouth of beautiful glistening teeth to take a bite of* SMITH] Still scared. Drop in. I mean it. Jiffy, he lives in the big stone mansion. Pomfret Manor. First turn left out of Cinder Village. Celebrities. Fifty bedrooms. Zoo. His wife is bald. A really big operator. Might find him handy to know. Everybody would go crazy over the bashful conservative way you are. Just wish myself I could be a wallflower like you. [*Taking a long look at* SMITH] Smithy, you're too quiet for comfort. Come on, you got a girl up here. I mean last Friday, you were cruising somewhere with Miss Martin.

SMITH   I beg your pardon.

TOMSON   I know it's terrible Smithy, the detective who was watching me stayed on watching you to see if I'd come back to work. I mean that's why don't hand me that beg your pardon, Miss Tomson stuff. You got some nice rural nest tucked in the woods somewhere. Is she beautiful. A hick. Maybe a farmer's daughter. Or maybe Miss Martin. [SMITH's *sad face suddenly stiffening*] Come on, Smith, I'm only kidding you. Like all quiet guys, boy. [SMITH *mumchance in this world of his where there is so much room for* MISS TOMSON] Anyway I better get back to my brother, see the way he's rocking back and forth, means he's bragging.

SMITH   Please stay.

CONDUCTOR   [*Offstage calling out*] Pleasantville Junction next stop, passengers for the Branch Line change.

TOMSON   Your stop's next.

SMITH   Five minutes yet.

TOMSON   Smithy, I don't understand you. You know that. What are you thinking.

SMITH   About a derailment in open country where we'd have to trudge through underbrush and snow to an empty farmhouse.

TOMSON   Trying our level best to conserve body heat by proximity.

SMITH   Yes. [*Expressing a scientific fact*] Your eyes are even bigger than I remember them. And the lashes longer.

TOMSON   Are you a traveler looking for a companion. [*With the big blue eyes burning across the derobes at* SMITH]

SMITH   You look dazzling, unemployed.

TOMSON   You pass out pretty interesting compliments. You're one of those skaters, Smith, who can zigzag like lightning across the ice. I really must be going.

SMITH   Can I see you again.

TOMSON   Sure. Tomorrow.

SMITH   I mean back in town. We could tear a claw off some lobster.

TOMSON [*Standing*]   Fine. I'll send you my new address. To keep this tall frame lean, I don't lightly turn down an invitation to the protein. [*Leveling her little hand pistol*] And don't fall through the ice with this little dish you're seeing. Thanks for the derobe. And Smithy, really have a good time, I mean it, so long.

SMITH   Goodbye, Miss Tomson.

TOMSON   Try Sally.

SMITH   Ha ha, Miss Tomson.

TOMSON   Ha ha, see you. [*Click clack of train, wail of whistle, stations flash by, solitary* SMITH *in his self contained world, wanting so much to stand in a crowd, lights dim, humming voices of "Annie Laurie"*]

SCENE 7. THE GOOSE GOES INN

Early evening in SMITH's *cozy bedroom, in this white clapboard country hotel. Hoots of an owl, gust of wind, bark of a fox. Snow heaped high outside through the nighttime woods and moonlit purple hills.* SMITH *standing in the blazing firelight*

rotating his arms in front of the mirror, in his long red under-
wear. Examining one or two sideviews of his body profile with
various little tilts of the neck. Taking up his tightly rolled um-
brella, assuming the en garde *position, making a few deep*
thrusts accompanied with growl of the human beast. Phone
rings.

SMITH [*With a momentary lapse of proportion turns on the phone using*
the low astride crouch and thrust of umbrella. He collects himself,
taking a quick look to rear and with a reasonably elaborate dignity,
hesitates to pick up the instrument, letting it ring. It rings. With his
natural but arch dignity he picks it up. Listens. Hangs up. And phone
rings again just as he taps his umbrella previous to taking up the en
garde *position. Phone continues to ring.* SMITH *with stony exaspera-*
tion returning to it and picking it up] I told you, no calls from Mrs.
Smith. What do you mean she's not calling. What is she doing.
You've just woken me out of a sound sleep to be flippant. Well tell
her to go away. I see. [*Slamming down phone. Waits looking at it. It*
could, of course, jump. Picks it up again] All right, Smith here. Tell
Mrs. Smith to come up.

SMITH [*Viewing his ridiculous redness. Climbs into his cozy little country*
bed and reaches out, switching off bedside lamp] I don't often talk
to myself but by Jesus the odious manage so well in this world and
people with principles get trampled, kicked and crushed to the bottom
of the pile. But live and let live. Miss Tomson didn't even want her
pay. Her train pulled out of the junction. She never even took a peek
or gave me a wave. Off to her house party and fun.

SHIRL [*Knock on the door.* SHIRL *offstage*] George. Are you in there.
[SMITH *submerging in blankets, mumchance*] All right. I really am
sorry what I said. I say the wrong things that come into my head and
wish you wouldn't listen. But you're so sensitive. [*Slight peeking up of*
the SMITH *periscope head*] Isn't it true. [*Opening door*]

SMITH [*Resubmerging in firelight glow. Eyes just showing from under*
blanket] Naturally one wants to feel welcome.

SHIRL [*Speaking through door as it stands ajar*]   You were. But do you have to take a young child seriously.

SMITH   A revolting degraded human being. No father wants to hear that. Get down on my knees with the toys and they tell me, get away, you're ruining our game.

SHIRL   They're just children, George.

SMITH   All I was trying to do was push one of the little trucks up the ramp. And they push me away. I never had toys like that as a kid. And they tell me, don't blame us, we weren't your father. Then lock me out of my own house.

SHIRL   I know you own the house, George.

SMITH   Just an ordinary decent reception was all I asked for.

SHIRL   You got that.

SMITH   I got insulted. Can see what open country, fields and woods with crystal lakes do for kids. Four little heathens.

SHIRL   Keeping God out of their lives was your idea. It's a long way in the snow here, George. Won't you come back.

SMITH   No.

SHIRL   Will you let me in.

SMITH   I'm thinking about it.

SHIRL   Do we cost too much. I'll economize. Let me in.

SMITH   You've got the door open.

SHIRL   [*Timorously entering*]   May I.

SMITH   You may.

SHIRL   [*Entering, moving her hand in front of her face*]   No light.

SMITH   I know.

SHIRL   Where are you, George.

SMITH   In bed.

SHIRL   Can't we have some light.

SMITH   Firelight.

SHIRL   Well, can I come in.

SMITH   You're in.

SHIRL   Should I close the door.

SMITH   Close it. [SHIRL *closing door*]

SHIRL   Is it all right with you if I sit down.

`SMITH   There's a chair. [SHIRL *accustoming eyes to light*]

SHIRL   I see it. Thank you, George.

SMITH   Any time.

SHIRL   [*Guiding her bottom to rest*]   Can I talk, George.

SMITH   Sure.

SHIRL   You know what I want to say, George.

SMITH   Beep beep.

SHIRL   What's that funny noise you're making.

SMITH   You mean, beep beep.

SHIRL   Yes, beep beep.

SMITH   Oh that's just beep beep.

SHIRL   Sounds strange coming out of the dark.

SMITH   Beep beep.

SHIRL   [*Slowly standing*]   George.

SMITH   Yes, Shirl.

SHIRL   [*Timorously approaching bed*]   George.

SMITH   I'm listening, Shirl. [SHIRL *stops halfway*]

SHIRL   I sound so loud in the dark.

SMITH   Beep beep.

SHIRL   Don't do that, George, please.

SMITH   Beep beep.

SHIRL   I know I deserve it, George.

SMITH   Deserve what? [SHIRL *moves to side of bed*]

SHIRL   Beep beep.

SMITH   Beep beep.

SHIRL   [*Leaning over* SMITH]   George, are we cars.

SMITH   You said it.

SHIRL   I wanted you to see my gold slippers, George.

SMITH   Too dark.

SHIRL   Yeah. But do you want to feel my gold slippers.

SMITH   [*Taking a crash dive under blankets with his twin periscope eyes focusing on this trembling tempting ship*]   Stand back.

SHIRL   [*Standing erect and fists clenched tightly*]   I know I deserve it, George. Do whatever you want to me.

SMITH   Pretty risky talk.

SHIRL   I want to be risky. [*Pulling open a long zip on back of her dress*]

SMITH   What are you doing, Shirl. [SHIRL *takes off dress*]

SHIRL   I'm undoing. [*Takes flying leap into bed*]

SMITH   Careful. Beep beep. I'm a car.

SHIRL   [*Sinking under covers*]   This is the way we used to be, George.

SMITH   [*Emerging from covers*]   I've just stopped for traffic lights.

SHIRL   Are you sitting up, George.

SMITH   I'm waiting for the lights to change. [*Submerging back down*] They've changed.

SHIRL   [GEORGE *and* SHIRL *two heads just showing above covers*]   We should have been like this more often, don't you think, George.

SMITH   Beep beep, I'm going again.

SHIRL   Should we have a crash.

SMITH   Are you suggesting I'm not a careful driver.

SHIRL   No, George.

SMITH   Well, watch it, beep beep.

SHIRL   I can see you, George. I can.

SMITH   He he. I can you too, Shirl.

SHIRL   We've wasted so much time, George, haven't we.

SMITH   Don't drive your car too close.

SHIRL   I want you to crash into me.

SMITH   Safety first.

SHIRL   George.

SMITH   What are these, Shirl.

SHIRL   Feel them.

SMITH   Wow. Headlamps.

SHIRL   Feel this.

SMITH   What is this, Shirl.

SHIRL   This what I want you to feel.

SMITH   I'd be a fool to feel it.

SHIRL   Be a fool and feel it.

SMITH   What a foolish feeling.

SHIRL   Just because you're feeling foolish. [*These two close packed sardines under the blanket*] You like it, George. [*Naturally* SMITH *does not know what to say considering the implications and backfires slightly with the emotional excitement of the time*] George, I like my bread and butter. [SMITH *going in for incoherent mumbling*] Fat belly George, what are you mumbling. [*The music of the distant parade* SMITH *has lightheartedly dreamt up, bass drum, drummers*]

SMITH   The parade.

SHIRL   George, don't slip out, it's a year since you were in.

SMITH   [*The last steam organ in the world trumpets for the merry go round*] Boom boom boom. Got the parade going.

SHIRL   George what parade, shut up, it's up. Enter me.

SMITH   Shirl, watch the underwear.

SHIRL   What made you wear red.

SMITH   A predilection.

SHIRL   Take it off, it rubs me.

SMITH   You're tearing the garment, Shirl.

SHIRL   Kiss my bazumma.

SMITH   Shirl, you're tearing the garment.

SHIRL   I'm pulling the zipper.

SMITH   It's tearing the garment Shirl and is caught in the hairs of my belly.

SHIRL   It rubs me—

SMITH   I didn't ask you come in here.

SHIRL   Shut up and take a handful of hair. Where have all the big strong men gone. You were so nice when you were a car. Drive, you bastard.

SMITH   Beep beep.

SHIRL   Drive.

SMITH   Stop telling me what to do, Shirl. I've got my own mind.

SHIRL   I'm the hottest handful you've had for months.

SMITH   Don't be too sure.

SHIRL   So you've been into others.

SMITH   That remark is false and your use of language regrettable.

SHIRL   Ha ha George.

SMITH   Ha ha Shirl, it's not funny.

SHIRL   Once more fast, George. My friends are waiting. Faster, now you know why I ride horses.

SMITH   [*Waves of red glowing light flooding over this little cozy room in the Goose Goes Inn and across the blankets now stony still. The hoot of a snowy owl out in the woods. The bark of a fox*]   Shirl, what do you mean your friends.

SHIRL   They're waiting downstairs.

SMITH   They're what, Shirl.

SHIRL   Waiting.

SMITH   [*Whisking back the blankets*]   Get out of this bed.

SHIRL   Hey, we're not finished.

SMITH I will not give myself to being used while your friends wait for you. Get out.

SHIRL [On her knees holding up the bedsheet around her] I'm not dressed.

SMITH [Sitting up left handed pointing to door, his head lowered, peering out under his outstretched arm] Get out. [SHIRL retreating barefoot to door wrapped in sheet]

SHIRL You're not pushing me naked into a hotel hall. George, you're not doing that. That's one thing you're not doing.

SMITH I am doing. [SHIRL shrinking away, grabbing up dress from floor] Out. Into the hall.

SHIRL No.

SMITH Go to your friends. Waiting for you. Bunch of ambitious little commuters. Oh, Shirl's upstairs having a throw with some guy. Don't make me a laughing stock.

SHIRL You are already. Everybody knows how you make your money. And they laugh, boy do they laugh. They laugh because they know.

SMITH You take it from me and spend it.

SHIRL I wish I didn't because it's horrible money. And they know what happens with that Nigger maid in that apartment. Don't try to fool me.

SMITH Simply get out of here before I lose my temper.

SHIRL [Dressing under the sheet] Don't look at me. [SMITH turning aloofly away] Always knew you were from the wrong side of the tracks.

SMITH A little fantasy of yours.

SHIRL   It isn't. You sneaked into society.

SMITH   I see. I'm in society now.

SHIRL   They saw you sneaking, don't worry. My friends know. Your phony little cultivated habits. Mosaics all over your stupid apartment. How they let you in the Game Club I don't know. And trying to make some baronial hall sowing trees up our drive. [*Digging her feet into her shoes*] My friends were wise to that, don't you worry. And I know more than you think.

SMITH   Good.

SHIRL   Can't find my things, my purse. I want the lights on.

SMITH   You came in the dark, you go out with all lights off.

SHIRL   You rat. I'm glad I can't see your face. It's the only way I could bear you fucking me.

SMITH   [*Snowy owl hoots way out in the snow. The little fox gives its high pitched bark*]   I think perhaps you've said enough.

SHIRL   [*Pulling dress over head*]   Tell me to get out. And I'm going. You'll hear from my legal counsel. [SMITH *leaning out and grabbing umbrella*]

SMITH   Can't wait. [*Slowly unraveling it*]

SHIRL   [*Struggling under dress*]   My friends are better than you are. And I know where all that other money goes. I can stop you building that edifice. [SMITH *opening umbrella*]

SMITH   I don't know what you're talking about.

SHIRL   [*Her back to* SMITH, *smooths down dress*]   I'm talking about one acre, foundations thirty feet deep, imported marble and the biggest mausoleum built in Renown cemetery. [*Spinning on* SMITH] Doctor Fear.

SMITH   Oh.

SHIRL   Yes Oh. That's who you are. Under that umbrella. Doctor Fear, who's building. Whose name is connected with it. None other than George Smith. [SMITH *lowering umbrella over countenance*] You can't kid my lawyer, he's smart.

SMITH [*Lifting up umbrella*]   Since I pay for him I'm glad to hear that. [*Down umbrella*]

SHIRL   I ought to have half of what you possess. I can stop you squandering what my children and I have a right to. That ghoulish monument is going to be stopped. [*Pulling on one of her elbow length black kidskin gloves*]

SMITH [*Up umbrella*]   You're amply supplied with money. [*Down umbrella*]

SHIRL   I want more. [*Slowly pulling on other glove*] Because you've got more. You're rotten with it. You tried to buy two thousand canes from an antique dealer.

SMITH [*Up umbrella*]   Two hundred. [*Down umbrella*]

SHIRL   And then walked out with a bronze pig worth a fortune. [*Fully dressed, leaning in toward* SMITH]

SMITH [*Up umbrella*]   Brass. [*Down umbrella*]

SHIRL   You admit it. And the poor man is hysterical.

SMITH   The whole world is hysterical.

SHIRL   You robbed him.

SMITH Nothing of the kind. Brass. Recent.

SHIRL Bronze and ancient. My detective said so.

SMITH I see. Some detective.

SHIRL Yes, as a matter of fact he is. And happens to be a college graduate, something you're not.

SMITH Ha ha.

SHIRL Go ahead and laugh. Where's my purse. You'll be laughing. Boy, you'll be laughing. I'll make you laugh. You'll laugh all right. Boy, you'll be laughing.

SMITH Ha ha.

SHIRL Laugh all you want. Go ahead. But I'll squeeze you dry. Drier than that mausoleum. Be the only time traffic will ever stop for you. Is when you're dead. [SMITH *lifts up umbrella. Four more hoots of the snowy owl. And whisperings of a winter snowy wind*] George, George, what terrible things am I saying.

SMITH You were saying, boy, you'll be laughing. And I'll squeeze you dry.

SHIRL George, I'm scared and shivering. What's making me shiver. [*Turning to look and touch the surface of the table and chair*] Turn on the lights. I'm scared the things I'm saying.

SMITH Can't you find your purse.

SHIRL No, George and I'm scared. Don't throw me out. I didn't mean that about legal counsel. [*Hoot of owl*]

SMITH Forget it.

SHIRL   I can't. What about the kids. God, legal counsel. Don't make me go to court.

SMITH   I'm not making you go to court.

SHIRL   They'll scream down at me. I know they'll scream down at me. A judge with white hair. He'll eat up my soul, George.

SMITH   Don't be silly.

SHIRL   Never make me go before a judge, George. As you lie there now promise me that. I'm scared. [*Trembling, sits on the table side chair*] Let me sit. I'd be accused. The judge would accuse me and it would be horrible. [*Whiff of "Annie Laurie"*]

SMITH   Shirl. [SHIRL's *heaving silence, her head bent.* SMITH *collapses his umbrella and rests it at side of bed*] Don't cry. I've got your purse here under the pillow. [*Holding up the gold mesh purse*] Dry up your eyes. I'll let no judge get you.

SHIRL   [*Half looks up*]   I'm sorry. Behaving like this.

SMITH   Shirl, all women cry. But outlive men. [*Turns to window*] Remember, out there under the snow, lies summer. Done that for a lot of years. Your purse is made of mesh like your slippers. [SHIRL *looks at* SMITH. SMITH *smiles softly*] I think you're right, the only time traffic will ever stop for me is when I'm dead. [*"Annie Laurie"*]

ACT TWO

SCENE 1. CONSERVATORY POMFRET MANOR

This March cool evening the end of winter, a wind rising across a forested countryside. In a cavelike anteroom, a white pedestal holding a large plant with a green flower arching over a pink love seat. The evening clothed figure of GEORGE SMITH *rubbing a leaf between his fingers. Sound of voices, laughter and music from other rambling rooms.* SMITH *leaning to sniff the strange flower. Faint strains of "Annie Laurie" on stringed instruments.* MISS TOMSON *enters slowly in the dim light. Stops.*

TOMSON Smithy. Well. You move on a lot of levels. [*Crossing to* SMITH *in her blue evening gown and string of pearls, hand outstretched*] What are you doing here. [MISS TOMSON *raising hand high momentarily and bringing it back to handshaking position to briefly shake* SMITH's *hand*] This is a high level.

SMITH Looking for you.

TOMSON   Well I've been looking for you. Someone said they saw you. Lurking around. I couldn't believe it. Said you arrived in a hearse.

SMITH   I accepted a neighborly invite to a jamboree, thought I might see you after all these months.

TOMSON   I'm around. [*Rumbling of thunder,* MISS TOMSON *looks toward heaven*] Gee, there's going to be a storm. Well, how are you. You look a little tired around the eyes. You even made the newspapers with a picture. How are you doing with your enemies.

SMITH   They have vowed to get me. I will escape by submarine.

TOMSON   Ha ha. [*Lightning flashes, silence, and the following fearful thunder*] Wow. Smithy, I'm a little scared of lightning. [*Unsure smile*] Guess we're safe all alone in this corner with this crazy green flower.

SMITH   How's Goliath.

TOMSON   Dead. [*Lightning*]

SMITH   My God.

TOMSON   He got shot. [*Distant rumble of thunder*] In a dog fight.

SMITH   I'm sorry to hear that.

TOMSON   He was winning too, against two dogs, just as big. All the best steak I bought him. Perfect report on his medical checkups. Never even had worms. Could have shown him in the dog show. [*Head turned askance*]

SMITH   Mustn't dwell on it, Miss Tomson. You look terribly good tonight.

TOMSON   You really mean it, Smith. Do I look OK.

SMITH [*Steps back, viewing* MISS TOMSON's *gown*] Yes. Even without seeing your feet.

TOMSON [*Shaking a leg and putting forth a bare foot*] There.

SMITH [*Mesmerized*] Exquisite. [*Quickly to one knee planting a kiss*]

TOMSON Gee, you're old world, Smithy. [SMITH's *smile*, MISS TOMSON *withdrawing her exquisite tootsie under her gown, her foot searching around for her shoe*] Can't find my shoe now. [*A flash and splitting crack of thunder,* MISS TOMSON *ducks and from this protective position taking up a subject which seems close at hand considering the almighty bolts lashing out of the heavens and in a high, hurried octave*] Smith, this true you putting up a memorial to yourself. [*Straightening up, lowering her octave and progressively slowing her words to an easy amble*] I read in the paper. Earthquakeproof. [*Rumble of thunder*] And the most elaborate ever erected. Isn't that kind of conceited. And expensive. What's the point. What does it matter what happens when you die.

SMITH It matters all the days you live.

TOMSON You call it living zooming around the countryside in a hearse. Aren't you rushing it a little. [*With a smile and a little fist thrusting it slowly and gently to the* SMITH *midsection*] Looking at you, Smith, like this you're a strange one. Who'd have thought out of that little operation you've got going for yourself, you'd be rubbing shoulders with me in Pomfret Manor. [*The passing* BUTLER *two handed white gloved with tray of drinks and canapés.* MISS TOMSON *turns, calls*] Hey, Gustav, where you going. We're starving and thirsting here.

BUTLER [*In tails. Offering his tray*] Madam. Sir. Oh. [MISS TOMSON, *then* SMITH *each taking a glass of bubbling wine and canapé*]

TOMSON [*To* BUTLER] What's the matter, you seen a ghost.

BUTLER No. Miss Tomson. Sorry, I mean I'm interrupting.

TOMSON   That's what we're here for.

BUTLER   I just need some investment advice. [*To* SMITH]

TOMSON   We're here for that too.

BUTLER   Aren't you Mr. George Smith.

TOMSON   Smithy, tell him.

BUTLER   I recognize you from your picture. You caught the big boys napping. [*Flood of loud voices, laughter, music from the other rambling rooms*]

TOMSON   And a lot of them are here tonight.

BUTLER   And maybe. Excuse me interrupting. What's the secret.

SMITH   Free the mind of emotional ingredients when looking for profits.

BUTLER   Is that right. Well, what do you know. My whole life I've been getting all emotional looking for profit. [*Offering tray*] Another drink. Madam. Sir. And thanks a lot. [*Memorizing to himself this easy way to profit as he leaves*] Free the mind of emotional ingredients when looking for profits.

TOMSON   [*Turning, watching* BUTLER *leave*]   Another tycoon is born. Smithy, you know what. You'll get sore if I tell you.

SMITH   No I won't.

TOMSON   [*Choosing a few seconds to reflect on the image of* SMITH *in his new light, as she gets set to tell him of his image in the old*]   I used to add money to the petty cash box because I thought you were really having it rough. You'd come out [*Opening imaginary door*] and when you thought I wasn't looking [*Peeking east and west, tiptoeing a few delicate steps. Reaching with her magic hands to pick up the* box] you'd take it [*Turning tiptoeing*] back into your office and [*Stopping, counting, making two little pincers with her fingers*] count it and come [*Turning, tiptoeing back wearing her eyes big as apples over her smile*] back looking so pleased because it was more instead of less.

SMITH   I never did.

TOMSON   [*Fists buttressed on her hips*]   Real sweet the way you used to look with that cash box. [*Self consciously taking fist down to stand like a lady*] Even cried one night over my pay check but next morning I thought what the hell, this is a jungle and paid it into my account. Thought I might get a letter like you, Dear sir, we would like to bleed you white, taking it in easy stages, so the blood lasts. Someone gets cross eyed trying to look in your window while you're undressing and they sue you for it. [*Rumble of thunder*]

SMITH   You're not bitter, Miss Tomson.

TOMSON   No, Smith. [*A waltz struck up in the distance*] Not bitter. Let's dance.

SMITH   I don't know how.

TOMSON   [*Putting down her drink on a side table and taking* SMITH's *and putting it there too*]   Come on. [*Performing a slow gyration*] Come on, Smith. [*Reluctant* SMITH *attempting a similar gyration four feet away*] You're doing all right. What else don't you know how to do.

SMITH   I beg your pardon, Miss Tomson.

TOMSON   [*Dreamingly beholding* SMITH *who looks as if he might suffice for one woman, provided, as they lived in the country, she gleefully brought him breakfast in bed*]   Do I look like I want a baby. A rocking chair. A porch in the country. To put the baby to the nipple. But what am I doing. I'm farting about with guys, rich without reason, rotten without rhyme.

SMITH   Miss Tomson I wish you were still working for me. [*Getting the slight hang of this newfangled dancing, moving in close*]

TOMSON   I know, it's sad. [*Dancing music stops*] Stops. Just as we were really beginning to go. Let's sit down in the love seat. [*Sits,* SMITH *standing.* MISS TOMSON *sighs*] These trying times.

SMITH   What would make you happy, Miss Tomson.

TOMSON   Gee, I'm glad I ran into you, Smithy. You ask such nice questions. A guy with a large soul. Not the small sneaky rats careening around these days. [*Wind, rain against windows, rumble of thunder*] This storm's really getting something. Good to be indoors. You got some gray hairs, Smith. Why don't you get married before you turn white. [SMITH *putting hand to head*] It's all right, your hair's still there. But don't be like me. My life is a shambles. My soul is just too big. I could never be faithful to one guy. Even if he was steady and dependable. [*Patting a place on the pink love seat beside her*] But, Smith, I like you. Sit down. You cheer me up. You look good.

SMITH   Thanks. [*Moving for seat*]

TOMSON   [*Flicking up her hand from her wrist as it rests in her lap, to halt* SMITH] Gee, stand. [SMITH *in his discreet manner standing, skidding one of his eyes down his person, along the lapels with a further momentary cautionary look downwards*] Your fly's not open, Smithy. Ha ha. [SMITH's *hand making an instant investigation*] No it isn't. [SMITH's *hurt look*] Oh, that was cruel. I'm sorry. You remind me of my first little boy friend who used to look up my dress every Friday after school to see if anything had changed. Easy joys of childhood. [*Taking a backward look in her life.*] What happens to all the little boys who want to play doctor or husband and wife in barns, on lonely rooftops, or down dark alleys. Where do they go when you grow up and guys have to take you to dinner just to touch your hand. But, Smith, do you think I'll ever have a chance. Be like other women. That's what I know, I'm crippled by what I want. Guys use you. If you love him. Give him everything and they want to get rid of you.

You're a chain around his neck. And I can't even find a real man. If I knew what one was. The rats win.

SMITH   That's not always true, Miss Tomson.

TOMSON   Guess you're just a sweet non dancing guy, Smith. You know, if you were a bum drowned in drink, unshaven, unlaundered and unpressed, you know I might say, Oh Jesus, Smith, you poor guy. [*Reaching out her palm*] Feed from the crumbs in the palm of my hand.

SMITH   How many crumbs.

TOMSON   Plenty. [*Lightning and thunder*] Boy, this storm's getting worse. [*Looking out of window and back at* SMITH]

SMITH   Miss Tomson. [*Flash of lightning*] Will you come with me. [*Thunder*] To a port in a storm. [*Lights go out. Wind bleeding in around the windows lashed with rain. The silence growing longer, two figures in the flashes of lightning*]

TOMSON   Gee. You're propositioning me.

SMITH   Sounds so stark and maybe even sneaky. In the dark. I have to ask because if I don't the world will go rushing on without us.

TOMSON   [*Low voltage smile and pointing finger*] Without you. I'm right out there rushing in front of the mob. [*Two figures silent as the wind and rain lash*] Smith. Smith, don't listen to me. You really want me to come to a port with you, don't you. I like that.

SMITH   Will you. [*Eyes locked for a long few seconds with those big blue ones of* MISS TOMSON]

TOMSON   Yesh. [SMITH *quietly slowly joining his hands crossed on each other in prayer*] It's sad.

SMITH   Why do you say it's sad.

TOMSON   Wasted all this time. I never thought you liked me.

SMITH   Oh God.

TOMSON   You do, Smithy.

SMITH   Yes.

TOMSON   I like you. I think. I do. Yesh. [*Standing*] Gee you look handsome.

SMITH   Because it's dark.

TOMSON   Smithy, hold hands. My car's out there just across the lawn. You're an endless surprise. You're trembling.

SMITH   [*Taking the hand of this blue sunflower*]   You smell so good.

TOMSON   Isn't it something. [*This sunflower raises up its blue pistils, two long blond arms*]

SMITH   [*Growling in deference to the jungles the world over*]   Grrrrr.

TOMSON   Smithy, what a marvelous sound.

SMITH   Grrrrr.

TOMSON   You're so close you could give me a heart beat.

SMITH   Bump.

TOMSON   Was that it.

SMITH   Yes.

TOMSON   Thanks. Bump. There's one for you. Help you get me to the car. [*Hand in hand, moving to the garden door*]

SMITH   Thanks.

TOMSON   Anytime. To hell with our coats, let's go. [*Hand on door*] Ready to run for it.

SMITH   Miss Tomson.

TOMSON   What.

SMITH   Will you come to my funeral when I die.

TOMSON   Smithy. You poor guy. Sure I will. But you're not going to die. [*Whiff of music "Gentle Annie"*] My epitaph will be written before yours.

SMITH   What will it be.

TOMSON   [*As she puts out her two hands and unturned palms and gently looks down upon her bosoms and up again with a little smile to* SMITH] Hers / were large / without hope / for tiny / hands.

SCENE 2. ROOM 604, DYNAMO HOUSE, OWL STREET

These forty hours later on this March cool morning. The new office, Room 604, Owl Street, with a window watching out on the endless white tiled wall of a warehouse. MISS MARTIN'S *desk at one end of the room near that naughty unpredictable door and at the other, behind an antique screen, a small desk. A little world there surrounded with its horsehair sofa, a chiming clock, a stand full of canes, an antique bathtub on fat lion's paws, a burner for coffee and light office cooking.* SMITH'S

*Personal Defense Diploma from the Game Club framed on the
wall. The phone ringing and a rapping at the door.* SMITH *in his
evening shirt tails and black socks briefly peering at a canvas
rifle case leaning against* MISS MARTIN'*s desk.*

SMITH   That you, Miss Martin. [*Approaching door gingerly*]

MESSENGER   Special messenger delivery.

SMITH   [*Opening door a crack, reaching a wrist through to take an
envelope*]   Thank you. [*Slowly closing the door in which it seemed a
small foot was put*] I beg your pardon, little boy. Your foot's in the
door.

MESSENGER   Yeah.

SMITH   Won't you take it out.

MESSENGER   Hey some people, I guess you don't get any appreciation.

SMITH   What are you talking about, sonny.

MESSENGER   A tip.

SMITH   What do you mean tip.

MESSENGER   Ain't you the guy with his picture in the paper again this
morning like you was last week. Well, you should give me a tip for
bringing a message. [SMITH *taking the red white and blue envelope*]
Here's the newspaper. [SMITH *taking newspaper*]

SMITH   Just hold it, sonny, I'll read it. [*Viewing newspaper and giving a
gasp*] Bye bye, sonny. [*Slamming door*] Goodness, if it isn't one thing
then it's another. [*Taking quick glance at envelope, holds it gently
away from his person with two pincer fingers and drops it. Stops at*
MISS MARTIN'*s desk. Stares wearily at canvas rifle case. Lifts it and
raises tired eyebrows as it thuds to floor. Waddling back to his couch*

behind screen, climbing under covers and the newly arrived news-
paper. Phone ringing with a fast urgency not usually heard from
telephones. Office door opening slowly. Phone stops ringing. MISS
MARTIN *tiptoeing in*] Good morning, Miss Martin, is that you.

MARTIN   Yes.

SMITH   Miss Martin, what time.

MARTIN   I'm late. They stopped the train in the middle of the bridge
for about an hour.

SMITH   I just asked for the time.

MARTIN   Twelve thirty.

SMITH   Thank you. Don't look. I'm indelicate. [*In his lower self*
communicating personal octave] Utterly frazzled. After being vaguely
champion. I think. Last night. Oh God. [*Phone ringing. Starts up to*
prevent MISS MARTIN *answering, lapses back down as she answers*]

MARTIN   [*Hand over phone speaker*]   Mr. Smith, it's *The News of the*
Truth asking for comments. What should I say about an air con-
ditioned mausoleum. They want to know if it's a new departure in
graveyard antics.

SMITH   Tell them they've got the wrong number.

MARTIN   [*Into telephone speaker*]   You've got the wrong number, sorry.
No. Yes. Mr. Smith. Yes. [*To* SMITH] They say they know it's not
the wrong number.

SMITH   Tell them it will be soon.

MARTIN   [*Into phone*]   Mr. Smith says it will be soon.

SMITH   Now hang up, Miss Martin. And bring in that red white and blue letter. [*Phone ringing again. Shouting*] Just say beetroot department.

MARTIN   Beetroot department. [*Listening to* SMITH] They're reading off a message. From J.J.J. [*Sitting taking down the shorthand*]

SMITH   Out with it.

MARTIN   Don't shout.

SMITH [*Hand to face*]   God.

MARTIN [*Reading from her shorthand*]   Dear sir, how dare you attempt to mail us such a thing. Do not refer to me as Junior. Or to the rest of us as [*Looks up, clears her throat, skips the words in question and reads on*] All of us have been acquainted with your kind before. And as married men with children we will not stand for your latest sauciness. Signed J.J.J.   P.S. You will hoot before long.

SMITH [*Left hand to forehead to clear the mind for rebuttal*]   Send the following telegram. Dear fellow, junior and the rest. I thought the incredibility of mailing you all an unsolicited piece of ass might amuse you. Toodle-oo. And P.S. Watch out for your short hairs. [*Look at the ceiling. A deep breath and an agonized cry*] Find that letter.

MARTIN [*Jumping to feet*]   I said don't shout at me.

SMITH [*Another reach up of the left hand to clear the mind of recent emotional ingredients*]   I'm sorry, Miss Martin. Find that letter.

MARTIN   I have found something.

SMITH   Let me have it.

MARTIN   I'm pregnant.

SMITH   No drolleries this morning, please. That letter.

MARTIN   Three months.

SMITH   Come on, Miss Martin, we must find this letter. [*Rolling out of his warmth. To his hands and knees as he pulls and disturbs various piles of paper about him, turning upon his evening clothes and upending them.* MISS MARTIN *extracting her rifle from its canvas case, gently holding it at parade rest, letting the barrel follow* SMITH *in his machinations round the office, as it would seem time was on* MISS MARTIN'S *side as* SMITH *crawls headlong into the screen sending it crashing over tub.* MISS MARTIN *in her winter coat standing silently at the door.* SMITH *looking under sofa and desk, two soiled feet sticking out. Backing out and ready to give the command to* MISS MARTIN *as he turns his head. He freezes at a familiar military sound,* MISS MARTIN *pulling back the bolt action of her rifle.* SMITH *slowly turning to view the lengthwise shadow behind him*] Miss Martin, what are you doing with that gun.

MARTIN   Listen to me.

SMITH   I'm listening. Put the gun down.

MARTIN   No.

SMITH   Miss Martin. I hope you're aware of what you're pointing at me.

MARTIN   I am. You're not going to turn rat on me.

SMITH   I beg your pardon.

MARTIN   No you're not.

SMITH   [*Straightening knees*]   Miss Martin, get a grip. [*Pulling his little items of loose dress closer about his person*] For God's sakes.

MARTIN   My finger's on this trigger, that's all I need.

SMITH   That's a high velocity twenty two caliber. Do you realize you could shoot me.

MARTIN Yes.

SMITH All right. Put it down then. I'll get you a glass of water.

MARTIN You think it's a joke.

SMITH [*Making with an airy shudder of the shoulders to encourage a lighthearted side of this situation*] I don't think anything's a joke. Just want to find the letter. [*Raising a tentative, pointing finger*] I think I just see it there behind you on the floor.

MARTIN You didn't even hear what I said. I said I was pregnant. Over three months.

SMITH This is no time to be hysterical. [*Beginning to make tiniest tentative motion to stand*]

MARTIN [*Leveling the gun just that extra bit more*] Don't move.

SMITH My eyeballs are rusted in the sockets. I feel terrible. [*Genuflecting head*] What a hangover. [*Reality closing upon* SMITH *as he looks up and back down this now unfortunately familiar barrel*] Just point the gun a little away.

MARTIN What am I going to do. [SMITH's *eye blink of what can anybody do in this naughty world*] If my mother finds out.

SMITH [*Slightly supplicating hands and word cascade*] Please put the gun down. Guns have a way of going off. I know you're an experienced shot. But my army revolver once went off in my holster and split open the toe of my riding boot.

MARTIN Shut up.

SMITH [*The dropping of supplicating hands*] Oh.

MARTIN You've ignored me all these weeks. You haven't been here for three days.

SMITH [*Raising of the supplicating hands*] Miss Martin, I've seen you nearly every day. We've talked. Chatted. Short of presuming upon you.

MARTIN You presumed on me in that cabin in the woods, when we were supposed to be trampling the flowers and shrubs.

SMITH It snowed. And I rescued you from a venomous spider.

MARTIN It wasn't. I read in a book it was harmless.

SMITH It was the way you were standing there. Helplessly and terrified. And once I got my hands, forgive me, on you, I couldn't stop.

MARTIN [*Sniffing*] You are an operator. I smell that Sally Tomson's perfume. You were at Pomfret Manor. She was there.

SMITH Miss Martin, I don't ask you where you go.

MARTIN Because you don't care.

SMITH Just let me put my trousers on, please. [*Making a move*]

MARTIN Stay right where you are.

SMITH I'm getting chilled and stiff here.

MARTIN Don't move.

SMITH I don't mind being shot but not without trousers.

MARTIN You lousy sneak. You've had a whole string of girls. And the look you've got, you're thinking of beating it. I can tell.

SMITH I don't know what to wear, Miss Martin. [*Feeble gesture toward his horsehair sofa*] I would just like to go over there and sit down.

MARTIN   Who's going to pay all the doctor's bills. [SMITH *wearing that look of please give me a moment to administrate this*] Who? [*A distinct increase in the rigidity of* MISS MARTIN'S *stance*]

SMITH   [*Substituting a calm sentence instead of the outright shout of don't shoot*]   Control yourself, Miss Martin.

MARTIN   You bastard.

SMITH   [*Slowly rising from the dog to the attempted upright bear position*]   I don't mind what you say but don't say it with the gun.

MARTIN   Back down. [SMITH *returning sadly to the dog position*] I've had nightmares nearly every night.

SMITH   Is it me. The father.

MARTIN   [*Renewing her aim from the hip*]   It's going to be a satisfaction to see you drop in your tracks.

SMITH   [*Sneaking a glance at his stockinged tootsies*]   I'm not in my tracks.

MARTIN   You will be.

SMITH   I mean, maybe it's me, all right. Why haven't you told me sooner.

MARTIN   Because I only saw the doctor yesterday, that's why. You skunk.

SMITH   That's unnecessary.

MARTIN   So's your damn burial vault. And the bulletproof car you've ordered.

SMITH   Well. All right. I mean is it any wonder.

MARTIN It's you.

SMITH OK. All right. It's me.

MARTIN Yes. You.

SMITH [*Raising the whitened right hand of truce. But in view of* MISS MARTIN's *implacability, disconsolately laying it on the edge of his desk over which so much written hardship has come. Taking the left mitt to examine where this body could take a few low caliber bullets in nonvital spots.*] Aaaa. Aaaa. [*Remembering to talk, for to leave any time between words now, that's where the bullets will fit in. Lips working but only sounds come out. Finally overcoming the dry arid mouth and his tongue functioning once more*] Miss Martin. I know you're distressed.

MARTIN Shut up.

SMITH I can't.

MARTIN Shut up.

SMITH Please, you've got to let me keep talking. You might shoot.

MARTIN That's right.

SMITH You can't shoot a talking man.

MARTIN Get your hand off that desk.

SMITH Of course. Couldn't you just hand me over my cod liver oil.

MARTIN No.

SMITH Can I have the morning newspaper.

MARTIN I can tell you what's in the morning newspaper. It's got your picture, right on the front page with plenty about your tricky shenanigans. You disappear every afternoon. While I'm stuck alone in this gloomy dump.

SMITH Miss Martin, I must have a bit of private life. But I don't want to see you unhappy.

MARTIN You see me underpaid, so how could you care if I'm happy.

SMITH I'll review your salary. Anytime. Make a memo right now, if you put down the gun. The way I'm dressed, to fall mortally wounded. The papers would be full of it.

MARTIN I'm the one who should worry. You'll be dead.

SMITH Oh dear.

MARTIN This gun is pointing at the biggest chamber of your heart.

SMITH What sort of a raise do you want. Pension. Anything. Mention it.

MARTIN Just keep talking.

SMITH I'd like to.

MARTIN Make it good.

SMITH You mustn't get the idea I'm made of money, Miss Martin.

MARTIN You're buying an armored car.

SMITH As I've said, considering the present situation. It's reasonable enough. Now please. There are just two of us here. [*Looking a little to the left, a little to the right to make sure, and back down that little barrel*] And if you just put the gun down. We'll get out of this wretched room, cross over to the bun and coffee shop. Sit over a nut ring or doughnuts, whichever you prefer.

MARTIN   Oh boy. I'll bet. [*Referring* SMITH *back to the ticklish topic*] I'm going to have a baby.

SMITH   If it's me—

MARTIN   [*Raising rifle to shoulder, taking aim*]   I'm going to shoot you. Right now.

SMITH   Jesus, don't.

MARTIN   I knew you'd rat.

SMITH   [*Raising hands to stop the bullet*]   Hold it.

MARTIN   You're a rat.

SMITH   [*With the edge of fingertips which slowly cease to wiggle and waver*]   Behind you, Miss Martin. [MISS MARTIN *not lightly to be distracted from this recent Mohammedan*] Is an apparition. I can see it. Hold fire. Just let me enjoy this vision before you shoot. Full of all the colors of the rainbow. And a mist, a light gentle rain. Like tiny tears that maybe an insect might cry. [*The little hush* SMITH *has brought down upon them. His eyes saying suddenly that there was sorrow as well as the ratlike attempt to escape. But his heart held a thimbleful at least, of straightforward goodness*] Just another ten seconds. Then shoot. After this, I want to go. Pray for me. I haven't got much religion but I believe. I'll just stay here on my knees for a moment.

MARTIN   Why don't you die like a man.

SMITH   I will. But please just look the other way. I'd like these few seconds to be private. Don't want you to remember me as if I were begging. Please, don't watch me praying like this. As a final wish, burn all the files. Sue my estate so you won't be without. Be blood for a blood test. Any reasonable judge will award enough for you and the little one. Now turn away. [MISS MARTIN *hesitating*] Please. And cough before you shoot, I need an advance signal before I meet my maker. He lives on a hill for miles around with buttercups sprinkled in the green. According to a recent remark in this apparition. [*Bowing his head. Tails of his shirt. A little peek from the* SMITH *as the* MARTIN *turns her head*] Good-bye, world. [*Uncoiling from his crouch. Shirt tails flying. Crack of the gun. Bullet crashing into his personal defense diploma. Gun smoking.* GEORGE SMITH *alive and well on top of* MISS MARTIN] OK, Miss Martin. It's all right. Just lie still. Just let's get rid of this gun. [*Pinning* MISS MARTIN's *arms gently to the boards.* SMITH *taking a deep sigh. Her eyes closed as she squeezes out the silent tears*] I haven't hurt you, have I, Miss Martin. [*Looking down on this victim who lives so wrapped up in her own little world*] Hello there, Miss Martin. [*Her head rolling to the side.* SMITH *leaning over to seize the telephone cord, dragging the phone to him across the floor*]

MARTIN [SMITH *dialing*]   Please, Mr. Smith, don't call the police. [*A surprised* SMITH *taking this new angle in the proceedings into stride*] Oh dear God, I swear I'll do anything if you don't call them. Don't have me arrested.

SMITH [*That all forgiver of sins, hesitates at the phone*]   I'm sorry, Miss Martin.

MARTIN   Oh no no. [*Rolling a bit under* SMITH *as he rides this brood mare*] Let me go. Please let me go. I'll have my baby. [*Lying still a moment*] I won't bother you. I swear.

SMITH   I'm sorry, Miss Martin.

MARTIN   Oh Mr. Smith, please forget everything I said. I'll be a good girl. I'll die in prison. My baby. I'm just a working girl. Please. Please. [*Renewing the struggle again to get up from under the disconcerted* SMITH] You knocked me out of my shoes. I'll put them on now. Where are they. I'll go out the door and you'll never see me again.

SMITH   Miss Martin. I'm just phoning to make a reservation. For a table in a little automat somewhere. And we can walk in cold and

hungry and buy coffee buns and goodies. Would you like that.
Would you.

MARTIN   Yes. ["*Eine Kleine Nachtmusik*"]

SCENE 3. BAR AND BEER RESTAURANT

*White aproned waiter passing across this restaurant on this
chilly rainy April evening. To a seated* SMITH *reading a newspaper in his sable collared great coat. Black briefcase at his side.
Sound of blackslapping and noisy voices at the bar. Waiter
comes up to* SMITH *in the pink lighted booth.*

RALPH   What's yours, buddy.

SMITH   I'm waiting for someone.

RALPH   Someone was looking.

SMITH   Oh.

RALPH   What's the name of your party.

SMITH   A Miss Tomson.

RALPH   Ha ha, not Sally.

SMITH   Sally.

RALPH   [*Sudden sober seriousness*]   Not the Sally Tomson. [*Raising a hand]* Tall, big blonde, etcetera. Here. [*Looks around for clear coast*] You mind if I sit down.

SMITH   Feel free. [RALPH *sliding into booth opposite* SMITH]

RALPH   Thanks. Wait till I tell you my story. Hey. Who are you.

SMITH   Smith.

RALPH   Ha ha, not George.

SMITH   George.

RALPH   Hey, not the George Smith. Boy. I'm glad I sat down. You don't mind, I mean someone with your accent might not like it. I don't want to seem personal, but Sally Tomson. You really expecting her.

SMITH   Yes.

RALPH   [*Back handed thumb at himself*] Well, I used to promote her brother. That's my story. Look where it's got me. Temporarily that is. Thought your face was familiar. I like to observe when others are not aware. [*Sound of siren*] Especially in this tough part of town. You appear to me to be a guy who likes solitude. By the way, it's Ralph.

SMITH   I see.

RALPH   Now let's jump to a conclusion. I mean you look just as I thought you would look. I witness no rings on your fingers. [*Eyes taking in the ten facts spread on the table*] This is indicative. [*Mind adding up the facts*] You're ruthless. Just like Sally. Sally doesn't kid around. Let's admit. Know what she says to me. On the telephone. Push off, crumb. I mean crumb. Push off. Right? Right.

SMITH   Perhaps.

RALPH   I had her brother on the threshold of stardom and she never even wanted to meet me. She doesn't even know me. As who can afford to now. And I was thinking, with a sister like Sally. [*Framing this image in the mid distance*] There they both were. The real beautiful people. Quality people. I got him into the social columns. And I end up in the unemployed. [*Stopping for breath*] Well for Christ's sake, you're George Smith. How could I imagine. I mean, just what I would imagine. [*Pause for a weak smile of the waiter become customer*] Gee. I'm out of words. For a second. Well, the recipe. [*Waiting for recipe*] Let's be frank. [*Waiting for frankness*] Come on. The recipe for success. [*Leaning in to get the ingredients*] Who did you sell up the river. I mean I don't mind telling a guy like you the lousy things I did. [SMITH *stony silent.* RALPH's *shrug of shoulders, slides out of booth and stand*] OK. It's just a reflection in passing. You know this was a great moment in my life. To meet you. No kidding. I'm impressed, everybody throws dough around to make themselves look good living. So what refreshment, a guy. Who wants to look good dead. Right? Right. [*Putting hands on hips waiting for* SMITH's *unforthcoming agreement*] I've seen it. [SMITH *wondering if he's witnessing a crack up*] Your mortuary. [*Waiting for some dawning light from* SMITH] The bone house you built. [*Again waiting for some dawning light from* SMITH *and putting forth a hand*] For your bones. Went up there the day after I read the mention. It's swell. Now what do you do.

SMITH   What do you mean.

RALPH   Why you send me an invitation to the bust out.

SMITH   I beg your pardon.

RALPH   Hey. The memorial opening. The shindy. Like they said in the paper. Sure. [*Holding out his blank hand from which he reads rapidly*] George Smith requests the pleasure of your company at the opening of his memorial at Thistle Plot, Buttercup Drive, the Renown Cemetery, November seventeenth at three thirty. Decorations will not be worn. Sally's brother showed me. The invitation you sent Sally.

Some touch. Decorations. So I don't have any. [*Leaning in close to whisper*] Hey, just off the record. You packing anything.

SMITH   I beg your pardon.

RALPH   A rod. You know. [*With his handmade gun pointed at* SMITH] Bang bang. Rumor's around you travel under armor. Just thought I saw a bulge under the jacket. I mean, none of my business.

SMITH   What's your earning power.

RALPH   Mr. Smith I'm glad you asked me that question. Really I am. [*Doing a quick skip and machinegunning out the five words*] Don't mind me, I'm nervous. [*Returning abruptly to his normal hasty hustling speech*] But it's just I don't want to damage our friendship by mentioning it with a figure right now. Even including tips. I could give you my job history.

SMITH   Shoot.

RALPH   Don't say that word. But listen. I know you're ruthless. But we could do a deal. I mean you could have the upper hand. [*Waiting for* SMITH *to take upper hand*] You think I'm the human condition at its lowest. The world needs guys like me. Can I pick up the telephone and call you sometime.

SMITH   No.

RALPH   [*Looking at entrance.* SMITH *turning round to look*]   Boy here's your party. Do me a favor. You never met me. [*Backing away as* MISS TOMSON *enters restaurant smiling. A dogwood flower pinned to her sealskin coat. Offstage humming "Annie Laurie"*]

SMITH   [*Rising, right hand making the motions of a handshake as* MISS TOMSON's *hand comes out and retreats, standing in their friendly uncertain tracks five feet apart*]   Hello, Miss Tomson.

TOMSON When are you going to call me Sally.

SMITH Sally.

TOMSON That's better. [*Regarding* SMITH's *regalia*] That get up. I got to laugh. You know, Smithy, you're so out of date it doesn't matter. You look like the international gentleman. That collar's the best sable.

SMITH [*Nodding to* MISS TOMSON's *coat*] That's the best seal.

TOMSON We're meeting here like two clothes racks.

SMITH You look so splendid.

TOMSON Just my image. [*Adjusting her flower*] The inner Tomson is in a sandstorm. While the outer Tomson skis down the sunny mountain, smiling.

SMITH Shall we bring the inner Tomson some refreshment. [*Motioning* MISS TOMSON *to a seat opposite him in booth*]

TOMSON [*Opening her coat, sliding in*] Let's.

SMITH [*A raised hand*] Waiter. [RALPH *waltzing across*] What's for you, Sally. [RALPH *with his little white pad and pencil at the ready, cocking his head in the direction of the sounds from* SMITH *and* TOMSON]

TOMSON Just a beer.

SMITH Mind if I have some wiener and sauerkraut.

TOMSON Feel free.

SMITH Beer for madam, beer, wiener and sauerkraut for me.

WAITER [*Intoning*] Beer for madam, beer, wiener and sauerkraut for sir. [*Bowing, retreating*]

TOMSON [*To* SMITH] Get him. He's been taking lessons. [*Twisting out of her coat*] I'm roasting. [*Contemplating* SMITH] Smithy? Did they do something to you in your childhood. [SMITH *wondering for a moment if he had a childhood*] I hear you've got a chauffeured, one way vision, bulletproof limousine. Someone trying to rub you out. You need friends.

SMITH Those are the ones who are trying to rub me out.

TOMSON Smithy, come on. Open up your coat. [SMITH *taking off coat around his shoulders*] Why would they want to air condition a sweet guy like you.

SMITH Bullets are the least of it, Miss Tomson.

TOMSON Oh.

SMITH One can always deal with those. It's the insinuation and discourtesy I find weighs heavy on my spirit.

TOMSON Gee.

SMITH I've missed you. You just disappeared. All these weeks. You never tried to get in touch. I even tracked you down or up to a penthouse, living under an assumed name.

TOMSON I know. Smithy, the doorman thought you were my father.

SMITH I see.

TOMSON Oh Smithy, sorry, you know, things happen. It was one thing after another. [SMITH *slowly pulling a glove on and off his hand*] You don't believe that. All right I'll tell you. You got a wife and four kids. A certain log cabin in a certain woods. [RALPH *nearing table*] And a certain secretary. [*Making a large curve over her belly*] Like this. You want me to go on. [RALPH *delivering dish of wiener and sauerkraut and the two beers held in the left hand*] You see, Smith, what you don't know about me is, I got principles. [RALPH *retreating behind* MISS TOMSON's *back. Lurking momentarily in the near distance*] What balls, sorry about the language. This vein of talk is a sure way of ruining the evening. But if I phoned you and said hello, George, I'm expecting a baby, what would you say. [RALPH *entering kitchen putting a mock index finger in each ear*] Sally that's great but I got four already. [A *little concern crossing* SMITH's *countenance*] Don't get scared, I'm not pregnant. See what I mean, you had a real look of fear.

SMITH Just concern. [*Slightly bowed head*]

TOMSON What's a matter, Smithy.

SMITH I ebb.

TOMSON You're not ebbing. You're just getting old enough now to take on a few perversions. And cavorts. Have a wiener. Some sauerkraut. You can blast off to heaven.

SMITH I beg your pardon.

TOMSON Nice to see you smile. [SMITH *grinding up his quite long tasty wiener*] You know I did try to get in touch. Phoned you. At that new office. I ask for George Smith and after a few seconds a pipe and drum band fades in and some crazy song away in the highlands or something. And at Merry Mansions I get that Matilda on the phone and she tells me its the tabernacle of the dark complexioned redeemer. [*Reaching out to take the sad* GEORGE SMITH *hand, leans her face over across the table to peer into the musty inner* SMITH *who has left-handed snapped up another wiener*] Smithy, we're kind of like old friends now. Give me a bite. [*Snaps off an end of wiener vulnerably protruding from* SMITH's *mouth*]

SMITH All these weeks. I even lurked in Grand Central Station. Thought you might catch a train.

TOMSON Oh, Smithy. I'm a weak character. Why keep up the pretense. [*Chewing merrily*] I'm going to try the wedlock. I said I'd go to your funeral. So if I ask you to my wedding, will you come.

SMITH   Miss Tomson, this is a terrible conversation.

TOMSON   I know.

SMITH   I nearly prayed to God. To say please. Send Sally Tomson back into my life. Wearing nothing but her pearls.

TOMSON   Oh God. [*Stops chewing and swallows a lump of wiener*] I told God I was going to be a good girl, I was going to climb into the wedding chains. Hands in the soap suds. Squeeze out socks, wax the furniture. Gee, I'm a terrible liar. Only thing my hand will go into is a glove holding a check book. The guy's a dynasty. If I want an ocean liner I whistle.

SMITH   Miss Tomson. What will you do for love.

TOMSON   [*Looking deeply into the generous Georgian windows of* SMITH's *soul*]   That's nice, the way you said that.

SMITH   What will you.

TOMSON   I don't know. What I always do. Cry. Be crying and whis-.tling. I'll make a stinking wife and I know it. I'm taking him for his money. I told him so. Sweet thing about him is he said he was marrying me for my brains. I thought that was so rich I accepted on the spot. After he'd been begging me for six months.

SMITH   You do have brains, Miss Tomson. [MISS TOMSON's *smile*] You have.

TOMSON   I got just little word combinations. [*Taps her luxurious blond head*] Coming out of here. Like the letter you get. Dear sir, I'll casserole you. Unless you cough twice every Tuesday. Gee, I don't love this guy. What good is my body to him. Or what's more important, to me. [*Offstage humming "Annie Laurie"*] You gave me my first honest job. And what lousy pay. Sorry I said that. But, boy, it was low. Even so I used to go home happy at night. No kidding. Woke up laughing. Because I had you so scared.

SMITH   I wasn't.

TOMSON   You were. You used to lurk behind your door for hours thinking up something to say to me. So it would look like you were running some big enterprise and your next move was going to have consequences everywhere. But I thought you were nice too. I really felt a few times, why don't I tell this guy the truth. But if you knew I was a big time celebrity, it would have made it awkward. Gee, Smithy.

SMITH   What.

TOMSON   I don't know. Even though telling you what I'm telling you. It was great strolling out in the fresh air tonight to meet you. Just like we were kids or something, meeting for a date. I think about you a lot. While the rest of us are skidding around, there you are in your own little world. It's so sweet. Why do you look so funny at me.

SMITH   I don't want to lose you.

TOMSQN   Gee, you've got moistening in the eyes. You're the most surprising guy.

SMITH   I feel I'm never going to be alone with you again.

TOMSON   Sure we are. We'll see each other. Let's not turn this into a funeral. Here's a hanky. This is just great.

SMITH   Sorry to behave like this, Miss Tomson.

TOMSON   Don't mind the drops of moisture, it's the guys who pray I don't like. [*Encouraging smile*] Nice to see you break down.

SMITH   Thanks.

TOMSON   Don't mention it. Smithy, why don't you buy horses and sport around the resorts. We might meet up. My fiancé had to go horsey after he got in this rut inheriting millions. [SMITH *understanding this problem*] That makes you smile. That's better. Smith, I don't know. I don't want to cut you out of my life. The part you were playing was swell.

SMITH   And small.

TOMSON   No. Important. But a guy, when you love him and you're his. Well, like a rag doll. Throw you in a corner when they're finished with you.

SMITH   I wouldn't throw you in a corner.

TOMSON   Smithy, Jesus. That's what I'm thinking. That's what I'm thinking. Wish my body was big enough I could spread it around and you could have it too. Send it over to you when you needed it. You're always hanging around in my mind, in your crazy old clothes. With your quaint little problems. [*Big long sigh*]

SMITH   Why do you sigh like that.

TOMSON   I only got these looks for so long. I got a career. Just to avoid getting shunted by guys. Then I throw the guys over because they try to own me. [*Opening her bag.* SMITH *staring at his hands.* MISS TOMSON *taking a white card out*] Gee, your invitation. It's great. Nice purple border. Would you autograph it for me. [SMITH *taking card, taking out his pen, signing his name*] Ha ha, I'm dying to get there. [*Shivers*]

SMITH   You're shivering, Miss Tomson.

TOMSON   Yesh. Funniest thing. Keep thinking I'm carrying black lilies up the aisle.

SMITH   I don't want to lose you.

TOMSON   Oh.

SMITH   I don't.

TOMSON   Gee.

SMITH   I don't want to lose you.

TOMSON   I know.

SMITH   You won't let me lose you.

TOMSON   Smithy.

SMITH   I want to tell you.

TOMSON   OK.

SMITH   That if I lose you I have nothing left.

TOMSON   You do.

SMITH   I don't.

TOMSON   You do.

SMITH   I could buy you.

TOMSON   Could you.

SMITH   Yes.

TOMSON   Gee.

SMITH   Can't give you a contract. But could give you laughs.

TOMSON Smithy, yesh, you give me a chuckle. True.

SMITH And it wouldn't be enough, would it.

TOMSON You are the most surprising guy. You don't know how close I'm to saying, yesh it's enough. [*Quietly surveying* SMITH] I'm glad I went to that port with you in the storm. [*Looking level across at* SMITH] I want to hand you one of my kidneys.

SMITH Would you.

TOMSON Yesh. I would. Because I don't want to lose you, Smithy. I don't. But I can't two time, I just can't. I'm funny people. I don't love this guy. But I'm not really taking him for his money either. Because the price is so high. A father on tap for my kids. To play with them on the rug with trains. If you were giving me money. I mean gee, it would be miserable for you having to part with all the cash I would need. [SMITH's *head slowly sinking,* MISS TOMSON *leaning toward* SMITH] Don't ebb. Jesus, don't ebb. I let the hair grow under my arms. [*Lifting an arm*] I did. Because you said that night you liked it. Not much to do to show affection. This is terrible talk. Between us. Because suddenly I'm not kidding. Maybe it's all because you haven't got brown eyes.

SMITH I have the lonely green variety. [*Standing and putting on coat*]

TOMSON Oh Smithy, gee. [*Bends head down*]

SMITH Miss T.

TOMSON [*Looks up*] Mr. S.

SMITH Can you hear that sound, Miss T.

TOMSON No.

SMITH It's me. Tiptoeing.

TOMSON   Where you going, tiptoeing.

SMITH   Out of your life.

TOMSON   Oh no. [RALPH *peeks a head out of kitchen door*] Gee, I sort of yelled, didn't I.

SMITH   You did.

TOMSON   [*Pulling on coat, sliding from seat to stand up*]   I'm leaving, Smithy. Should we shake hands.

SMITH   [*Standing, taking* MISS TOMSON's *hand to shake.* RALPH *watching from kitchen doorway*]   You won't miss my funeral. When the bullets blot me out. [MISS TOMSON *making a fist, swinging it slow motion through the air at* SMITH's *jaw*]

TOMSON   You give them hell, Smithy. Make your bark more scary than your bite. Then you avoid using the teeth too much. [*Backing away*]

SMITH   Don't go.

TOMSON   Going to go. Tiptoe. Before you do. But would you do one thing for me.

SMITH   Yes.

TOMSON   I know it doesn't sound sane.

SMITH   Tell me.

TOMSON   Send me one of your shirts.

SMITH   Sally.

TOMSON   I mean it.

SMITH   What for.

TOMSON   Please. Do it.

SMITH   All right.

TOMSON   A dirty one. I'll wash and iron it.

SMITH   Miss T.

TOMSON   Would you do that? Really. For me.

SMITH   Yesh. I will. Sally.

TOMSON   Thanks. But please don't kid me, Smithy. [*Offstage humming* "*Annie Laurie.*" MISS TOMSON *walks out from restaurant.* RALPH *comes up behind* SMITH. SMITH *watching as she becomes a dark apparition, a silhouette in the night outside*]

RALPH   Beautiful girl like that. The legs alone. You know something. I don't know the real Sally. But you know something else. [SMITH *turning slowly to confront* RALPH] They say she slept with a different guy for every year of her age. [SMITH's *stony silence*] Want to know how old she is. [SMITH's *stiff slap to* RALPH's *face.* RALPH *reaches up to feel it*]

SCENE 4. MISS MARTIN'S MOTHER'S APARTMENT

An evening the end of April. The wind blowing and whining around the windows of ANN MARTIN's *mother's apartment away in the wilds beyond Fartbrook.* MISS MARTIN's *mother*

*seated in a deep chair, her hands resting on the lace arm rests.
A card table set with snacks and condiments. The doorbell
rings.* MISS MARTIN *entering from kitchen wearing a brown
dress in her condition.*

ANN MARTIN   Momma, I'll go. [*Opening door*] Mr. Smith, I thought
you were never going to come. What happened. Your feet. [SMITH
briefly regarding his feet]

SMITH   I kicked a vending machine to pieces when it failed to produce.
Toes too swollen to get into a pair of shoes.

ANN MARTIN   Oh dear.

SMITH   Meant only to give a little kick but the impertinence of the instruction signs, machine fully automatic, I kicked it, I'm afraid, to
pieces. And it produced.

ANN MARTIN   [*Further ushering* SMITH *into room*]   Come in, we're going
to have a few sandwiches. I hope you like tongue. [GEORGE *in his
sandals and white socks, switching his paper carryall from hand to
hand*] And I want you to meet my Mother, this is Mr. Smith.

MRS. MARTIN   [*From her chair where she sits, her two arms laid out on
the rests, her thumbs rubbing her two first forefingers*]   I'm so glad to
meet you, Mr. Smith, Ann has told me so much about you.

SMITH   [*Briefly regarding feet once more,* MISS MARTIN *twisting a little
string bow at her belly*]   I'm afraid these sandals, Mrs. Martin, are
the result of an accident. [*Forgetfully putting forth his hand*] I'm delighted to meet Ann's mother. [MRS. MARTIN *raising a lank hand up to*
SMITH, *one awkward shake*] Ann's been such a splendid help to me
through so many unforeseen difficulties. [*Taking a couple of backward
paces*]

MRS. MARTIN   You can see, Mr. Smith, we're very modest here. [SMITH
sneaking a look at the modesty prevalent] I've always had to look

after Ann since my husband died. Ann, take Mr. Smith's coat. [ANN MARTIN *helping* SMITH *to divest the luxuriously lined sable collared overcoat*]

ANN MARTIN   Sure, Mom, I was just waiting till the greetings were over.

MRS. MARTIN   [ANN *laying* SMITH'S *coat over a chair at door*] Ann, that's not the way, hang up Mr. Smith's coat. [MRS. MARTIN *regarding the stranded* SMITH *once more*] We just put up the card table, Mr. Smith, with some snacks on it. Not much, Ann and I are not big eaters, until well, you know, until Ann . . . [ANN MARTIN *clenching two tight fists*]

SMITH   [*With the tiniest of bows*]   I quite understand, Mrs. Martin.

MRS. MARTIN   Well, may as well be honest.

SMITH   Of course.

MRS. MARTIN   [As SMITH *stands further stranded from chair, wall or table*] Ann, you know, was the apple of her father's eye.

ANN MARTIN   Mom, please, Mr. Smith doesn't want to hear all that.

MRS. MARTIN   Ann is such a spoilsport, Mr. Smith. Maybe you'd like a glass of beer.

SMITH   Yes, that would be fine Mrs. Martin.

MRS. MARTIN   Ann, get Mr. Smith a bottle of beer. [ANN *exiting to kitchen*]

SMITH   I notice a piano through the door there, Mrs. Martin, does Ann play.

MRS. MARTIN   We gave her lessons. You know how children are, Mr. Smith, they don't appreciate those things until it's too late. You are musical, Mr. Smith.

SMITH   No, not really, Mrs. Martin. Just like to listen.

MRS. MARTIN   I'm sure you must like classical.

SMITH   I'm fond of several classical pieces.

MRS. MARTIN   So is Ann. [*Calling out in direction of kitchen*] Would you bring in the cream spread, Ann. [*To* SMITH] You like cream spread.

SMITH   Yes. [ANN MARTIN *carrying a little tray with a plate of crackers, the cream spread, bottle of open beer. Placing it on card table and pouring beer into a glass for* GEORGE SMITH. ANN MARTIN *handing beer to* SMITH *who takes it and looks behind him to spot an edge of chair, and to* MRS. MARTIN *before seating himself*] May I.

MRS. MARTIN   Make yourself at home. [SMITH *surveying room sees a picture on a side table, father and mother and daughter*] You're looking at the picture, Mr. Smith. Taken of us when Ann was just six, always eating frankfurters, never eat anything that would stick to her ribs. Her first ride on the roller coaster. That's her father. He was an engineer. He worked on the bridge across the bay where the train runs. He was killed working on it.

SMITH   I'm sorry. [ANN MARTIN *passing the sandwich plate to* SMITH *who nods thanks*]

MRS. MARTIN   Long time ago now. Ann has been my whole responsibility.

SMITH   I understand, Mrs. Martin.

ANN MARTIN   Please, Mom.

MRS. MARTIN   Don't interrupt me while I'm talking, Ann. Mr. Smith knows and understands. That's why I've had him come out here. [MRS. MARTIN *sustaining* ANN MARTIN's *burning stare, turning again to this besandaled traveler who takes a needy sip of beer*] I know you're a gentleman of the world. Well, I understand that too. I can be modern in my outlook. But when you see everything you've worked for just go in one night of carelessness, one moment when a girl's defenses are down.

ANN MARTIN   Mom, you promised, you told me you wouldn't.

MRS. MARTIN   Now, Ann. Mr. Smith understands. He's a man of the world, you're not. You're an innocent young girl, don't pretend to Mr. Smith boys flocked after you, because they didn't. But Bobby from downstairs is a boy who has wanted to marry you since you were eight years old [*Measuring off a vertical eight years*], now that's a long time, and Bobby is nicely situated now. He's moving right up. [SMITH *looking up*] But that chance is gone. How would Bobby explain you off in this dress sticking out a mile as you went up the aisle, why his job wouldn't be worth a cracker.

ANN MARTIN   Mom, you promised me you wouldn't.

MRS. MARTIN   I know what's best, Mr. Smith understands, don't you, Mr. Smith. [*Waiting with tapping fingers for* SMITH *to understand*]

SMITH   Yes.

ANN MARTIN   What do you expect him to say, Mom, when he's out in this burg. Who wants to marry Bobby. I wouldn't let him touch me if I were a corpse.

MRS. MARTIN   Enough of that smart talk. A lot of girls appreciate his prospects, [*Upturned hand to* SMITH] I'm sure Mr. Smith understands. [*Leaning forward to* ANN] What about your condition. Doctor Vartberg doesn't live on charity. You weren't raised on charity.

ANN MARTIN   But you've got Mr. Smith trapped here, what do you expect him to say.

MRS. MARTIN   You don't feel trapped, Mr. Smith, do you. [SMITH's *eye flicking over the several tons of chains*] You're completely free. To go right now. I'm only explaining Ann's position as I see it as her mother. We have to be adults about this. [SMITH's *clearing throat*] Ann until she was eighteen was not allowed out past eleven o'clock. I always sat up until she came home. Right in this chair. And made it my business to meet any of Ann's boyfriends. They were all clean cut young boys. From good homes. This neighborhood wasn't all like it is now. Some of those houses on the shore were owned by prominent people. I organized some bridge games, and met them personally.

ANN MARTIN   God, Mom, stop. [*Taking beer bottle and pouring tiny remainder into* SMITH's *glass*] Here's some more beer, Mr. Smith. [*Turning*] Shut up, Mom.

MRS. MARTIN   Don't speak to me like that.

ANN MARTIN   Mom, Mr. Smith came out here of his own free will.

MRS. MARTIN   And your free will is responsible for your predicament, my dear girl. I knew when you were staying away those nights there was going to be trouble. I knew it. Don't think I didn't know what was going on, because I did. I suppose, Mr. Smith, you must have a lot of girl friends, don't you. To keep a cabin in the woods busy.

ANN MARTIN   Mom.

SMITH   As a matter of fact, Mrs. Martin, I have very few friends of either sex. I'm very fond of Ann. She's been an extremely faithful and dedicated secretary. I don't know what I would have done without her on several occasions.

MRS. MARTIN   You got her pregnant on one of them.

ANN MARTIN   Mom, if you don't stop I'm leaving this room.

MRS. MARTIN   Leave then. Go ahead, Mr. Smith, I want to hear you talk. If there are two sides of this. [ANN MARTIN *turning, leaving, slamming door,* SMITH *clearing throat in the silence left by the slam*]

SMITH I see your point, Mrs. Martin.

MRS. MARTIN Of course you do. Easy to see, isn't it. [SMITH *reaching for a tidbit, thinks better of it, withdraws hand*] That poor girl, out like a balloon, who's going to marry her now. She could have had Bobby Richards downstairs who's doing well and able to set her up. Now what do you want her to do. You think Bobby's mother doesn't know about this. That the whole building doesn't know that since she began to show she's had to leave an hour early so she wouldn't meet anyone in the elevator. I'll tell you, Mr. Smith. Ann won't, but I will. You could have prostitutes with your money. And left our Ann alone.

SMITH I'm sorry, Mrs. Martin. I understand that you should feel this way but I don't think remarks of that kind help matters.

MRS. MARTIN Oh you don't, well let me tell you a thing or two. [ANN MARTIN *at the open door, moisture collected in her eyes, hands down at her sides, veins standing out on her wrists*]

SMITH Mrs. Martin I don't want to be responsible for Ann getting upset.

MRS. MARTIN Oh you don't. You've upset her enough already. For the rest of her whole life. She might just as well go out there on the bridge where her father lost his life and jump. You did it to her. You could have found some cheap tramp. Thousands of them. [SMITH *looking at the sad* MISS MARTIN. *She moves back to get his coat.* SMITH *slowly rising*] And you have to pick on a respectable girl to do it. A married man with children. Aren't they enough for you, haven't you got a wife already. And this building you put up to put your dead body in. I'll tell you a thing or two, sure get up, stand up, sure, Ann, sure, get him his coat, exactly what I expected from your kind, all educated with fine manners and accents. [ANN MARTIN *standing askance, tearful, stiff, forbearing silent*] As if we weren't good enough for you. My daughter comes along and you use her body for your pleasure and throw her in the gutter. [SMITH *slowly putting on the coat*] Go ahead, get your fancy coat on and get out but you won't hear the last of this. [MRS. MARTIN *moving forward in her chair*] I promise you. And take that bag with you. [SMITH *picking up his little parcel*] If you want to know, residents of this apartment wouldn't be seen dead with a broken paper bag and an outfit like that, if you want to know. [ANN MARTIN *gently leading* SMITH *to door*, MRS. MARTIN *haranguing* SMITH's *back*] Good-bye, good riddance. But you'll hear more, don't you worry. Decent people know how to deal with your kind. [ANN MARTIN's *hand on his arm, looking up with sadness into the* GEORGE SMITH *eyes*] Let him go, Ann, he's not doing any fast talking. Not now with me, he isn't. Next time he won't be so fast with an innocent girl from a good background and respectable people. [*Door closes*, ANN MARTIN *turning from the door. Standing staring at the silent mother*]

SCENE 5. ROOM 604, DYNAMO HOUSE, OWL STREET

A dark suited GEORGE SMITH *slumped in his sofa chair, staring down through his legs at the world in the middle of May. A tinkle of late afternoon chimes from the clock, four o'clock. Stacks of letters piled on* MISS MARTIN's *desk. A cane at his side, shoes on his feet. At the open office door* SHIRL *raising a hand to knock. Hestitates, looks at* SMITH *and crosses silently, gently, to where he sits. Till her feet stand before his downcast eyes.*

SHIRL You can look up, George. I'm not going to be unfriendly. [SMITH's *eyes staring at* SHIRL's *legs before him*] I was passing. Saw your chauffeur waiting. I knew it was your car. Everybody knows it. Thought I'd come in and see where your office was. [SHIRL *looking* round, *the tiniest shake of her sad head*] The man's closing the building. [*Softly, tenderly to this man* SMITH] What are you still doing here. Your door is open. Are you waiting for someone.

SMITH [*Looking out across the floor*] No.

SHIRL You look so tired, George. [*Reaching with her hand to touch* SMITH, *stops halfway and withdraws it slowly back*] Come back, George. [*Looks down on his hair*] And I know, George, you can't come back. You never give in, do you. Sit in your own worst terrible sorrow, all alone. What I want to say to you. Even though I'm not saying it. That I don't care, I won't mind, I'll forgive even as I ought to be as cruel as you, I won't be. [*Her hand on her breast*] I have a mother's bosom. [*Her hands open, reach, close and* SHIRL *lets them rest at her sides*] You foolish thing. Built up your hard stone castle to shut us out. Because of simple little words I said in fury. Just to put a whiplash around your heart which had been flailing mine. Because I know. You do. You want so much for traffic to stop for you. When you're dead. I know you do. [SMITH *looking up into* SHIRL's *eyes and she slowly retreats away*] How have you been, George. Really, tell me. I want to tell you something. The law is not going to come between us. Do you hear what I'm saying. The law is not going to come between us. Even though I have to starve with the kids. You hear what I'm saying.

SMITH Yes.

SHIRL And do you think I mean it.

SMITH Yes. [SHIRL *steps away. Looks back,* SMITH *stares down through his legs. At the door* SHIRL *turns for one last look and goes. Lights grow dim, all blue cold and old. A faint tapping. Humming voices "Annie Laurie."* MISS TOMSON's *voice speaking*]

TOMSON Hear that bell, Smithy. And that humming. [*The open empty door*] Here. Yesh. Come back to work. [SMITH *looks up. Reaches and puts on radio, humming music "Annie Laurie" from radio*] Look and see, Smithy, I'm here outside. Thought you'd like to hear from me. [SMITH *looks toward the door, waits for the voice and looks back down again*] Here. I know you've got no one now, so I just thought I'd come back, wasn't doing anything this afternoon just past four. So here I am. With a whole load of change for the petty cash. Smith, don't turn into one of those guys who after pulling some ruthless deals sits back in the warmth of luxury looking everywhere for love. God will forgive you for everything else, Smith, sure he will. He knows you've got no philosophy, no conscience. And you know, Smithy, that I don't care you don't. I sort of like it. Look where my principles got me. I was robbed. What about tea. For two. And chocolate cake. Just past four. [*Voice fading*] Past four/past four. [*Fading into a knock on the open door*]

HERBERT [*Leaning into the room*] Sorry, Mr. Smith. Thought I better come and tell you it's raining a bit. Could be a storm. Traffic will be thick.

SMITH Thanks.

HERBERT [*Steps into room*] You look tired, Mr. Smith. After the Game Club you might kinda like to come home with me. Wife's always glad to see you. Good home cooking, plenty for everybody, you know if you're not doing anything after the club.

SMITH Thanks, Herbert. Tonight's Sally Tomson's engagement party. Thought I might go.

HERBERT Read about it in the paper. She got some publicity. Anyway, you want a rain check on the meal.

SMITH If I may.

HERBERT Sure. [*Music on radio fading. Announcer's voice*]

ANNOUNCER Every fifteen minutes your local up to the minute news, over your station of the stars. Several arrests have now been made resulting from the raid on the drink clip joint where police alleged customers were doped, beaten and then robbed.

HERBERT I tell you this town, Mr. Smith.

ANNOUNCER And a bulletin just received—

HERBERT Be waiting downstairs, Mr. Smith.

ANNOUNCER Sally Tomson [HERBERT *hesitates and waits*] the model and sometime actress whose wedding was to take place shortly to Claude Grace—heir to the mercantile fortune—was killed this afternoon on highway twenty two south of Bedford when her car she was driving hit a tree. Miss Tomson was dead before arrival at Bedford Hospital—she was alone at the time and no one else was involved in the accident. End of bulletin—your station of the stars—weather man says—clear skies changing to rain—

SMITH [*Waves* HERBERT *away. Fade in "Gentle Annie." Fade in* MISS TOMSON's *voice*] Four past four, that's what I was saying, Smithy, just a little while ago. I'll be one splash in a rolling sea, and bubbles and wreaths are left. But maybe you'd like to know that at night seals sing, they come up out of the water with their big sad eyes. Good news/ In the sweet/By and by.

[*Curtain, Tears, Applause, Royalties*]

The Saddest
Summer of
Samuel S

CONTESTANTS

HERR DOCTOR

SAMUEL S

WAITER

ABIGAIL

VIENNA, AUSTRIA

ACT ONE

SCENE 1 PSYCHIATRIST'S OFFICE
Thursday afternoon

SCENE 2 A CAFÉ
Later that afternoon

SCENE 3 PSYCHIATRIST'S OFFICE
Thursday afternoon—seven days later

ACT TWO

SCENE 1 SAMUEL S'S FLAT
Friday afternoon—one day later

SCENE 2 PSYCHIATRIST'S OFFICE
Monday afternoon—three days later

ACT ONE

SCENE 1

Vienna, Austria. Thursday afternoon this late cool August, up forty six stone stairs from a gray narrow street. This room with its wide desk alight with lamp and quiet green summer sun from a polished window and garden below where fat pigeons perch eating lilac leaves. The great bell of St. Stephen's tolls five times and dims itself away over the city of Vienna. HERR DOCTOR *seated at his desk writing with pencil on a yellow sheet of paper. A rap on the door.*

DOCTOR   Come in.

SAMUEL S [*Dressed with a military excellence and socks matched with tie, opening and closing the door with jaunty precision*]   Doc, how does one ever learn to take off an enemy's underwear and sell it back to him thread by thread. [*Taking off cap and hanging it on hook of closed door*] Or is the whole secret just wasting time on the bank of some river back in one's childhood thinking that there is a whole lifetime to be lived.

DOCTOR Good morning, excuse me, good afternoon. Be seated, Herr S.

SAMUEL S Woo hooo, Doc, you losing touch.

DOCTOR Perhaps.

SAMUEL S [*Plonking himself in the brown leather chair worn with elbows, backs and bottoms of patients*] Well, to business. Do you think this Countess is giving me the runaround. I mean to say she must need it. But she appreciates me. We were at the opera last night. Under the chandeliers. She's seven years older than I am. But no spare fat. Just like a reptile. I mean that makes me a spring chicken. Which she's trying to slip between her elastic jaws. Christ, everything I do fails. Three lessons I gave on American hospitality. Just when I get to lesson three, giving them a Harvard president's tea and how you light a match on the sole of your shoe, I knock over a whole tray of Dresden and a full teapot onto two clients' dresses. Now the Countess was a good sport. She rolled right across the floor laughing. But that was the end of my lecture tour through the upper class of Vienna.

DOCTOR [*Adjusting lamp*] The light, it's not in your eyes.

SAMUEL S [*Pushing away the interruption with an impatient shake of head and wave of hand*] The Countess thinks it's monstrous that a man of my sensibility, wit and knowledge should go to waste on the world. And I say ah, but Countess, you appreciate me and that is enough. After the opera she invites me to her flat. Says come in, come in, she plays a requiem on the Gramophone and I'm saying boy this is just swimming. She busts open a bottle of champagne and pours me a viertel. I'm thinking this is it, I've broken through the culture and will soon have her in the bedroom. [*Momentary hand and face up to heaven*] Thanks a bunch, God. Then she says what on earth is the matter with us, living in some kind of dream world, who cares if we go to the opera, who cares if we are superiors in this village which used to be a city. I say I care. And a few minutes later I'm standing on the sandalwood scented landing with the door slowly closing in my face. Boy, no more attempts at screwing unless it's for marriage and kids. Doc, here I am. [HERR DOCTOR *slowly rises. Watched by* SAMUEL S *he stops and stands*] Five years. [HERR DOCTOR *slowly walks behind* SAMUEL S *seated in his chair who, as* HERR DOCTOR *disappears out of his side vision, stares ahead over desk and his words begin to tumble out slower and slower*] Still skiing down the spiritual slopes toward what I hope are the buds of May instead of the acorns of September. [SAMUEL S's *brief silence as who knows,* HERR DOCTOR *might have fallen through a trapdoor in floor.* HERR DOCTOR *reaching out to put his hand on the back of* SAMUEL S's *chair to restart this otherwise reliable waterfall*] Unless I'm straightened out soon and know where I took the wrong turning and got shunted off to celibacy-ville—[*Gripping the full perception of* HERR DOCTOR's *hand, turns his head*] Get your hand off my chair.

DOCTOR   Why.

SAMUEL S   Because I'm paying to sit here and while I'm sitting here and paying it's my chair. So get your hand off.

DOCTOR   [*Nod of head agreeing the constant in this economic equation*] Very good, Herr S. I will remove my hand.

SAMUEL S   That's the way it's got to be, Doc.

DOCTOR   Certainly, you are quite right, Herr S. Please continue. [*Turning his back to* SAMUEL S]

SAMUEL S   I've got to pull in the outposts of life. The dreams, ambitions, the distant deals. So that some passing grabber swishing his scimitar doesn't lop them off. I look for love and recognition and get punched in the eye by guys with power and money. In my life the time always comes. Like clockwork. If I'm hired I get fired. Not because I mix up the statistics or infract a rule. But because I go to work neither late nor soon. That I bow gently. Speak softly. Dress in my own fashion. Regard life with a gimlet eye. And I do what they tell me. And sometimes they will kill you for that.

DOCTOR [*Turns round with a small nod of agreement to* SAMUEL S] Yes.

SAMUEL S Well, I want to end up just being alive. [HERR DOCTOR *returning to his seat*] The only thing that matters at all. So now I'm feeling the way carefully while there are still teeth left in my head. Doc, beware reaching for that pretty little flower. Growing on the sunny mountainside. It's always connected to a buried electric cable to send you flying clear across the grassy field. I always reach out.

DOCTOR We must sometimes reach out, Herr S.

SAMUEL S Not no more. I'm at an age when the flesh begins to go its own way. [*Reaching for reins*] And the spirit struggles to hold it back. I mean that's why I'm in this town, age is a virtue. But the sounds of the rest of the world. [*Tapping the top of his skull*] You've got to tap your skull to let them in. [*Sitting up as he moves forward in his seat*] Now Doc, the landlady. The one who's raising the snails on the vine leaves in the cellar. She was knocking. On my door. I call her now Agnes Anxiety. I mean, Doc, I can't stand it. This morning she came in. One good eye glinting at me across the table. Takes off her clothes to here. [*Drawing his hands across his waist*] And I take off mine the rest of the way down. She's on her side of the table and I'm on mine. Even after I've chased her five times around it. She's in good condition. I can't catch her. So we end up, she's huffing and puffing, I'm near apoplectic. She's naked from the waist up, I'm naked from the waist down. Together we make a nude. And conducting this foolish conversation across the dregs of my breakfast. She tells me not to call her Agnes Anxiety. I ask her why we can't have a normal sexual relationship. And she tells me I frighten her.

DOCTOR Would you like to discontinue your relationship with her.

SAMUEL S You mean antics. No. If that's what God is giving me for my recreation, I'm not religious enough to ask for a change.

DOCTOR You have asked her why she will go so far and not further?

SAMUEL S   Sure. She says she likes to see me enjoy myself. And she has nothing else to do before lunch.

DOCTOR   I see.

SAMUEL S   She likes to hear me talk. I do a sort of war dance. Flip my kneecaps around. Makes her grin. She has a big black hole between her upper incisors. As well as hairy legs. One eye. Breasts like harvest moons. But what I want ist verboten. God. What am I doing here. It's an international museum of failure. And I'm the prize exhibit. Well one thing's for certain. When the time comes for suicide I will have no qualms leaving the Viennese to clean up the remains. But Doc. Anyway, to their eternal credit, the Viennese are not Swiss.

DOCTOR   Thank you, Herr S.

SAMUEL S   Summer's going to be over. I can't face another winter like the last one. Waking up in the morning with my toes icicles rapping the floor. Dragging my heels through the streets. Begging palm fulls of coins from aquaintances. People raise whole families. Where do they all get the money to live. How do they do it. I can't keep my head above water.

DOCTOR   The Countess offered to help you.

SAMUEL S   To buy me. With conditions.

DOCTOR   And you could not accept the conditions?

SAMUEL S   No. People say one thing and they mean another. I was being bought so that every once in a while when she was feeling down she could give me a kick in the teeth.

DOCTOR   Perhaps she did not see, Herr S, that you like to take chunks out of the hand that feeds you.

SAMUEL S   Hold it, Doc. That's aggression.

DOCTOR A mild opinion.

SAMUEL S You're not allowed to give opinions.

DOCTOR I am allowed. But if you so wish I will refrain from opinions.

SAMUEL I take the biggest chunks I can out of the hand that feeds me. I avoid starving that way. Squirming under the thumb of the Countess would give me an appetite. Joy at another's misfortune is one of the biggest doses of goodness that people gore themselves on in this town.

DOCTOR You regard her offer as misfortune?

SAMUEL S No. Just the conditions which made me reject it. [*Lifting up his pistol like index finger to point at* HERR DOCTOR] You're worried about your fees. On the Countess's railroad I'd turn into a gravy train.

DOCTOR I have not mentioned fees.

SAMUEL S You're worried about what I owe you.

DOCTOR I know you will pay when you can.

SAMUEL S That's right.

DOCTOR May I ask what were the Countess's conditions.

SAMUEL I don't know.

DOCTOR You said you rejected them.

SAMUEL S Sure. I did. I know human nature.

DOCTOR Herr S, permit me to say—

SAMUEL S   What.

DOCTOR   I would like to say—

SAMUEL S   Let me save you the trouble. There are some people who've got a kite to fly in every different wind. I've got one kite and can only fly in certain winds. So I said wham bam, no thank you, ma'm. [HERR DOCTOR *tilting his head at this wham bam slam ma'm*] Because I just know from previous experience in my life that whatever I said to the conditions would have been the wrong thing. Especially if it concerns something I want. That much I've learned. Just like when I was a kid. At a friend's house when I sat down at the table with his family and had soup. And I wiped my mouth with the napkin which was the only pointer on graciousness my mother knew and stood up to go home. They asked me where I was going. I said home, why, is there more. Doc, I'm still getting the soup. While everyone within farting distance is golfing down fish and entrees. This same kid tells me if he told his mother he didn't believe in God she would drop dead. I ran home. My mother was ironing in the kitchen. I said, hey ma, I don't believe in God. She said, is that right, pass me that sprinkling bottle. My first insight. People are just too busy for beliefs. Five years ago I had a plan to straighten myself out. Here I am thousands of dollars later with one more insight. That you grow older faster staying in the same place.

DOCTOR   May I speak, now.

SAMUEL S   Sure.

DOCTOR   It is remarkable you are still with us on this earth, Herr S, with much life still before you.

SAMUEL S   If I can't get married and have kids I don't want to live it.

DOCTOR   People live with much less.

SAMUEL S   I'm the patient, Doc. Cut out the opinions. Let's forget other people. It's me. My problems. I can't hold a job. My landlady takes off her four sweaters, I drop my drawers. We have our little disaster. You don't know how it is, Doc. [*Raising his hand to eye level, palms turned down*] There's just one big bright desert that lies out across these unfolded freckled hands. And a voice whispering from the horizon. Hello there, you, when will you ever be cured, be cured, be cured. Only hope now is for me to sail into old age on an ocean liner full of bullion.

DOCTOR   And you, Herr S, the captain.

SAMUEL S   Doc, you're learning.

DOCTOR   Thank you a bunch, Herr S. [*Reaching for his cigar holder*]

SAMUEL S   Why do you chew on that cigar holder.

DOCTOR   I have given up smoking and it helps me—

SAMUEL S   Do something with your mouth.

DOCTOR   If you wish, yes.

SAMUEL S   Very infantile trait.

DOCTOR   I am not above infantile traits.

SAMUEL S   Well, always bound to be one or two misunderstandings in everyone's joy tugging at the breast. [*Sighing, reclining back in chair, head toward ceiling*] I feel like I'm smoking a cigarette during the Great Cambrian Ice Age. [*Fade in faint strains of choir*] Feet propped up on the North Pole, blowing smoke rings around the moon. A breather on the long trail of failure. Right from boyhood school days. Before I knew there was nectar. When my young heart was beating like a humming bird and not to know there was nectar. Too busy tripping over the tiny little customs that make people like you. Now if there's nectar. There's too many years of watching where

I was going. Holding outstretched hands ahead, keeping off the obstacles. Knocking over the nectar. Doc, how much longer is it before I'm cured. Before I can ask someone to marry me and have kids.

DOCTOR   You know, Herr S, I cannot answer that.

SAMUEL S   Oh Doc. [*Puts his brow in his uplifted hand and sighs*] In the old days there was always friends to visit on an empty afternoon. Instead of dancing lonely. Wearing only. The cobra skin belt. And the camel hair pulse warmers. I've given up all my phony liberal feelings, letting healthy prejudice sneak back into my life. Isn't that good, Doc. You must be full of them. At least I'm going to get that pleasure in before I die. Maybe I should go on the stage.

DOCTOR   Yes, I see, Herr S. [*Slowly shaking his head up and down at these constant detours*] And if you will continue, please.

SAMUEL S   Well, I was born in Pawtucket, Rhode Island, in the U.S.A. on a fairly cool October day, my mother moaned with surprise as she saw her belly give rise to this yelling nine pound prize. Which grew up on what I did not know was the wrong side of the tracks. On which I got my toes continually trimmed as I stood there looking at the goodies on the other side.

DOCTOR   [*This gentle, tired Doctor*]   Do not joke, please, Herr S.

SAMUEL   Well, you won't tell me anything. I'm just going back over it to see where I went wrong. And took the train to Celibacyville. I mean Doc, this is five years I'm coming here twice a week. I lie in bed in the morning adding it all up. It's the price of an expensive car. A thing I have never owned in my whole life. I mean I could have polished it twice a week for fifty minutes. From the Countess I refuse a ticket on the biggest gravy train that ever whistled by. I want to get straightened out. [*Shouting*] And it shows I am not straightened out.

DOCTOR   Please don't shout, Herr S.

SAMUEL S You afraid the neighbors will hear.

DOCTOR [*In his high octave of patience*] Continue.

SAMUEL S Now answer me. Are you afraid the neighbors are going to hear.

DOCTOR No, Herr S, I am not afraid the neighbors are going to hear. Do please continue. But let me warn you, you are showing all the symptoms of being cured.

SAMUEL S [*Standing on the tundra in the Great Cambrian Ice Age*] Don't say that Doc. I'm so lonely. Really, really lonely.

DOCTOR I do [*Two little head nods*] understand.

SAMUEL S A long road down. Right from my first romance. I used to follow a girl whose profile I watched all day long in school, follow her home afternoons. Found out what her father did. The amount he paid for his electricity. When they told me at the counter of the electric company I just stood there whispering it over and over. Mysterious beauty. Twenty six dollars and thirteen cents. I was nearly caught on the pebbles of their driveway. Trying to see what they ate for dinner. Fried eggplant. I went to their grocer, twelve cents a pound. The license plate of the truck taking it to Pawtucket ZR-48 671. [*Eyes staring back into these years of lonely, feverish fortitude*]

DOCTOR You would have made a remarkable scientist, Herr S.

SAMUEL S You mean income tax inspector. Traced all her relatives when they came to visit. What they did for a living. Watched her uncle forty miles away watering his lawn. After two years of learning more about this girl than she knew herself, I said hello to her. [*Waits as he waited that day for her answer*] She looked right through me as a piece of polished glass. Doc, the soul bruises like the body. And you turn away from the world. End up standing in the middle of a great big zero. Right by that doorway. The black one. Always left open. Step through and never come back again. Just go down without stairs and as you begin to fall, chase back through your life, shouting out in the street for the ones you knew longest of all. They had hair and hands you touched and sat around, just sat around, and you were a child and had anybody touched me and said, now don't you fret, now don't you mind, little boy, little boy. [*Fading strains of boys' choir. In the silence that's left*] I don't know, Doc, maybe I've had enough for today. I think I'll go get a cup of coffee and kick around a few private imponderables. [*Rises pointing a finger across desk*] But don't you do anything else for the rest of my hour. Right? [*Collecting his cap from hook*]

DOCTOR   If you so wish. Of course. It is your hour, Herr S.

SAMUEL S [*Holding cap by peak*]   It's my hour. I've got to have it this way.

DOCTOR   Very well.

SAMUEL S   Because when I go out of here down those stairs I got to feel while I'm out there that back here these twenty minutes of yours are mine.

DOCTOR   You may be assured, Herr S.

SAMUEL S   OK. [*Flips on cap. Opens door*] So long.

DOCTOR   Till next time, Herr S.

   [SAMUEL S *exits. Boys' choir*]

[*Curtain*]

SCENE 2

Twenty minutes later. Dingy, careworn interior of café. Juke-box. Two round little tables, tops held on wrought iron stands. SAMUEL S *seated.* WAITER *comes.*

WAITER Guten abend, Herr S.

SAMUEL S Einen grossen Mokka und ein Kipferl bitte.

WAITER Bitte schoen.

[WAITER *departs.* SAMUEL S *raising his framed paper, reading. Girl comes in slowly, looks around, goes and sits at other table, in her hand a map which she opens.* WAITER *comes out with coffee and kipferl and glass of water and serves* SAMUEL S. *Goes to girl's table*]

WAITER Was darf es sein.

ABIGAIL [*In her brown open necked patterned silk short sleeved blouse, leather skirt, saddle bag slung over one shoulder and deerskin ankle boots*] Can I have a coffee, please.

WAITER Yes.

ABIGAIL And a, let me see, a roll or something like that. Roll. Or a cake.

WAITER [*Leaning inquiringly*] Eine Torte.

ABIGAIL [*Looking over at* SAMUEL S's *table*] Like what he's got.

WAITER [*Looking at* SAMUEL S's *table and back again*] Wie bitte.

SAMUEL S Ein Kipferl.

WAITER [*To* SAMUEL S] Danke. Nicht immer so einfach mit den Aus-
laendern. [*Exits*]

ABIGAIL You speak English.

SAMUEL S That's right.

ABIGAIL Thanks for helping me.

SAMUEL S My pleasure.

ABIGAIL [*Her clean hands. Nails bitten down, a gold ring on one finger
set with blue turquoises round a pearl. Her fresh fruity fragrance.
Smoothing out her map of Vienna, peeking closely at a point she
marks with her fingers*] Excuse me, maybe you can help me, I'm sort
of lost.

SAMUEL S But certainly. [*Removing his cap*]

ABIGAIL I want to find the Habsburg hearts.

SAMUEL S You go out this door, turn left. Turn right. Turn left again,
right again and second left, the church which will be standing in
front of you will contain the Habsburg hearts.

ABIGAIL Boy. You know Vienna. I've only been here three days. I get
lost soon as I walk off main street. You're American.

SAMUEL S That's right.

ABIGAIL Oh my God. [*That little bounce of her bouncy arse*]

SAMUEL S What's the matter.

ABIGAIL It can't be, you're not, are you.

SAMUEL S Not what.

ABIGAIL Samuel S.

SAMUEL S You don't know me.

ABIGAIL You are. [SAMUEL S *impaled on this arrow of recognition*] Gee, I mean I've never seen a picture of you but somehow I wouldn't miss you anywhere. [SAMUEL S *staring mumchance, suspicious*] Gee, I hope you don't mind. [SAMUEL S *mumchance*] You're wondering how I know. You know a friend of my uncle's. This friend talks about you all the time. My uncle's a professor at NYU. When we, that is, my girlfriend Catherine and I, were planning our trip, he said you were one of the points of interest in Europe.

SAMUEL S [*Taking a shaky sip of his coffee, breaking off a piece of kipferl*] Despair is the word.

ABIGAIL [*Standing a little way up out of her chair to tell the world*] Gee, it's true, that's just, ha ha, like what he said you might say. [*Sitting back*] Gee, if only my girlfriend Catherine was here, she isn't going to believe it. I'm sorry if I'm sort of excited about this revelation. I even have your address.

SAMUEL S I've been evicted.

ABIGAIL Oh gee, sorry. By the way, I'm Abigail.

SAMUEL S Hi.

ABIGAIL Hi. This has sort of made my day. Would you mind if I joined you.

SAMUEL S Yes.

ABIGAIL   Oh. God. I'm sorry, maybe you don't want to be tangented.

SAMUEL S   What do you mean.

ABIGAIL   Deflected. Tangented. [*Shooting her hand off on a little brief tangent*] Zoom. You know. Career off. Away from your purpose.

SAMUEL S   What purpose.

[*Enter* WAITER *bringing* ABIGAIL *coffee, kipferl and glass of water*]

ABIGAIL   Any purpose. You know. A purpose is round. A tangent goes off it.

WAITER   [*Serving* ABIGAIL]   Bitte schoen.

[WAITER *exits*]

ABIGAIL   Haven't you got a purpose. [SAMUEL S *giving the gimlet eye to the uppercut question, wondering if it requires the knee block or hand upon the balls to stop the breeze from rocking them unduly*] Everyone should have one.

SAMUEL S   Have you.

ABIGAIL   Sure.

SAMUEL S   What.

ABIGAIL   You mean right now? The near future? Lifetime? I have one for each. They're round. A bunch of balls.

SAMUEL S   Right now.

ABIGAIL   Well, if you mean right now, sort of right now or right now meaning sort of all around now, sure, I've got one. I want to grow outside myself. Or do you mean right now. Hey. Come on. Let's not do this. Sounds crappy. I'm a tourist.

SAMUEL S   Do what.

ABIGAIL   Fence.

SAMUEL S [*Calling to* WAITER]   Zahlen bitte.

WAITER [*Entering*]   Zahlen. [*Taking his pad from his belt, tearing off sheet and placing on table*] Fuenf fuenfzig.

SAMUEL S [*Putting out his coin,* WAITER *slapping back change from large black purse*]   Das stimmt.

WAITER [*With graceful lightning sweeping change off table into his black pouch*]   Danke schoen.

[WAITER *exits.* SAMUEL S *slapping back his cap on his head and leaning to return framed newspaper to hook on wall. Rising from his chair*]

ABIGAIL   Hey. Please. Don't regard me as one of those.

SAMUEL S   One of what.

ABIGAIL   Oh gee, I don't know. Just someone that you think isn't worth talking to. It's not for me. My uncle. He'd be so thrilled to think I met you. Can I explain. Please. [SAMUEL S *sitting back in his chair*] Gee. [*Putting three fingers against her cheek*] I'm afraid of everything I'm going to say. Would it be all right if I just rearranged my thoughts. I'll only be a second.

SAMUEL S   I'm waiting.

ABIGAIL [*Folding her hands at her mouth, frowning down at her coffee*]

Ah. That's better. You see I know too much about you. You don't know anything about me. You're at a disadvantage.

SAMUEL S   What do you know about me.

ABIGAIL   I mean don't you know you're talked about like that. Things you do.

SAMUEL S   I do not know.

ABIGAIL   Well you are. Like you were a racing car driver. [As she drops her voice for this aside] Only maybe you hold the record for walking backwards.

SAMUEL S   What things.

ABIGAIL   OK. You really want to know. That you watch red ants walking across your carpet in your house and you got them tamed. That you never let religion rob you of your appetite or sense of humor. That you give lectures on American hospitality, gee I laughed at that. Boy. Do they need it. No kidding. Maybe you might not like me knowing this, that you go around with this elegant Countess. All that stuff impresses my uncle and his friend. You know. But what impresses me. Is. I thought it was good. How you go through Vienna and how when they cheat you with the short change. You bow politely and say quietly. You have cheated me, aufwiedershen. I've been wanting to say that, if I knew enough German, the whole time I've been here. I heard about the clothes you wear and the cap. That's why I thought it was you. Catherine, my friend, and I were going to look you up together tomorrow. No kidding.

SAMUEL S   That right.

ABIGAIL   Catherine and I, we've got different cultural interests. She wants those horses prancing around and to mope through palaces. I like that but I'd rather just walk around. One thing I saw in the museum. Looking at all the stuffed birds and animals and you suddenly come across a glass case expecting to see stuffed reptiles and they're alive. I love snakes. So well groomed. You like them?

SAMUEL S No.

ABIGAIL Well, guess that takes care of snakes. I just happen to know a lot about snakes. [*Takes a sip of her glass of water*] You know you're really not helping me. When you asked before about my purpose. My purpose now. Well it's to realize myself. We've come for three months. Sometimes I wished it was for three days. I nearly headed back loads of times. Then something would crop up. I mean, you see, like this. You cropped up.

SAMUEL S I'm here. I didn't crop up.

ABIGAIL Whoops. Whoo hooo. Wrong turning there. I mean, could I ask you something. Like. Have you got a purpose.

SAMUEL S To get through the day until it's over.

ABIGAIL But that's just living, that's not a purpose.

SAMUEL S It's mine. I'm staying alive.

ABIGAIL OK. I'll allow you that. But what about your whole life. What's going to be the purpose of that.

SAMUEL S That I had a life.

ABIGAIL Well I guess at your age you just sort of give up. And it doesn't matter. But, boy. Let me tell you. It matters to me. I majored in humanity right through college. Until I decided what the hell, if you're going to understand humanity like we got in America then you got to get to Europe and catch up on the inhumanity. I mean, they grab the money right out of your hands. You can give France back to the Romans. What creeps. Lovers. All they want to do in bed is get your jewelry off you.

SAMUEL S   Hmmmmmmnn.

ABIGAIL   What are you saying hmmmmmmnn for.

SAMUEL S   I'm just saying hmmmmmmnnn.

ABIGAIL   Well hmmmmmmnnn then. I was expecting something different from you.

SAMUEL S   Something a little bit more profound. My only profundity is that I would like to do dirty things to you.

ABIGAIL   I think that's insulting.

SAMUEL S   You do.

ABIGAIL   I do. You sound like a crummy European. What kind of an American are you.

SAMUEL S   How many kinds are there.

ABIGAIL   I don't know, but you don't seem like the kind of American I know.

SAMUEL S   Why not.

ABIGAIL   Well if you want to throw around insults, I know how to do that too. I mean thanks for ordering the roll for me, but you know you're kind of old, you know, like you should be dead or something. Like those shoes you're wearing. And the tie. I mean you're not all that thin. And the collar doesn't match your shirt, which is sort of an English affectation but is really just what a crummy English civil servant would wear.

SAMUEL S   You know what an English civil servant wears.

ABIGAIL   Yes, it so happens, the kind who thinks his balls are bells to ring for tea. Well, boy, excuse me for ever talking to you. I really am sorry.

SAMUEL S You're pretty insulting.

ABIGAIL You're damn right I am. I'm kind of fed up with this stupid superiority. In fact, you might have been around but I'm smarter than you think. [SAMUEL S *slowly shaking his head up and down*] And don't shake your head up and down. I came to Europe to enlarge my area of human understanding by digesting a little of the kind of old hat ideas over here. Only I'll be honest, also to meet guys.

SAMUEL S So you wanted to meet guys.

ABIGAIL That's right.

SAMUEL S Hmmmmmmmm.

ABIGAIL Oh hmmmmm. What's that supposed to mean.

SAMUEL S Whatever you want it to mean.

ABIGAIL You know I think I know what you're thinking. You think I'm stupid.

SAMUEL S I've said nothing.

ABIGAIL Just the way you start to look away, as if you knew everything. Well I've read all the great books. And I think they all stink.

SAMUEL S Please continue.

ABIGAIL And I took a course on human relating. And I've got news for you. I thought that stunk too. Only I wouldn't sneer at it like you might.

SAMUEL S Please continue.

ABIGAIL   Don't be so damn superior. With that please continue stuff.

SAMUEL S   This is pretty serious behavior. I hardly know you.

ABIGAIL   Boy, I know you.

SAMUEL S   Are you trying to pull my leg.

ABIGAIL   I just wouldn't be bothered trying to pull your leg.

SAMUEL S   Well I'll make a pronouncement.

ABIGAIL   You do. I'm mad. You think you're so superior.

SAMUEL S   You're just a rootin' tootin' good old American college girl, who's going to grow up and be different from ma and pa. Age will teach you a lot, when things will turn out just as you thought they wouldn't.

ABIGAIL   So we know you're grandpa wisdom. But you don't know the least thing about me, what I'm really like. I know I'm not good looking enough, so I have to talk to someone weird like you. Who could be my father. Or even my uncle whose friend thinks you're the cat's meow. Well I guess I was wrong to pay you the compliment of being a man.

SAMUEL S   What are you.

ABIGAIL   Well I'm not a cockteaser. But you're a desperate snob. You look like you've been trying to look down your nose at everybody you've ever met. Or else I expect kissing someone's ass. I think you're just a bully. [*Looks up for* WAITER] Waiter! [WAITER *appearing*] I want my check, please.

SAMUEL S   Zahlen bitte. [*Sitting, his hands caught on the table spread eagled, as he looks down to see them there, and slowly draws them away*]

WAITER [*Coming over, looking down the bridge of his nose at the remnants of* ABIGAIL's *table*] Ein Kaffee, ein Kipferl, fuenf shilling fuenfzig.

ABIGAIL [*Putting out her note,* WAITER *withdrawing his enormous black wallet,* ABIGAIL *waving him away*] Oh keep it. [ABIGAIL *rises*] I don't have time to waste while you cheat.

WAITER Danke sehr. [*Exits*]

SAMUEL S Wait.

ABIGAIL What.

SAMUEL S I'll walk you to the Habsburg hearts.

ABIGAIL Oh don't you bother.

SAMUEL S I could enlarge your experience of European inhumanity for you.

ABIGAIL [*Stopping, deliberately turning back at* SAMUEL S, *shooting the bullets quietly out*] Don't worry. You have. And let me tell you something, while we're on the subject. Why don't you go home. Back to the States, if you know so much. You know why you don't. Because the competition would close you out. They would close you out so fast, boy, you wouldn't know what happened to you. [SAMUEL S *standing listening. The bullets passing through him. He holds the blood carefully in with a dignified hand and gently lowers himself to his lonely seat at the table. Bows his head slightly to look at his hands.* ABIGAIL *putting her hands slowly to her lips as she watches*] Hey, gee, I'm sorry. I didn't mean to hurt your feelings like that. I'm only kidding.

SAMUEL S You've bested me.

ABIGAIL Hey, gee.

SAMUEL S   You've bested me, that's all right, I asked for it.

[*Fade in choir music.* ABIGAIL *taking her few seconds to reorganize the thought*]

ABIGAIL   Well, I'd like you to come.

SAMUEL S   It's all right. I'll stay.

ABIGAIL   But it's not politeness. I really want you to come with me.

SAMUEL S   You want me to come.

ABIGAIL   I do.

SAMUEL S   No one has ever had the courage to say that to me before. But I'm staying.

[*As* ABIGAIL *sees this sad heart wanting to be alone with its own sorrow*]

ABIGAIL   OK. [*Exits.* SAMUEL S *with head bowed over his hands encircling his black cup of coffee.* ABIGAIL *enters. Stops. Stands.*] I'm at the Hotel Sacher.

[SAMUEL S *motionless.* ABIGAIL *exits. Fade in bridge music*]

[*Curtain*]

SCENE 3

HERR DOCTOR's *office. Seven days later. Five booming bells.* HERR DOCTOR *at his desk. Door opens. Enter* SAMUEL S.

DOCTOR   Good afternoon, Herr S.

SAMUEL S   Wow, Doc. [*Hanging up cap behind door*] My cerebellum is ringing.

DOCTOR   Sit down.

SAMUEL S   You don't mind. [*Hands folded behind back, head bent forward, paces back and forth in a short line*] I'll just skate around here for a minute.

DOCTOR   Of course.

SAMUEL S   I scrambled my synapses on slivovitz. Just put everything back in place with a little centrifugal force. [*Spinning around in front of desk, stops suddenly*] Ah, that's better. It's all there. I really got a tug on the medulla oblongata. [*Sitting*] That's why I missed my session Thursday. Hey, what did you do.

DOCTOR   I sat here. [SAMUEL S *raising a finger at the* HERR DOCTOR] Devoting my thought to the patient to whom this time belonged.

SAMUEL S   [*Nodding*]   I believe you, Doc. Well, I got smashed last week. Really walked into the blades. I forgot the rule, do not try to look big making others feel small. I met this girl. Just by accident. She knew about me. At least that I was the most colorful twisted personality in Europe. I thought that that gave me the upper hand. But she just flashed around and kicked me one right in the soul. I'm getting on, Doc, I mean when am I going to get married and have kids. I don't want to go around a dirty old man.

DOCTOR   A dirty old man, Herr S, can be married with ten children.

SAMUEL S   Ah, Doc, you stepped into it. You expressed an opinion.

DOCTOR   Please continue, Herr S. [*Picking up his cigar holder, putting it in his mouth*]

SAMUEL S   Did you have a big ample mother, Doc.

DOCTOR   Did you, Herr S.

SAMUEL S   Yeah, I weighed nine pounds when I was born. The whole world should have loved me right from babyhood. Instead of sneaking out from underneath the thick green group of trees to shove me around in the clearing. [HERR DOCTOR *rising from desk*] Where you going, Doc.

DOCTOR   I am just changing my seat. Please continue, Herr S. [*Walking behind* HERR s *and sitting near the door*]

SAMUEL S   I've got you smiling, Doc.

DOCTOR   Please continue, Herr S.

SAMUEL S   You smiling, Doc.

DOCTOR   Perhaps.

SAMUEL S   You don't think it's good for me to see you chuckling.

DOCTOR   Perhaps.

SAMUEL S   Maybe you don't want me to see you sucking the cigar holder. I saw your hand freeze as you were reaching for it. I make you tense, Doc. If I can make you smile you might last after all.

DOCTOR   Yes.

SAMUEL S   I actually cried, Doc. Does that mean I cracked. I mean when this girl, half my age, flashed around with a bolo punch.

DOCTOR   The bolo, Herr S. What is it.

SAMUEL S   The bolo is the one comes looping into the solar plexus. The one you're not expecting. I crumpled. Couldn't fight back. Does it mean I cracked.

DOCTOR   No.

SAMUEL   Well, what should I do. The day I met her. I thought wait a minute. When she slammed in with the punch. Maybe I should slam her back one. [*Putting up his fists with left lead and right for the coup de grâce, and dropping fists to lap*] Then I thought, better beat it this time. She's got my number. Then I thought. Well that's good. If she has my number it means we can get to know each other. And I can go swinging through the trees in her jungle. But Doc, it's worrying me, I'm looking for them younger and younger. What's the matter. [HERR DOCTOR *takes the cigar holder from his mouth to express an opinion.* SAMUEL S *spinning to partially confront* HERR DOCTOR] I demand you come around to this side.

DOCTOR   [*Rising and returning to his side of the desk, watched with the eagle eye of* SAMUEL S]   Very well.

SAMUEL S   Now. Do you think getting my hands on this young bimbo that I'm trying to rub off some of her yeast mold to keep my own fermentation going.

DOCTOR   May I please know what is a bimbo.

SAMUEL S   Want me to conjugate it in Latin.

DOCTOR   English will do.

SAMUEL S   Well, what is a bimbo. Conjugate it in life. A bimbo is a small, tan and skinny thing. With a brain which switches off like a light when you take it to bed.

DOCTOR   Thank you, Herr S.

SAMUEL S   Rid the mind of knowledge when looking for pleasure. Or start thinking and find a lot of pain.

DOCTOR   This bimbo. When did you meet her.

SAMUEL S   Right after the last session. Just like that, in my café. My mind was leaping around like a volcano. All the time I'm trying to play it cool, play it cool. And she left me sitting there sailing across the Bering Strait in an eggshell. Then I thought it out. Went into hibernation. I figured what have I got to lose. I asked her out. She brings her girlfriend. A big fat pig. So I thought right, let's bounce some fat off and canter round the Prater. I was amazed they could both ride like a nightmare. But I couldn't shake off the fat one. We made another date the next day. I was like a baby tiger leaping out of bed. Charging across the floor, killed fourteen of my pet ants. I was so hysterical I didn't even give them a funeral. I was remembering all her good points. The long young hair. You know those white eyeballs, Doc, the kind that look like a cool clear breeze is blowing across them. The lashes long, dark and silky. I was thinking, Christ how do I dump the girlfriend Catherine who was making big eyes at me. Fat Catherine was not to be shifted. Or dynamited. Then I was thinking loyalties flow deep between girlfriends. Until they want the same man, when wham, no longer a bead of sweat. In which to sail friendship. So we're standing in the Heiligenkreuzerhof, in front of the garden wall of the Praelatentrankt. I ask this Abigail to a meal. She says sure. I say fine. Pick her up at the Sacher. I'm just about to leave and she says Catherine's coming. I said right back Catherine is not coming.

Catherine was standing right there. I just know that American thing, and I can't stand it. That whine. You know. And that very morning, I got a windfall from my rich friends in Amsterdam. Agnes Anxiety brings me the letter. She was suggesting in the doorway we have our usual little overture, which I'm hoping might lead to an opera. In bed. So I say is that so, well well, Agnes. You mean all the outer garments will be shed and that you will grab me and I will grab you and we will, in short, tangle. She says not so loud so someone might hear. So I'm thinking in this glut time of females, why not let the whole world hear, anyway I was on my way to sing an aria. Needless to say, Agnes Anxiety was not thinking of having a duet for which for a change I couldn't care less. She started taking off the sweaters. I said thanks a bunch. But no thanks a banana. Which I think I'm going to be peeling elsewhere. [HERR DOCTOR *turning with a little smile to the window*] What's a matter, Doc. I say something.

DOCTOR   Continue.

SAMUEL S   I thought something was the matter.

DOCTOR   Please continue.

SAMUEL S   Three of us are standing there in the Praelatentrankt. So this is it. I say Catherine is not coming. And she says she, Abigail, is not coming. So I say goodbye, she says goodbye. I'm walking away. And she says good riddance. That smashed me right between the shoulder blades. And that was that. I stretched the ethical rope some more and so when I finally take the drop the noose beheads me. Doc. She's one of God's creatures. Why can't I compromise. I axe down all the bridges behind me. I'm just staying alive by leaving an image of myself on some acquaintance's mind. There in the square. I saw all those shuttered windows. Looked up into the leaves of a tree. Felt a few rays of warm sunlight on my face. And a sentence comes into my head I never thought in the five years I've been here would ever get there. The Austrians are graceful of spirit. [SAMUEL S *reaching and taking a tome into his hands from* HERR DOCTOR's *desk, spinning past the pages with his thumb*] I'm an animal. Who hasn't even got into the zoology books yet. I got beheaded. Went quietly loping along the back streets. Then crawling my way down the Kaerntnerstrasse. The early bird whores taking up positions. Pale blue and pink sweaters. Cool evening. Some of them when they smile have beautiful teeth. I go in the bar around the corner where they know me. I sit down, the waitress asks me if I'm sick I looked so white. I said I'm about to scramble my synapses on slivovitz and give myself a self inflicted kick into exile. Or else end up in the blue pair of plimsoles playing the electric piano by the ice cold sea. I didn't wake up until two days later. Last thing I remember was standing on the table. Giving a bow after a dance called the goofs gavotte. That's a drunken antic of mine with the plenty use of the hips and shins. I scared the hell out of the proprietor, only he knows I bring in business. I gave a demonstration of American football, lesson three, the place kick, using a glass of slivovitz for the ball. I kicked it all over their faces. Put my usual questions, do you each have something to love you. Do you each have a cherished care. I took off my jacket. Said my poem, Sprinkle me/ With anther dust/ Sprinkle me/ With lime/ Sow me/ Beneath the buttercups/ After all/ The pantomime. Sounds good in German.

DOCTOR   You are a talented man, Herr S.

SAMUEL   I'll let that opinion by.

DOCTOR   Thanks a bunch.

SAMUEL S   Ha ha. You know I had a grand time. I had a cigar in one hand. Took off my yellow suspenders. Wrapped them around me neck. And you know how I really kill the Viennese. Just when they want to kill me.

DOCTOR   No, Herr S.

SAMUEL S   I sang four spine soothing Mozart arias in a row. Without missing a semiquaver. Collecting people in from the street. Jamming the doorway and sidewalk. Boy I went up in a cloud of smoke. I demonstrated a baby's arse with my squeezed up belly. And the last thing I remember before waking up two days later was singing my closing number, I'm going up shit's creek/ With no engine/ No sail/ No boat/ And would they all wave goodbye. When I woke up I was lying under my table, suspenders still entangled around my throat. In my hand holding a nun the shape of a little black doll, I thought I was in hell. And threw it across the room. And a little white piece of paper floats down. I struggle to my knees. Get it and I read, You should have your brains examined, yours truly, an Austrian citizen. Oh Doc. Jesus. You know I can't take this tightrope walking across the abyss. Each time I get on the other side I feel I'm setting forth for Odessa across the frozen wastes with a collection of assorted combs to sell. My liver is still squeezing the poison out drop by drop. Also I'm minus my passport. Which I had to leave behind because I couldn't pay the bill. Nothing ventured. And everything lost anyway. Doc, I should have a son. I should have a daughter. This thing between my legs is only giving me the willies. Brains fried. Eyes looking in instead of out. Ears barely tuned to the outside world. I go back to my flat, take a wad of toilet paper and stuff it around the doorbell. Bury the telephone under a gigantic pile of dirty laundry. Black out all the windows, switch on the electric light and go back and forth soaking myself in the hot bath until I come back and sit here. Just so the time can tick by. [*Whistle blowing outside*] What's that, Doc.

DOCTOR   A whistle.

SAMUEL S   The police?

DOCTOR   Not the police, Herr S. It is a child. Who has a little whistle. She plays down there in the garden. I often watch her. Little girl in white gloves with big blue eyes. She lives on the first floor. She blows the whistle just before her father comes home.

SAMUEL S   Never heard her before.

DOCTOR   I usually have my window closed.

SAMUEL S   Christ, why am I so suspicious.

DOCTOR   It is what makes you so charming, Herr S.

SAMUEL S   Hey, watch it, Doc. Little sneaky aggression there.

DOCTOR   Perhaps.

SAMUEL S   Maybe I've had enough for today, Doc. But I want to sit here until my hour is finished.

DOCTOR   It is your hour, Herr S.

SAMUEL S   I know it's my hour. I know it annoys you. I just want to sit here and say nothing. Because I'm not getting anywhere saying things. What is it, Doc, no one will let me have the good jobs, the good women. I mean, look at the big international agency in the town. I mean to say, there is a big breast. Sure I want to gnaw at it. But when anyone sees me eyeing it and coming close, they say go on, we're chewing here already, go get out of here. Those are the grabbers at life's banquet. And I'm elbowed to crawling around under the table scooping up the crumbs. Trying to avoid the heels they're slamming down on my outstretched fingers for laughs. Doc, when no one else wraps arms around you like a mother [*Wrapping his arms around himself*] you've got to give yourself a big bear hug of sympathy. That holds you tight and safe from harm. What do I do, throw myself panting on this girl's chest and locked in sweat say marry me, wash my socks, grind my coffee bean, tint my toast the lightest, the warmest shade of brown. And I could never get a woman to commit a domestic chore in my honor. My friends' American wives taught me that if I asked for an egg fried, some coffee, toast, I'd get the egg. Nicely greased and neatly slipped off the pan into my lap. Coffee. Of course, a generous pouring over the wrist. So died the dream to be king. Alone at table, a dozen kids squabbling in another room and when the tea comes with the bacon, perhaps the egg too, the wife says, ah your nibs, is the repast to your liking, would you be wanting now a little hot up of the tea, another rasher of bacon. And Doc. Will I ever be king. To say another rasher of bacon. Ever be husband to have a wife. Be a father to have a son. [*Turning a sad gaze to window, to the faint hymn of the practicing boys' choir in the nearby church, as they sing "Jesu Joy of Man's Desire"*] Had a dream. God at his last board meeting said, Gentlemen, the principles of Samuel S are to be tested. With a comely bimbo. Who will offer Sam one piece of ass unencumbered by the usual strings. And to be preceded by a good cup of Viennese coffee. If he is not tempted to indulge the ass she will then clean up the flat and wash his dishes. If still he is steadfast, she is then to take all his dirty laundry, wash, starch and iron the bloody lot, serving him with two eggs fried with one boiled Gutsratwurst flapping in sauerkraut on a steamy plate. His stomach will easily survive this mixture according to our dietitians and if still he does not jump her, we will fly in an angel to give him apprentice character guidance, following which he shall be voted assistant to assistant treasurer of our operation, styled with the title of Saint Stubborn Sam of the Sealed Lips and Crazy Celibacy.

DOCTOR   And thanks a bunch, God.

SAMUEL S   Yeah. OK, Doc. [*Gets up, walks to hook to take his cap and plants it on his head*] Today is Thursday. What time is it, Doc.

DOCTOR [*Tilting up his desk watch with his hand*]   Five minutes to six o'clock.

SAMUEL S   I've overstayed my time. You didn't tell me.

DOCTOR   No.

SAMUEL S   Well, I tell you when you exceed your position.

DOCTOR   Perhaps.

SAMUEL S   Out once more into the shenanigans. With the arse of my mind broken. August. Vienna. Nearly near Mongolia. See this line, Doc. If I walked west on it, I'd go right through Munich, Paris, and if I could swim I'd crawl up on a pier in Halifax, Nova Scotia. Well,

I'll leave you with one of my little homilies. Pursed lips can look like an arse hole. So long.

DOCTOR   Till next time, Herr S.

[*Curtain*]

ACT TWO

SCENE 1

Friday afternoon, one day later. Flat of SAMUEL S. *Curtains pinned across window. Under pile of dirty laundry a telephone is buried. A bed. Packing cases stacked with books, sheaves of paper, parcels, an area of wall pinned with pictures and newspaper clippings. A table strewn with books, cooking utensils, paper, bread, cake and clothes. An armchair covered with a sheet and towel. Stack of books within hand's reach. A stool at makeshift desk piled with papers.* SAMUEL S *sitting naked to waist under a light bulb reading.*

SAMUEL S [*Taking his finger from his book, pointing it out toward table and touching the edge of the table to make a little bridge*] Hello. Come on. There's a little bridge. Now don't be like Samuel S and hesitate to cross bridges. That's it, you come on right out there. Right across. Ah, zat's so. Ah. You come to big uncle Sam here. That's it. Step on to that sentence there. That's it. Walk right over that paragraph, plenty more, put you on another chapter to tramp around.

[*Knock at door,* SAMUEL S *rigid, silent, another three knocks,* SAMUEL S *waiting in the silence, five knocks in a row*]

ABIGAIL [*Off stage*] Hello in there. [*Silence*] Hello in there. I know you're in there. I can see the light. I heard you talking. It's me, Abigail.

SAMUEL S [*Coming up out of his chair, pulling white sheet up around him, standing, reconsidering, sitting back down again*] What do you want.

ABIGAIL I want to talk.

SAMUEL S I don't, I'm undressed.

ABIGAIL I just want to say something.

SAMUEL S What do you want to say.

ABIGAIL I don't know yet. But I want to talk.

SAMUEL S I don't want to go through the whole thing again. You beat me. That's enough.

ABIGAIL That's pig headed and stupid. Why don't you face up to things.

SAMUEL S Face up to what.

ABIGAIL I want to get to know you.

SAMUEL S Think of one reason why I should get to know you.

ABIGAIL You could rest your head on my shoulder.

SAMUEL S [*Wiping his brow with the edge of sheet, sits. Contemplates, gets up and goes over and stands at door*] How old are you.

ABIGAIL   Old enough.

SAMUEL S   I'm nearly twice your age.

ABIGAIL   Then stop acting like a child. Open the door. I want to be friends.

SAMUEL S   That's the most ominous relationship in the world.

ABIGAIL   What's the matter with you. Are you a coward.

SAMUEL S   Yes, what are you.

ABIGAIL   I'm Jewish. Three quarters.

SAMUEL S   Well I'm anti Semitic, four quarters.

ABIGAIL   OK. I'll improve your prejudice for you.

[SAMUEL S *undoing latches to the door, holding the sheet together around him with his teeth. Enter* ABIGAIL *dressed in brown, a patterned silk shirt and leather skirt, a large saddle bag slung over her shoulders, feet in deerskin ankle boots.* ABIGAIL *stopping halfway into the musty dim sitting room and letting out a high pitched whistle*]

ABIGAIL   Holy cow.

SAMUEL S [*Standing at ajar door*]   You wanted to come in.

ABIGAIL   I've read about poverty in Europe but this is really for the books. The outside looks like it's been through a war. [*Looking around her*] And this was one of the battles.

SAMUEL S   If you don't like it here's the door.

ABIGAIL   Don't be so touchy. You know. And maybe would you close the door.

SAMUEL S [*Closing door*]   I don't ask people to visit me, if they do I take no responsibility for their feelings when they get here.

ABIGAIL   You're a charlatan. Real charlatan.

SAMUEL S   As I say, there's the door.

ABIGAIL   I have a good mind to walk right out of here. The only reason I don't is because this is the filthiest place I've ever seen. This place is really dirty. Something should be done about it. What have you got the light on for. And the curtains blocking out the daylight. It's three o'clock in the afternoon.

SAMUEL S   As far as I'm concerned it's midnight.

ABIGAIL   Can I sit down. [*Sitting*]

SAMUEL S   Sit down.

ABIGAIL   You know. Boy. You were rude. I mean can't you understand. That Catherine has feelings. I mean she doesn't know any German at all and if I just go off in the evenings like that she just makes life miserable when I get back to the hotel.

SAMUEL S   I invited you.

ABIGAIL   I know. But I just couldn't leave Catherine standing there. I would have paid for her. Or she could have paid herself. I mean we had a kind of pact. That every other day we would do things together. And that was one of the days. You had to pick. Well anyway, I'm sorry for what I said. I met some friends of yours. They told me you were under treatment. If I knew, I wouldn't have said what I said.

SAMUEL S   People say what they want to say. And they always mean it. And then do exactly opposite.

ABIGAIL   [*Looking down at her hands*]   God am I embarrassed. I don't know what to say. Could we open up a window.

SAMUEL S They're sealed.

ABIGAIL I'm not used to these European smells.

SAMUEL S This air's been here for four months and I can see no good reason to change it. Fresh air makes me sick.

ABIGAIL Do you like living primitive like this.

SAMUEL S No.

ABIGAIL Why do you.

SAMUEL S Because I haven't the money to live any other way and nobody else will clean it up.

ABIGAIL You should clean it.

SAMUEL S I don't feel like cleaning it.

ABIGAIL Forgive me for suggesting.

SAMUEL S [*Standing solemnly by his makeshift desk piled high with sheafs of paper*] Why did you come here.

ABIGAIL You want to know.

SAMUEL S I want to know.

ABIGAIL To give you a lay. [*From her head down, this little bimbo slowly but surely raises up her sweet face to flash her beams right on that strange outpost of* SAMUEL S]

SAMUEL S Hey watch that. [*Caught in his little eggshell on the Bering Strait as this volcanic wave comes crashing at him from the horizon*] I mean you can't say that.

ABIGAIL [*As she sits on her surfboard riding down on* SAM *s' eggshell*] I said it. Sam.

SAMUEL S [*Slumping on to stool at his makeshift desk*] Let me sit down for a second. This situation needs thinking out.

ABIGAIL [*Standing up*] Mind if I stand up.

SAMUEL S No, stand up. [*Getting up and rushing over to push away the conglomerate around*] Wait, let me fix you some space.

ABIGAIL That's all right. I'm standing.

SAMUEL S No no, just a second, you need space. Push this stuff away.

ABIGAIL No, really, that's all right.

SAMUEL S Just get rid of this towel and underwear.

ABIGAIL Don't go to any trouble.

SAMUEL S It's no trouble. [*Dancing attendance. The careful procedures of the undergraduate. To look white, right and scrubbed, and wearing drawers fragrant as the fir forest over one's Christmas decoration*]

ABIGAIL [*Viewing the antics of this curious sudden host you wouldn't want to be meeting in a cave on the hillside back in the dawn of ages*] Maybe it's easier to sit. [*Sitting*] Can I call you Sam.

SAMUEL S Anything you like. [*Carrying sheets and underwear to the repository where phone is buried and stuffing them there with his foot. The little black phone wire leading in there. Who knows who might be ringing under all the dirty laundry and sniffing the speaker at the other end of the phone.* SAMUEL S *looking to find more untidiness to put right at this moment of plentysome bombardment stops, caught in the sights again of the field gun, staring down the barrel as* ABIGAIL *gets ready to fire]*

ABIGAIL   I heard you wanted a lay. Sam.

SAMUEL S   Let's lay off that subject for a minute.

ABIGAIL   Gee, can we go on having a conversation like this. If you want I'll withdraw the offer.

SAMUEL S   [*Spinning round stung on the ass by the asp*]   Don't do that.

ABIGAIL   Well, it's kind of undignified if I have to ask you again. I better stand again. [*Standing, belly in, chest out. Turns to look at her arm*] Gee, look that little muscle is throbbing just there over the elbow. [*Holding up her arm toward* SAMUEL S] Want to see. [SAMUEL S *finding his way back through the jungle, now slumps on stool again, sinking back on desk and papers to reach up a hand to wipe the moisture from his brow. In this sea green room*] Are you going to say something. Sam.

SAMUEL S   Have a piece of cake. There on the table. It's stale but no mold yet. I'm covered in a cold sweat.

ABIGAIL   You admit everything.

SAMUEL S   Because I've got to come to terms with everything.

ABIGAIL   Boy, Sam, I'm going to sit down again. [*Sitting*] If I have to wait while you come to terms. And you expect people not to give you a kick in the tonsils in the meantime. For your own good, when are you going to wise up.

SAMUEL S   I've got my ways of fighting.

ABIGAIL   Only if you know you've got somebody you can beat.

SAMUEL S I see.

ABIGAIL Christ, I'm sorry I said just what I said.

SAMUEL S That's why I'm here for five years. To get straightened out. So I can take those remarks.

ABIGAIL God, five years.

SAMUEL S Could take another five years.

ABIGAIL You can afford that.

SAMUEL S I'm not affording it. I'm broke. Living on the handouts from some rich friends who can't face the pain of refusing me.

ABIGAIL [Looking down at her bitten nails, remembering the cake, reaching to take it, biting it. Widening eyes, ready to make a complaint, thinking what the hell this guy's got enough troubles without complaining about the gâteau, swallowing the cake, looking to see if SAM is looking. He's not. Gently putting back the rest of the cake on the table. SAMUEL S looks up. Sees] Whoops. You caught me.

SAMUEL S That's all right.

ABIGAIL You know. Sam, you're an honest person. Even the way you give me stale cake to eat. Guess I should adapt. I mean my whole reason for coming to Europe was to widen my area of experience. And did we walk into it. Right at Le Havre. I mean an hour off the boat heading for Paris, a French truck driver tried to lay me and Catherine. He said it would teach us about Europe. I told him his breath stank. Then he made a rude suggestion. I was sort of amused but Catherine slapped his face, he didn't know we knew so much French. He nearly tried to kill us and then he threw us out of the truck. I think Europeans are pretty lousy and uncouth. You've gone European. It's wrong.

SAMUEL S   What's right.

ABIGAIL   They should grow up in Europe. They think they have spiritual values. They should get wise.

SAMUEL S   You think so.

ABIGAIL   Yes, and you should problem solve. Plenty of people who are mental cripples work out of it after a while. Take me.

SAMUEL S   Well, take you.

ABIGAIL   [Settling in, flapping over her hands to look at her array of nails] They tried to make me a child prodigy at the piano. My parents are rich. I grew up in a greenhouse. My mother tried to suck my father dry. But before she finished, another doll came on the scene, both trying to suck him dry, which, while they were fighting, gave me a breather. I mean you want to hear all this.

SAMUEL S   Please continue.

ABIGAIL   Cut out that superior stuff.

SAMUEL S   I'm just listening. Continue.

ABIGAIL   I've had my problems. My mother's built like a mole. I mean she wasn't always like that but it was like she was taking the fat off my father and putting it on herself. That's an awful image to imagine. My father said he really loves me, you know like a man really loves a woman, that kind of stuff. So I said it was abnormal. He socked me. I told him, well I don't want to be abnormal. My father is a sort of a good guy, he would understand, you know, laughs and jokes and stuff. He really has a sense of humor. So we were able to joke. His problem is he's only half Jewish. [SAMUEL s staring across the present Bering Strait. A distant booming bell tolling four] Is that four o'clock.

SAMUEL S   That's four o'clock.

ABIGAIL   Wow. Time flies in this room. Well you see, Sam, I'm out of
Baltimore. I don't know, maybe it doesn't look it, my father was raised
in the back of an ice cream parlor, I mean his parents couldn't speak
English, I mean if my girlfriends met my grandparents my social life
wouldn't be worth a gumdrop. I went to a snooty college, I mean if I
didn't have money those girls would have told me where to get off, I
can tell you. America is riddled with snobbery. I mean you haven't
been back. You don't know.

SAMUEL S   I know.

ABIGAIL   You think so. Well you should go and see how things are
shaping up over there now. I mean it's masses. Real masses. I mean
my eyes, I don't know how they got opened. But they're rolling them
out of the colleges. By the thousands. You don't know. My uncle's
friend said you isolate yourself. Gee, think of all those brains cluttered
with education. I got so scared. I emptied out my knowledge. Lost my
virginity. That shocks you.

SAMUEL S   If you want to think so.

ABIGAIL   Boy, you're difficult, but I'm talking like a waterfall to you.
My uncle's friend is one guy's opinions I'm impressed by and he said
you were one of the strangest items in Europe. How you in your own
personal life had built up the dimensions of some great historical
figure, ha ha, I mean I'll level with you, I think it's sheer balls, but it's
a real amusing situation you got going for yourself if that's the way
it is. You know some people get their kicks with hi fi but you, ha ha,
an historical figure, well maybe what the hell. I thought it was impressive. Then. You want the truth.

SAMUEL S   If you want to tell me.

ABIGAIL   Well then when I saw you, I was disappointed. I mean right
away something told me it was you. And something was saying oh gee,
I hope not. But it was such a surprise meeting you like that. Then
as you sunk in. Even though we kind of got on the wrong terms. I

thought, what. This old fashioned guy. My father could compete with him. You realize I'm giving it to you straight from the shoulder.

SAMUEL S   I realize.

ABIGAIL   Then when I socked you with a couple of remarks. And you showed your sorrow right there in front of me, I said either this guy is pretty sick or something or else he's really special. When guys cry in America it's sort of gooey with words coming out as well. But you weren't really crying. Just big tears rolling out independently. You know. [*Looking up to point*] There they are. Right top of the cliff, a little gang of leprechauns are pushing them over and they come pounding down slow motion like and you watch like it was a wonder or something. That's why I want to get to know you. Because I think you are the most interesting person I have met in Europe thus far. I think I can learn something from you.

SAMUEL S   Is that all.

ABIGAIL   Well yeah, that's all. But you're sort of an uncorrupted person. I mean I don't know what I mean. But. Oh God. I'm a woman. And you're a man. And gee we're in Europe and we're alone. I mean doesn't that get you all excited.

SAMUEL S   I'm excited.

ABIGAIL   Well, Sam.

SAMUEL S   Well what.

ABIGAIL   Well I told you why I'm here. I'm embarrassed. Do I have to say it again. Like I said you can give me knowledge. I can give you a lay.

SAMUEL S   Is that all.

ABIGAIL   Sure that's all. What did you expect.

SAMUEL S   I want to get married.

ABIGAIL [*Coming forward in her seat*]   Holy cow. Are you crazy.

SAMUEL S   And have children.

ABIGAIL   Boy. [*Standing*] Maybe we should change the subject. I mean
marry. [*Pointing to this antique historical, seated sheet wrapped figure*]
You. Jeepers. I mean you're not asking me, are you. I was only talking
about a lay.

SAMUEL S [*Shouting*]   I don't want a lay.

ABIGAIL [*Shy whispering*]   Wish you wouldn't shout. I can hear. Maybe
you want me to go. I'll go.

SAMUEL S   I won't do anything to stop you.

ABIGAIL   You mean you really wouldn't stop me. Well boy you better
face facts in the auction of life. And take what you can get. With a
young girl like me you wouldn't stand a chance. You got gray hairs,
means your reserves are running low. [*Holding up her upturned palms
as she slumps back in chair*] You can't even fall back on distinction.

SAMUEL S [*Staring at those two burning brown eyes, heart pounding in
his chest*]   By the world's rules I'm a failure. But I live here. I mind
my own business. I don't have visitors. The reason you're here is
because no young Ivy League guys are giving you a tumble. You're not
exactly ugly but from the chin up no one could say you were a prize-
winner. Although, crazy enough, I think you're damn pretty but I
know what kids your own age think. The smart talk doesn't become
you one bit. It's unpleasant and bad manners.

ABIGAIL   Wait Sam.

SAMUEL S   You wait.

ABIGAIL   But Sam, this is the kind of talk I thought would come from you. I'm glad I came. I know I was being smart saying that about laying and all. I just felt awkward coming along like this. I might have got here and found you with someone or something. But they told me you did this, went under, like a submarine or something and no one heard from you for days. [*Waiting an answer. No answer from the historical figure*] I don't think you are a failure.

SAMUEL S   What am I.

ABIGAIL   Well like you said about me. People your own age might look down on you. But to me you've got maturity not even my own father has.

SAMUEL S   If you saw me sitting in a café just me as I am you would ignore me.

ABIGAIL   You're the most stubborn damn person, for Christ's sake.

SAMUEL S   That's right.

ABIGAIL   Aren't guys trying to escape marriage. You're just looking for a wife and kids now so you won't be lonely in your old age. But me, I want to kick the gong around some more before I get all tied up. And if you really want to know, I want to be screwed by the great minds of this century. [*Silence.* ABIGAIL *slowly leans forward and puts her head in her hands and elbows on the table*]

SAMUEL S   Most of them are dead.

ABIGAIL   [*Another silence*]   Boy this is a seminar Sam. Have you got some coffee. [*Standing up*] I'll make some [SAMUEL S *perceptibly straightening up, like hearing the call to a fire somewhere and he a member of the local volunteer fire department in a town where this means you get in on a twice yearly barbecue*] What's the matter did I say something wrong.

SAMUEL S No.

ABIGAIL You got such a funny look. Have you got some coffee.

SAMUEL S You're outraging American womanhood.

ABIGAIL What do you mean. Just because I said I'd make the coffee. [SAMUEL S *mumchance in the prospect of coffee*] Say, what do you take American women for. We're not cripples you know. [ABIGAIL *waiting for* SAMUEL S *to say American women are cripples*] I'll even clean up for you here. You couldn't have cleaned this place for at least a month.

SAMUEL S Three months eighteen days.

ABIGAIL Wow you've got it counted. Well show me where. I'll make the coffee.

SAMUEL S I'll have to go and get some coffee.

ABIGAIL Oh, OK.

SAMUEL S If you can loan me the money.

ABIGAIL [*Eyebrows puckering, she goes into a little purse in her saddle bag left in her chair, hands across to* SAMUEL S *a fifty shilling note.* SAMUEL S *watched amazed by* ABIGAIL, *tucks in sheet like a shirt in belt, pulls on jacket over and ties scarf at neck. Heads for door, stops as if remembering something, then continues out.* ABIGAIL *takes a look around. Lifting up carpet and whistling at the dirt. Leans over and smells the cake. Goes over to a mirror and looks at herself, takes out a comb and runs it through her hair. Stands still a moment. Goes over to door and listens. Comes back to center of room. Takes off shirt, takes off brassiere and puts in her handbag, puts shirt back on, takes off drawers from under skirt, puts same into handbag, wriggles her body to settle the clothes upon her again and goes looking for the broom, to a closet, opening door and the stack of books inside comes tumbling out, she picks up books, and sets about with a little neatening and sweeping. Finally settling on clearing a little space on table. Lock turning,* SAMUEL S *entering with a loaf of bread and bag of coffee beans, sniffs the air.* ABIGAIL *standing with broom licking the edges of her lips.* SAMUEL S *putting the coffee beans on the cleared space of table. As she turns and smiles]* Doesn't that look better Sam. Got a whole square foot of clear space on table. Just picking up the papers and stuff. Gee you know it's so quiet and sort of lonely here, it makes me sad. I need to wash my face now, I got so much dust over it. *[Pointing]* That way to the bathroom? *[*SAMUEL S *nodding, his eyes following her little fiery ass as it spreads wings to fly and exits wagging under its animal skin to the bathroom. Two goodly tough tendons behind her knees in the smooth backs of her legs.* SAMUEL S *taking cap and slapping it on hook behind his door, taking off jacket, coming to center of room and just standing doing nothing at all at all.* ABIGAIL *enters. Standing in opening to bathroom]* Sam, this place isn't very soundproofed. I could hear in the next apartment. Maybe you heard me peeing.

SAMUEL S   There was that music.

ABIGAIL   *[As she walks through the disarray]*   Well I'm not one of those dames who flushes the can while they pee so no one can hear them peeing. You have to pee, everybody does, so they hear you, so what. *[Lifting up a sheet of paper, looking at it]* Of course, it might be different if I was having a noisy crap, I might be embarrassed by the sound. Does it worry you.

SAMUEL S   My worries are silent.

ABIGAIL   Well mine are noisy. *[Searching and pushing through more papers at random]* I was raised a free farter. Maybe I don't belch much. It interested me though which of my girlfriends ever farted on a date. They would never admit it. I lost four boyfriends that way. Three with prospects. Can you imagine just being human, one little innocent fart and.

SAMUEL S   And.

ABIGAIL   And that's all.

SAMUEL S   Here's your change.

ABIGAIL   [A little wave of hand]   Oh don't bother, that's all right.

SAMUEL S   Here's your change.

ABIGAIL   God you're touchy. [Taking change. Putting change back in purse and bag]

SAMUEL S   I have conditions under which I take money and conditions under which I don't.

ABIGAIL   You slay me. You really do. [Leaning back against the table, propping her hands along the edge and casually staring at SAMUEL S's eyes. Her lower stony lip carved out of her face. Nose wrinkling as she stares and SAMUEL S stares back. Let's have a little music here. As a little friendship wavers at the corner of ABIGAIL's lips and her eyes finally look down and away]   You outstared me, Sam. No guy's ever been able to do that before.

SAMUEL   Is that so.

ABIGAIL   Is it too much to ask you to address me as Abigail. You haven't once called me Abigail.

SAMUEL S   Abigail.

ABIGAIL   Not like that, after you've said something to me. Boy. I get myself into the most awkward situations. [A moisture in ABIGAIL's eyes. She lifts her face to look back at SAMUEL S. She takes two steps forward with a shambling pigeon-toed awkwardness. Her wrists and hands go up to her throat. Her fingers unbuttoning the top of her *blouse. And the next*] Sam you said I was no prize winner from the chin up. [*Opens wide her shirt*] How am I from the chin down.

SAMUEL S   Jesus Christ.

ABIGAIL [*Pulling zip on skirt*] And here.

SAMUEL S   You're all right.

ABIGAIL   And here farther down. And up.

SAMUEL S   All right.

ABIGAIL   And now. [*Drops skirt round ankles and standing facing a most steamed up* SAMUEL S *as she holds open her shirt*] How am I all over. A surprise package.

SAMUEL S   Let me sit down.

ABIGAIL   Sam. We're really going to do it.

SAMUEL S   No we're not. Wait a minute. You forgot what I said about marriage.

ABIGAIL   We can't worry about that now. Look at me. From the chin down. Really, how am I.

SAMUEL S   Something.

ABIGAIL   Really?

SAMUEL S   To remember. Right into old age. And later in the hereafter.

ABIGAIL   You've got a sense, Sam, of humor I never thought you had.

SAMUEL S   Humorous of you. To think so.

ABIGAIL Take off your clothes, Sam.

SAMUEL S Dance.

ABIGAIL Sure. [*Her fancy gyrations slowly doing the Bronx gavotte with a mixture of the Ethiopian trance dance.* SAMUEL S *charmed by this fixation. Rises to his feet to begin his awkward impetuous divestation of the garments which go flying as they leave his person and float down to casually rest themselves over the disarray as one of the better minds of this century is about to see to other things.* ABIGAIL *comes close.* SAMUEL S *making for the bed first as he pulls back the sheets, followed by* ABIGAIL *standing behind him*] You're not hairy. [SAMUEL S *taking her in arms for a squeeze of elfin body*] Gee, you're stronger than I thought. [SAMUEL S *rolling on top of her. The creaking of the horsehair and she rolls over on top of him. And she looks him in the eye, and he looks her in the eye. The eye game*] You're not going to do anything, are you.

SAMUEL S No.

ABIGAIL [*Creeping inches away from this walrus. And turning and stretching on her back, staring up at ceiling*] You must be the worst rat who ever lived. You don't know what that can do to a girl.

SAMUEL S I know.

ABIGAIL [*Eyes closed, eyelids tightening, merest tremble of her lip*] You couldn't.

SAMUEL S You don't know what screwing without a future can do to me.

ABIGAIL [*Shifting up on her elbows as she rolls over face down. Her eyes widening. Slight shake of her head*] I can't marry you. What would a girl like me do for maybe the thirty or forty years after you were dead. But I could stay right here with you screwing for two whole months. And I wouldn't mind making coffee and things like that every once in a while. Holy cow. What am I telling you. I mean, God, who do you think you are, like if you could fart in B flat or something.

SAMUEL S That's right. [*Lifting the covers with an elbow and letting go with a neat semiquaver, reverberating in the room and waking neighbors lightly late afternoon napping with this human music*]

ABIGAIL [*Sitting up on her elbows*] Wow. You're a tuning fork. No kidding that was B flat, Sam. You may think that's just funny but that's impressive.

SAMUEL S Marry me and I'll give you an organ recital.

ABIGAIL I know you could. I believe you. But why can't you just be content with getting what you're getting. What I'm offering. Haven't I got one of the best bodies you've ever seen. While you were getting the coffee I took off what I had underneath so I could show you fast all at once. Isn't it the cat's meow.

SAMUEL S I'm panting.

ABIGAIL Well don't think I'm going to stick around.

SAMUEL S Don't.

ABIGAIL I won't don't worry.

SAMUEL S For you this is just a tourist itinerary. For me it's a shovel full of sod slipped on my coffin.

ABIGAIL [*Moving up a notch in her crouch, brown hair dropping forward round her cheeks*] Sam. Listen. I'll be honest. It's asking me to sign up with a loser when I've still got maybe three or four years to find a boy or guy who's better off than I am or somebody who's made out as good as my father. Besides, I like sleeping some more with different guys. I mean it's no kidding. Maybe they all can't use their ass holes like trombones but it's funny and interesting with all the pricks you

come across. Some curve into left field, some into right. Crazy the
way no two pricks are the same. The end is like different kinds of fruit,
some like an apple, ones like pears, yours is like a cherry.

SAMUEL S . Thanks a bunch.

ABIGAIL   Some cherry. No kidding. I mean guys don't know. They
think they're debasing me. I got news for them. My interest is highly
scientific biological. I could tell them things. Gee, listen to me. A
seminar again. Come on. Yours goes into center field. First one I
ever saw did that. You can never tell the direction or the real size
till it's hard. Let's not waste it like this. How about it. Huh. I'll blow.
Warm air, ha ha, in your ear.

SAMUEL S   No one is saying you can't make it stand up and sing.

ABIGAIL   I've come all the way to Europe to get really laid, Sam.

SAMUEL S   I came all the way to Europe to get really cured.

ABIGAIL   Couldn't I cure you.

SAMUEL S   I've put two docs out of action already trying to cure me.

ABIGAIL   Haven't I got big but dainty breasts.

SAMUEL S   And my present doc is ready to sail for Hungary any day
down the Danube.

ABIGAIL   To hell with you. I'm going to sleep. Good night. And get
your hand away.

[*Tolling of bell. Five tolls and fading as it tolls on. Lights fade.
Music softly. Tram screeching down in streets. Car passing, hearing
it long before it arrives and long after it goes, whirring away on the
lonely cobbled road. Suddenly* SAMUEL S *leaping awake in bed with
a scream, lights on, tearing back the blankets, his hand shoot-*

ing down to his thigh and to grab in a thatch of hair and pull it away from the leg. A ring of bleeding teeth marks on his thigh]

SAMUEL S   What the hell are you doing.

ABIGAIL   Biting you.

SAMUEL S   You crazy?

ABIGAIL   Yes.

SAMUEL S   Blood all over my leg.

ABIGAIL   Don't worry, you won't die.

SAMUEL S   Jesus Christ, you're not safe. [*Gliding from the bed. Casting a glance behind at this werewolf and vampire, eyes glittering from a hood of bedcovers. The hurried movement one finds suddenly in the knees along with a slight trembling trying to stand still. Rivulet of blood right to the ankle bone upon which* SAMUEL S *looks.* SAMUEL S *dabbing wound with a towel]*

ABIGAIL   You want me to go. Will you call me a taxi. I mean it's nearly dawn.

SAMUEL S   You can stay till the trams start again. [*Sitting. Wrapped in a sheet in his chair. Lights off]*

ABIGAIL   I want a taxi.

SAMUEL S   Go get one.

ABIGAIL   [*The sigh and hear the heave of her little body flinging herself on her side in the bed]* OK. I bit you. Don't you ever have the urge to bite. Maybe you're too educated. Well I'm primitive. Maybe I just like the taste of blood. Besides you should have fucked me.

SAMUEL S   I'm finished screwing for screwing sake.

ABIGAIL   Bully for you. What did you take your clothes off for. You got a dirty mind.

SAMUEL S   You're right. I have. And maybe you don't know that a woman's shyness will make you do all sorts of things, even to screwing her.

ABIGAIL   Boy you know how to hurt right back, don't you.

SAMUEL S   Maybe. A woman should take all the guff a man wants to give.

ABIGAIL   That sounds like you all right. Oh Christ. Oh God. Oh Jeroboam. Oh Sid. Oh Joe. All you good guilty college guys I've been turning my nose up at. I mean you think you're going to get a dose of maturity. Boy. You talk about insights. You gave me one. I prefer a guy who can't get it hard to a guy who won't even use it. I've got a headache. I need an aspirin.

SAMUEL S   I'll get you one.

ABIGAIL   Don't bother. The pain's fine. [*Gray light creeping in. The first tram grinds by. Outside Vienna goes to work, creak of horsehair from the bed.* ABIGAIL's *little face a white oval in her dark hair turning toward him. Her legs tucked up to make a ball in the bed*] Sam. What's the matter with you. Could you tell me. I say all kinds of things but it's like bouncing bricks off an iceberg. I don't have any confidence at all. This is going to sound crazy but I like you. [*Another tram*] But do you really believe what you think. Because that's the way a woman thinks. I mean, Christ, what do I think. At this stage six o'clock in the morning. Catherine back at the hotel who'll be itching to know every detail. I guess you already assumed because I've been so outspoken that I'll go talking about you to the outside world. That what you think.

SAMUEL S   No.

ABIGAIL   Ho hum. Tell me did you ever crap on an airplane.

SAMUEL S   No.

ABIGAIL   On a plane zooming about twenty thousand feet or something in the air and you think, wow if it ever dropped you wouldn't want to be somewhere down there underneath quietly listening to background music. I'm nuts. Holy God. How's the wound. Blood's showing right through the sheet. I feel awful. I didn't know I bit that deep. Could I make a bandage or something. Didn't brush my teeth since yesterday, breakfast is that bad. [*Slowly climbing from the blankets, a blanket around her. Putting an uncertain foot on the floor. Stepping toward* SAMUEL S *wrapped stoic in his sheet. His left hand holding the stained thin cotton fabric pressed against his thigh.* ABIGAIL *gently lifting back the sheet from this whitish leg*] Can I see. My teeth do that.

SAMUEL S   Your teeth did that.

ABIGAIL   God am I sorry. Please at least let me take care of it. [*Staring at the wound her hands rushing up to her face. Her narrow back bending to make a line of white bumps through the blanket down her spine. A long groan, her face in pain. A shiver in* SAMUEL S. ABIGAIL *slumping to her knees. Little person crumpled up so small*] Sam can you help me. I need help. The first thing that ever happened to me was with my dog. I did it with my dog. I got bitten. You ought to know, has that doomed me. [SAMUEL S *tightening up his sheet around him as the icy fingers of weirdery reach out to tickle him about the earlobes and gently under the cheeks of the arse, smashing an icy wind up against this area*] Sam, aren't you going to talk. You embarrassed or something. Oh God, ha ha ha, excuse me for laughing, I bit other guys. It worries me but sometimes it was so funny I was convulsed. You look worried.

SAMUEL S   I'm worried.

ABIGAIL   Should I be worried.

SAMUEL S   I don't know.

ABIGAIL   I don't feel sick but I guess I am. [*Footsteps pounding across the landing*] What's that.

SAMUEL S   Herr Professor from upstairs.

ABIGAIL   What's he doing so early in the morning. Making real pounding.

SAMUEL S   He's carrying up blocks of ice. He's experimenting. With an ice that will never melt.

ABIGAIL   Like the match that always lights.

SAMUEL S   That's it.

ABIGAIL   I wrote my father letters from college while I was in the nude, and I told him that's the way I was. In the nude. I don't know, I still feel absolutely normal. Do you. Sam.

SAMUEL S   I don't know.

ABIGAIL   Why you wrapping up like that. Afraid I might bite it on you.

SAMUEL S   Could be that I'm not feeling like being an entree after your hors d'oeuvres.

ABIGAIL   You have the mind of a child, you know that.

SAMUEL S   I know.

ABIGAIL   You mean you're content with that.

SAMUEL S   I'm content.

ABIGAIL   I think you're a voyeur too.

SAMUEL S   That could be.

ABIGAIL   You got your eye full. To my nothing. Being a child and a voyeur doesn't look good at your age. [*Rising in her blanket and padding on the bare feet back to bed*] I don't know why I'm wasting time lecturing you. Except if nothing else is resulting from this relationship we might just as well spread around the advice.

SAMUEL S   The poison.

ABIGAIL   Well sure. [*Spins around from where she kneels on bed*] Hey, what do you mean poison.

SAMUEL S   That's what you're splashing at me.

ABIGAIL   Let's change the subject, holy cow. But I wish I knew what angle you look at life from. [*Pulling the covers tightly around her*] It's chilly. [SAMUEL S *reaching under his thigh to brush away a drop of blood. The same reddened knuckle to his nose to wipe a chilled bead of sweat*] What are you thinking all silent, Sam.

SAMUEL S   I was thinking I was chairman of a billion dollar bank.

ABIGAIL   What if I came in asking for a loan.

SAMUEL S   I'd give it to you.

ABIGAIL   You would. Gee. How is this going to end, Sam.

SAMUEL S   It's going to, that's all.

ABIGAIL   I feel all switched around now. Don't you have any advice to give me.

SAMUEL S   What do you want to hear.

ABIGAIL Well, if there's something wrong. With me.

SAMUEL S What I say doesn't matter.

ABIGAIL [*Rising from bed in covers. Two hands knotted tightly against her throat*] You pompous prick. And don't you ever dare tell anybody what I told you.

SAMUEL S You think it's so worth telling.

ABIGAIL Just don't ever tell anyone, that's all. I know the kind of crap these psychiatrists like to hear. They revel in it. They got dirty minds.

SAMUEL S You think so.

ABIGAIL I think so.

SAMUEL S A minute ago you were asking for help.

ABIGAIL That's right. But you can't give it. You take but you can't give. I scare you, don't I. Well if you want news, you're beginning to scare me. I might be nuts but you're a monster. You don't know a thing about me. Not a thing. Get that straight. Have you got it straight.

SAMUEL S I've got it straight.

ABIGAIL Just so long as you have. And you think something's gone on with my father.

SAMUEL S I've said nothing. I've got it straight, I don't know a thing about you.

ABIGAIL That's right. You don't. Because my father and I love each other. [*Rigid in the cold tundra of this moment. Staring back into her own life. And coming back suddenly in her little eggshell across from this sentinel iceberg, upon which she might climb from this arctic sea and cling to as she would slowly freeze away.*] Oh God Sam. Oh God. Please, have you got anything to drink. Please. [SAMUEL S *in his sheet going to his bathroom.* ABIGAIL *reaches out and takes her shirt and puts it on under blanket.* SAMUEL S *returning with a bottle and filling a glass. He holds it near and* ABIGAIL *reaches out to take it out of his hand. She puts tumbler to her lips and drinks it in a gulp. Holding glass out for more.* SAMUEL S *bending his wrist over the bottle and pouring. She throws it back again. Sitting there empty whiskey tumbler in her hand, the morning light sparkling in her tears.* ABIGAIL *leaning across to push the empty tumbler on the table, her wide dark eyebrow raised, lips tightened, hand momentarily put to twist a strand of her hair round her finger. Thighs together, shielding herself from eyes, she slides off bed and opens and picks her underwear out of her saddle bag. Shaking the flimsy black silk. Turning her head to* SAMUEL S] Don't watch me dressing. [*Nearby factory whistle blowing. Seven o'clock bell slowly faintly booming, the outside Vienna awake.* ABIGAIL *standing in her deerskin shoes at his corroded mirror pulling a comb through her hair. She takes up her bag, moves the strap across her shoulder and near a churning shaft of sunlight dust, finally stands by the doorway*] Goodbye. And I regret about the wound.

SAMUEL S   You know how to take the tram.

ABIGAIL   I know. Einmal zur Oper, bitte.

SAMUEL S   Sehr gut.

ABIGAIL   Wish there was a little more of this sunshine in this situation. I'll send you a postcard. You know. Oh forget it. Goodbye. [SAMUEL *is closing latching door. Turning back. Stands a moment in the middle of room, goes over takes coffee pot, puts in coffee, puts it on the stove*]

[*Curtain*]

SCENE 2

HERR DOCTOR'S *office. Three days later. Herr Doctor standing at his window, hands behind his back. Enter* SAMUEL S.

SAMUEL S   Doc, get set. This is the momentous session. [*Putting cap on its hook. Stops halfway across the room.* HERR DOCTOR *continues to look out his window*] Doc. I'm going to give you a case of the willies. I've got one big massive dream carried safely here trailing a sizzling fuse. And an explosive insight. [HERR DOCTOR *motionless, back to* SAMUEL S *as he still stands at window*] What's up, Doc. Why you standing. Like that. Usually you're sitting at your desk. Someone spying on you from across the garden. Big purge of doctors who overcharge in Vienna, I hear.

DOCTOR   [*Turning from window to confront* SAMUEL S]   Do please sit down, Herr S. [SAMUEL S *going to his seat*] You are limping, Herr S.

SAMUEL S   Tell you all in good time, Doc. I've really got some things for you today. Which have been zinging around the pons varioli since Saturday, and they're crowding right up the ninth and fifth nerves. You must remember those, the ones you expose in the dogfish. Well. It's happened. I just turned down flat my first real free piece of ass with no strings attached. To which I was trying to attach strings. Just dangling there in front of me for one whole night. You listening, Doc? And I've also got a big dream to tell you. Jesus, the icy fingers. Like big jellyfish in an ocean of fear. You know Doc, the whole world wraps them around you when the gradient is down and down. I've got to get up and run. Fast as I can go. Grab two liters of sour milk to set the stomach right. Say goodbye to the landlady's snails, goodbye to the Countess. Goodbye goodbye to weirdery everywhere. Who's the doctor, who's the patient. Where's the willies. They're here. Willies everywhere.

DOCTOR Herr S.

SAMUEL S Hold it Doc, I'm going to tell you about all the silent little children who commit suicide in Austria. And all these matronly Viennese women with their young boys.

DOCTOR Herr S.

SAMUEL S Hey Doc, you're interrupting me. Hey, you look worried. You ought to go back to smoking cigars. I mean you can afford it out of fees.

DOCTOR Herr S.

SAMUEL S Was ist Doc.

DOCTOR I would prefer if you did not speak German to me, Herr patient.

SAMUEL S Hold it, something's wrong, Doc.

DOCTOR Yes, Herr patient.

SAMUEL S Maybe you heard I'm organizing a union of patients for lower fees. Heh heh. Sit down, Doc.

DOCTOR What I am going to tell you, Herr patient, is something I do not want you to misunderstand. You are an extremely intelligent man and I do not think you will.

SAMUEL S I'm listening, Herr Doc. What's your problem.

DOCTOR Herr S, you are driving me nuts.

SAMUEL S   Whoa.

DOCTOR   A sign that you are well and truly cured.

SAMUEL S   Wait Doc.

DOCTOR   Please. If you will. This hour is free with my compliments. Therefore I should like to continue.

SAMUEL S   What are you going to do with all the money you've got.

DOCTOR   Herr S, you well know over these five years my fees have gone up and yours have not.

SAMUEL S   Sure. But what, Doc, do you do with the money.

DOCTOR   Herr patient, may I suggest that that is my business.

SAMUEL S   Well, it keeps me awake and agonizes me and if I knew it would help, that's all.

DOCTOR   I invest it.

SAMUEL S   In what.

DOCTOR   Please, Herr S, I've answered your question.

SAMUEL S   No you haven't.

DOCTOR   What's the difference what it's invested in.

SAMUEL S   Well if it makes no difference why not tell me.

DOCTOR   I invest it in manufacturing.

SAMUEL S   Manufacturing what.

DOCTOR   Chemical products.

SAMUEL S   What chemical products.

DOCTOR   I think perhaps our session is over, Herr S.

SAMUEL S   No it isn't. I want to know what you've put my money in. Or I'm sitting right here until I do.

DOCTOR   Very well Herr S. I invest in oral contraception and munitions.

SAMUEL S   OK.

DOCTOR   Does it answer your question.

SAMUEL S   Yup.

DOCTOR   I am glad to hear that.

SAMUEL S   Well Doc, you're really going to miss my shooting the shit to you. You're smart to kick me out into the cold world. Three more months of me and you would be sitting there a salt pillar.

DOCTOR   Perhaps, Herr S.

SAMUEL S   [*In his chair his hands spread out on the leather arms*]   Can hear your watch ticking there, Doc. Well anyway. You're no longer a punching bag. If you were a pillar of salt I'd break my fists on you. Mind, I'll just sit here. I mean it's free. It has a lot of meaning for me.

DOCTOR   I understand.

SAMUEL S   Like a glass of beer back in the States. When they say it's on the house, buddy. That's the one tastes best of all. You almost wait for it, through all the others. [*Turning to* HERR DOCTOR] By the way you can put your hand on my chair.

DOCTOR [*Taking a step toward chair, reaching out a hand*]   Thank you, Herr S, a bunch. I presume it is on the house.

SAMUEL S   Well, this final session has given me the biggest insight of all. That if I am ever cured I'll never know it.

DOCTOR   I have left your books I borrowed there. [*Books stacked on desk*] You may stay, Herr S. If you will permit me to go. I catch a train. Miss Ortz will let you out.

SAMUEL S   Sure. Doc, I'm going to send you the money.

DOCTOR   I know you will, Herr S.

SAMUEL S   I won't be seeing you again.

DOCTOR   No, Herr S. It's goodbye.

SAMUEL S   One last thing before you go, Doc. Do you think you'll ever be cured.

DOCTOR   No, Herr S.

SAMUEL S   Doc, you won't believe this but you're a good guy. Thanks anyway for what you tried to do.

DOCTOR   Herr S, I will express an opinion.

SAMUEL S   Sure.

DOCTOR   You are a strange person. And it is a pity you would turn me into a pillar of salt, for I could listen to you much longer. [*Extending his hand*]

SAMUEL S   Sorry, Doc, I never shake hands.

DOCTOR   May I bow.

SAMUEL S   Sure.

DOCTOR   Goodbye, Herr S.

SAMUEL S   So long, Doc. [HERR DOCTOR *exits.* SAMUEL S *sits, his head falling forward as he stares into his lap. He touches the edge of* HERR DOCTOR's *desk with his fingertips, presses his hands forward and slowly stands, his hands resting on either side of the stack of books, his shoulders hunched, and looks down at them. Inclines head*] Christ, I'm dying. [*Shoulders like wings*] A failure. Running down the tracks chased by a train. And you think that you don't want your friends to know you died screaming in fear but that you were brave, kept your mouth shut and said nothing at all. Like a summer fly waltzes out and wobbles in the winter. After this saddest summer.

[*Curtain*]

ABOUT THE AUTHOR

J. P. DONLEAVY was born in New York City in 1926 and edu-
cated there and at Trinity College, Dublin. He is the author of
four novels, *The Ginger Man, A Singular Man, The Beastly
Beatitudes of Balthazar B,* and *The Onion Eaters;* a short novel,
The Saddest Summer of Samuel S; and a collection of stories,
Meet My Maker the Mad Molecule.

THIS BOOK WAS SET IN DE VINNE ORNAMENTED,
BAUER BODONI, BODONI BOOK, AND ELECTRA TYPES
BY AMERICAN BOOK–STRATFORD PRESS.
IT WAS PRINTED BY HALLIDAY LITHOGRAPH CORP.,
AND BOUND BY AMERICAN BOOK–STRATFORD PRESS.
DESIGNED BY JOEL SCHICK